MW00721001

The Soviet Agrarian Debate

Other Titles in This Series

Westview Special Studies on the Soviet Union and Eastern Europe

The Soviet Agrarian Debate:
A Controversy in Social Science, 1923-1929
Susan Gross Solomon

The first decade of Soviet cultural life was marked by a pluralism unmatched in the subsequent history of the USSR. In many fields of art and science, Party and non-Party "proletarian" and "bourgeois" intellectuals worked side by side, vigorously debating questions of substance and method. In this first major study of a Soviet field of social science in the post-Revolution period, Dr. Solomon examines the controversy that divided social scientists studying the economy and society of the Soviet peasant during the 1920s.

The intellectual disagreements in post-Revolution Soviet rural studies were exacerbated by social, political, and professional differences among the contending scholars. The infighting between the groups was bitter. Yet in contrast to recent studies of other Soviet professions in the 1920s, the author finds that in rural studies Marxists and non-Marxists had much in common. Her findings suggest that the coexistence of the "old" and the "new" in Soviet rural studies might have lasted for some time had not external political forces intervened in late 1928, acting as a pressure on the field and eventually causing its demise.

Susan Gross Solomon received a doctorate in political science from Columbia University and is now associate professor in the Department of Political Economy at the University of Toronto. Dr. Solomon studied at Moscow University in 1968-1969.

Published under the auspices of the

Research Institute on International Change,
Columbia University
and the
Russian Institute, Columbia University

The Soviet Agrarian Debate

A Controversy in Social Science, 1923-1929

Susan Gross Solomon

Routledge
Taylor & Francis Group

LONDON AND NEW YORK

First published 1977 by Westview Press

Published 2019 by Routledge
52 Vanderbilt Avenue, New York, NY 10017
2 Park Square, Milton Park, Abingdon, Oxon OX14 4RN

Routledge is an imprint of the Taylor & Francis Group, an informa business

Library of Congress Cataloging in Publication Data
Solomon, Susan Gross.
    The Soviet agrarian debate.
    (Westview Special Studies on the Soviet Union
and Eastern Europe)
    "Published with the cooperation of the Research
Institute on International Change, Columbia Uni-
versity, and the Russian Institute, Columbia
University."
    Bibliography: p.
    Includes index.
    1. Agriculture and state—Russia. I. Columbia
University. Research Institute on International Change.

ISBN 13: 978-0-367-29591-2 (hbk)

To my mother, Anne Romoff Gross, and
To the memory of my father, Clarence Reuben Gross

Contents

Tables and Figures

Preface

The first decade after the Bolshevik Revolution was a heady one for social scientists studying the Soviet countryside. As the fledgling regime attempted to deal with the large, traditional rural sector it had inherited, the study of the peasantry acquired a legitimacy it had never before enjoyed. Bathing in the aura of that legitimacy, rural scholars introduced new approaches and essayed new methods of research.

Between 1923 and mid-1928, at the very time when rural studies was burgeoning in the Soviet Union, the field was rent by an intensely fought controversy between agricultural economists and rural sociologists. The intellectual issues in the dispute cut close to the bone; the contending social scientists argued over the rank ordering of research problems and the relative merits of the methods used to study those problems. To a considerable degree, the dispute reflected the fact that the Soviet field of rural studies, like its American counterpart in the same period, was in the process of broadening its traditional focus—economic issues—to include sociological concerns.

But the Soviet debate in rural studies involved much more than a change in the substance of the field. It was a struggle for power between the "old" and the "new" in a post-Revolutionary context. The agricultural economists, who were neither affiliated with the Communist Party nor Marxists by conviction, constituted the establishment in rural studies. The rural sociologists, who were committed to Marxism, were younger men struggling to make a place for themselves in a field with a long history. These two groups vied with each other for the right to define the content of their field and to lead its community of scholars.

The rivalry between tradition and novelty was not unique to the field of rural studies. Throughout the 1920s similar contests were taking place in a number of fields in Soviet art and science. But the controversy in rural studies had certain distinctive features. The substance of the field was very close to the core concerns of the regime, and prominent rural scholars were called upon from time to time to tender advice to government task forces and commissions. Consequently, major shifts in official policy toward the countryside left their mark on the work of the rural scholars—the more so since the Soviet state was the sole patron of rural research. The tangency between official rural policy and social research on the peasantry raises important questions about the impact of social factors on science.

This book is an examination of the debate among rural scholars—its social and organizational setting, its course, and its impact on the field of rural studies. To the extent possible, I have tried to conduct the examination from the vantage point of the 1920s. For in this case, hindsight may obscure more than it reveals. In late 1928, soon after the controversy was resolved, the field of rural studies was shaken by the Cultural Revolution, which consigned many received truths and established scholars to oblivion and celebrated the "research" conducted by men whose primary credentials were political rather than scholarly. In light of this denouement, the reader might understandably conclude that the protagonists in the rural studies controversy were but players on a stage, acting out a scenario whose end was predetermined. Detailed analysis of the context and content of the debate among rural scholars does not support such a conclusion. On the contrary, as I shall argue, the evidence suggests that until 1929 the coexistence of the old and the new in rural studies was viable and that the precise balance between the two was very much an open question.

I am delighted to be able to acknowledge in print the gratitude I feel to a number of colleagues and friends.

My greatest debt is to Seweryn Bialer, who guided the progress of this work from its origins as a doctoral dissertation. At critical junctures he intervened with wise counsel and support. I am particularly thankful to him for his having coupled encouragement with probing criticism.

The contributions of two other scholars deserve special mention. In his capacity as editor of *Minerva,* Edward Shils read several drafts of an article that summarized the major findings of this study. His critical comments forced me to make the argument more explicit and precise. Mark B. Adams, as reader for the Studies of the Russian Institute of Columbia University, shared with me his knowledge of and feel for the history of Soviet science. In more instances than I can recall, it was his remarks that sent me back to the sources for additional support.

In the early stages of the work other scholars figured importantly. During the course of a ten-month research stay in Moscow in the academic year 1968-1969, biweekly interviews were held with the late Sergei Mitrofanovich Dubrovskii, whose near-total recall of the events in which he had participated made the period come alive. Comments made by the historian Viktor Petrovich Danilov, often cryptic at the time, became important clues to the real scenario in the field of rural studies. Later, when the dissertation was being written, Moshe Lewin gave generously of his encyclopedic knowledge of the Soviet countryside in the 1920s; as chairman of the thesis committee, Harriet A. Zuckerman made helpful comments on the sections dealing with the sociology of science; and Janice Gross Stein gave, as she has continued to do subsequently, cogent criticisms of the logic of the argument.

When the final version of the study was being written, I delivered lectures to the Institut pour l'Histoire et la Socio-Politique des Sciences at the University of Montreal and to the Department for the History and Sociology of Science at the University of Pennsylvania. Special thanks are due the members of these two centers for their thoughtful reactions. In the same period, useful suggestions were received from Sheila Fitzpatrick and Franklyn Griffiths.

In the preparation of the book, I benefited from the support of several institutions. I owe thanks to the Center for Russian and East European Studies of the University of Toronto for sponsoring my exchange year at Moscow State University and to its former director, H. Gordon Skilling, for his much-valued friendship; to the Research Institute on International Change of Columbia University for its sponsorship of this study, and to its longtime director, Zbigniew Brzezinski, for a stimulating introduction to the study of Soviet politics and for his continued interest in the career of a former student; to the Russian Institute of Columbia University and its director, Marshall Shulman, for sponsoring this book; and to its publications officer, Beatrice Stillman, for her interest in the progress of the work. Generous financial support for the project was provided by the Center for Russian and East European Studies and the Office of Research Administration, both of the University of Toronto, and by the Canada Council.

I am grateful to Gloria Rowe and Audrey McCullough, who typed the final manuscript, and to William Freeman and Diane Mew for their careful editing. Tatiana Tontarskii of the U.S. Department of Agriculture Library was especially helpful in the assembling of rare materials for the study.

Last but not least, over the years my husband, Peter H. Solomon, Jr., has shared with me his fascination with the study of Soviet politics and his deep pleasure in the doing of scholarship. His unwavering conviction that this book should be published buoyed me up in trying moments, and his willing assumption of a series of tasks ranging from editorial to domestic left me with no excuse for not completing the manuscript.

S.G.S.
March 1977

Glossary

bedniak—a poor peasant.

desiatin—measure of land area, equally 2.7 acres.

dvor—peasant household. The basic social and economic unit of peasant society, consisting of the family and its farm.

Gosplan *(Gosudarstvennaia planovaia komissiia)*—State Planning Commission. A major government agency.

guberniia—province. The largest administrative unit in Tsarist Russia. Replaced by the *oblast* in the Soviet period.

kolkhoz *(kollektivnoe khoziaistvo)*—collective farm.

Kombedy (Komitety bednoty)—Committees of Poor Peasants. Set up in June 1918 to extract grain from the rich peasants. Disbanded in the same year.

kulak—a rich peasant.

Narkomzem *(Narodnyi kommissariat Zemledeliia)*—People's Commissariat of Agriculture.

NEP *(Novaia ekonomicheskaia politika)*—New Economic Policy. Refers both to the policy inaugurated by Lenin in 1921 and to the period it remained in force (1921-1929).

obshchina—peasant commune.

seredniak—a middle peasant.

sovkhoz *(sovetskoe khoziaistvo)*—state farm.

uezd—district. A subdivision of the *guberniia*.

volost'—small rural district. A subdivision of the *uezd*.

zemstvo—local governing council in pre-Revolutionary Russia.

Part 1
The Problem and Its Setting

1. Introduction

The period of the New Economic Policy (1921-1929) was a memorable chapter in the history of Soviet culture. To this brief period belongs a series of outstanding achievements in the arts and sciences. Even more important, Soviet cultural life in the twenties was characterized by a degree of intellectual and social pluralism that far exceeded that of any subsequent period in the nation's history. NEP, as the period was known, was the heyday of heterodoxy in Soviet culture. In field after field, intellectuals argued questions of substance and method, convention and innovation. The variety of views expressed in these disputes testifies to the social diversity of the intelligentsia. For most of the 1920s Party and non-Party, "proletarian" and "bourgeois," antiestablishment and established intellectuals worked if not together, at least side by side, in cultural institutions. In late 1928 this intellectual and social pluralism was brought to an abrupt end by the so-called Cultural Revolution, or the seizure of power in culture by "proletarian" intellectuals.[1] When that revolution had spent its force less than four years later, Soviet cultural life bore but a superficial resemblance to what it had been for most of the NEP period. By 1932 the cultural institutions that had enjoyed a fair measure of autonomy in the administration and conduct of their work were firmly under the control of the Party. The intellectual community had been purged of many of its most brilliant members, non-Party and Party alike. And the content of most fields of culture had been radically altered; traditional concerns deemed "counterrevolutionary" were set aside in favor of new preoccupations that fitted the Party's definition of truth and beauty.[2] Among Western students of Soviet history, it is customary to regard the Cultural Revolution as imposed from above, brought about by the intervention of the Communist Party in the conduct of the arts and scholarship.[3] According to this view, the fundamental hostility in Soviet cultural life of the 1920s was that between the cultural professions, which were struggling to preserve their autonomy, and the Communist Party, which was seeking to extend its hegemony over every sphere of Soviet life. The debates *within* the cultural professions under NEP are treated as having had at best a secondary impact upon the fate of culture. To those who hold this view, the period 1928-1931 was but the final act in the drama. As David Joravsky, the most eloquent spokesman for this position, recently put it, at that point the Party "turned from fostering to forcing."[4] It bent every effort to control culture, and, in the face of such intense political pressure, the intelligentsia capitulated.

Recently some Western historians have begun to reassess the Cultural Revolution—its origins, its conduct, and its impact upon Soviet cultural life. Among the most important features of that reassessment to have emerged to date is the hypothesis that the events of 1928-1931 derived much of their initial impetus from below, that is, from within the ranks of the intelligentsia.[5] Those who espouse this view have stressed the fact that throughout NEP the cultural professions were rent by conflicts between "bourgeois" and "proletarian" intellectuals. These conflicts were particularly bitter, the historians explain, because divergent political commitments were overlaid with differences in the professional standing and orientation of the disputants. In many a profession, young communist intellectuals new to their field and somewhat ambivalent about its norms found themselves subordinate to noncommunist intellectuals who occupied the major posts and who regarded themselves as the guardians of professional standards. According to the scholars who espouse the new view, the infighting in the cultural professions in the 1920s was inherently explosive. In the pre-1928 period, so runs the argument, that infighting was contained only because the Party discouraged the escalation of conflict; in 1928, when the Party ceased its policy of active discouragement, the communist intellectuals, deeply resentful of their inferior status and position, converted the conflicts into open warfare.[6] The proponents of the new interpretation of the Cultural Revolution do not deny the importance of the Party's intervention in cultural life in the period 1928-1931, but they emphasize the primacy of the tensions that existed within professions prior to that intervention. Indeed, the foremost exponent of the new view, Sheila Fitzpatrick, maintains that the infighting of the pre-1928 period was so serious that even had the Party not intervened, Soviet culture would have been sapped of its vitality.[7]

At first glance, the difference between the two interpretations of the Cultural Revolution appears to be one of emphasis. Both interpretations accord some importance to the factors of Party intervention and professional infighting; the two accounts seem to diverge only over the weight assigned to each factor. Further reflection suggests, however, that the difference between the accounts goes well beyond the question of emphasis or accent. It is rooted in a fundamental disagreement about the cohesion of the cultural professions in the NEP period. Underlying the traditional view is the assumption that the intellectuals engaged in the disputes were united by a sense of professional solidarity that transcended their express differences. The new view, on the other hand, seems to assume that the cleavages that gave rise to the disputes within cultural fields were so fundamental as to outweigh the tendency to professional solidarity. The disagreement on this point is important, for it raises the more general question of the viability of the NEP experiment in culture. The more recent interpretation of the events of 1928-1931 would suggest that the coexistence of social and intellectual opposites in the twenties was so uneasy that some sort of crisis in cultural life was likely. The traditional view would imply that the NEP experiment did have a chance of success both because there was consensus among intellectuals over the value of pluralism in cultural life and because a feeling of solidarity within the various cultural professions overrode any particular disagreements.

The difference of opinion on the question of the viability of NEP in the area of culture points to the need for detailed examinations of the bases, extent, and dynamics of the controversies that divided intellectuals in various fields. The existing literature on the NEP years does not include such inquiries. Soviet scholars writing on the period have yet to raise the question of the cultural professions.[8] And Western historians have only begun to study the disputes that occurred within the cultural professions;[9] until recently, they have been more concerned to explore the organization and content of Soviet art and science in the 1920s.

A comprehensive study of the intellectual controversy in a field would be oriented around a series of related questions. First, there are the questions about the divisions among intellectuals. How did those working in a field divide according to intellectual position, social profile, professional orientation, institutional affiliation, and political commitments? Were the cleavages overlapping or crosscutting? Second, there are the questions about the cohesion of the profession. How much intellectual consensus was there? On what level did that consensus operate? On what factors was it based (agreement on substance, method, important questions, criteria of good work)? How much social solidarity was there in the profession? Were the disputants primarily loyal to their subgroups or to the profession as a whole? What bases for solidarity existed (institutional affiliation, distribution of power and authority in the field, the sharing of professional norms, training)?

A full assessment of the patterns of consensus and cleavage among Soviet intellectuals in the 1920s would require the study of a series of cultural professions. This book is a study of the infighting that occurred in one field of social science—that of rural social studies. There has to date been no full-scale study of Soviet social science under NEP; the two principal views of the origins of the Cultural Revolution described above are based on research in the natural sciences and the arts.[10] It may well be that we shall find in rural social studies a pattern of dispute that differs substantially from either of those presented. As a single case study (the first in social science) this book is designed not to furnish generalizations but to raise questions about the extent to which the category of culture into which a field falls (the arts, humanities, social sciences, natural sciences) defines the nature of the disputes that occurred among its practitioners.

The Case

Social inquiry into the rural sector has had a long history in Russia. As early as the 1860s social statistics on the countryside were being collected systematically;[11] in the 1880s and 1890s talented individuals were doing secondary analysis of the statistical data;[12] and by 1910 some courses in rural social studies were being offered in agricultural academies, polytechnical institutes, and universities.[13] It was, however, the Revolution of 1917 that provided the real impetus for the development of rural social studies. The Bolshevik seizure of power brought with it unprecedented interest in the rural sector, upon which depended both the economic prosperity and political stability of the new regime. With the Soviet government now assuming the role of patron and client of all the sciences, the field of rural social studies grew rapidly. New research and teaching centers were founded, new journals were created, and talented young people were recruited into the field. Ambitious research projects were undertaken, and a range of methods of social research were employed, with varying degrees of sophistication.[14]

For the first half of the 1920s, the most vital—indeed, the only fully articulated—area of rural social studies was agricultural economics. Institutionalized in specialized academies and institutes, Soviet agricultural economics in the NEP period was microeconomic in focus and practical in orientation. The major topic of study was the internal organization of the small-scale family farm, and the results of the research were directed at least as much at practicing agronomists as at economic scholars.

In the second half of the 1920s, the field of rural social studies was expanded to include research on questions of rural social stratificaton which had not been dealt with by the

Russian agricultural economists of the day. These questions, which focused attention on interfarm relations, were at the core of the specialty known as "rural sociology," although this label was not used by the Soviet researchers who pioneered the new direction in inquiry. Within a short time the sociological perspective in rural studies gained widespread acceptance in Russia.

The emergence of the new orientation to the study of the countryside constituted for Soviet rural studies a dilemma similar to that facing American rural studies at about the same time.[15] At the heart of the dilemma lay the relationship between the economic and sociological approaches to the study of the rural sector. Which perspective would have priority in the field of rural social studies? How, if at all, could the two approaches be combined?

The relationship between the new and the traditional approaches in rural studies was defined during a protracted controversy among rural scholars. The participants in the dispute were divided into two main groups. The first was the Organization-Production scholars, who were agricultural economists. Prominent in the field since the early years of the twentieth century, this group was the establishment in rural studies. Throughout the NEP period it continued to occupy positions of importance in rural studies, despite the fact that its members were not Marxists by conviction. The second group was the Agrarian-Marxists, whose research lay in the area of rural sociology. Committed Marxists, these scholars were considerably younger than their rivals and, for much of the 1920s, occupied positions subordinate to them. Thus, the differences between the groups in intellectual orientation were overlaid with differences in age, professional standing, and political sympathies; consequently, the struggle over the definition of the main lines in rural social studies was at the same time a rivalry for prestige between new and established cadres of rural scholars.[16]

The controversy in the field of rural social studies was a protracted one; it began in 1923 and was not resolved until mid-1928. Even the resolution did not bring surcease from strife. Late in 1928 the field of rural social studies experienced the Cultural Revolution. Marxist credentials became a prerequisite for any scholar who proposed to do social research on the countryside, and the Communist Party became the final arbiter of truth in the field of rural inquiry. With these developments, the most productive period in the history of rural social studies in Russia came to an abrupt end.[17]

For a consideration of the questions in Soviet history to which this book is addressed, the case of rural social studies has certain advantages. First, the controversy between the contending groups is well documented. Confrontations between the disputants were recorded in the stenographic reports of public meetings and scholarly working sessions, and the issues were aired at length in printed journals and monographs. The value of these ample records is enhanced by the fact that during the 1920s public discussion of the Soviet countryside was relatively frank and free of circumlocution. This extensive documentation will facilitate our assessment of the consensus and cleavage among rural social scholars. Second, within the course of a single decade, the field of rural social studies experienced not only a protracted controversy but also the direct and sudden intervention of the Communist Party in the conduct of inquiry. This will make it easier for us to evaluate the relative impact of professional infighting and political intervention upon the fate of rural social studies.

Implications for the Sociology of Science

In addition to its importance for the questions of Soviet history that lie at the core of this book, the study of Soviet rural inquiry in the 1920s should be of interest on several counts to sociologists who study the enterprise of science. First, our examination of the development of rural social studies in Russia will entail an analysis of the impact on the field of the infighting among scholars. Therefore our study may be seen as part of the growing literature on the impact of intellectual disputes upon the evolution of science.[18]

Research on this question done by sociologists of science suggests that the course of scientific development in a field may be substantially affected by intellectual dissensus among its practitioners. Controversies have been found to exert considerable impact upon the content of a field, sometimes altering its priorities,[19] at other times leading to the growth of new specialties.[20] Disputes have been discovered to affect the behavior of scientists, both in their roles as bearers of ideas[21] and as members of the same social community.[22] Intellectual disagreements have also been known to affect the organization of science—the distribution of authority within a scientific community and the structure of research activities.[23]

The dispute among scholars studying the countryside was an integral part of the development of rural social inquiry in the USSR. Indeed, the field expanded its boundaries against the background of a heated and lengthy controversy among its practitioners. A new perspective in rural studies emerged, put forward by a group of young scholars who were in revolt against the traditional conception of the field in which they had been trained. The emergence of this new perspective raised two questions that were to underlie the substance of the scholarly dispute. What was to be the relationship between the traditional and the novel approaches to the study of the countryside? And what was to be the relationship of the established and the new cadres of scholars working in the field?

A comparison of the state of rural social studies in 1923, when the dispute began, and mid-1928, when the controversy was resolved, reveals the way in which these two questions were settled. Looking at the details of that settlement, we shall first ask how the controversy affected the intellectual content of the field. Did the dispute affect the rank ordering of scholars' concerns, exert pressure for new studies, or stimulate the development of new methods of research? On balance, did the controversy lead to the broadening or narrowing of the boundaries of rural studies? And second, we shall inquire how the dispute affected the community of scholars. Did it lead to a redistribution of status and authority among those studying the countryside? Did it change the patterns of communication and work in the scholarly community? In answering these questions, we shall attempt to the extent possible to pinpoint those features of the dispute (its duration, the centrality or marginality of its issues for the field as a whole, its implications for education in the field, and its bearing on public policy)[24] that were responsible for the effects observed.

Our treatment of the controversy in Soviet rural studies should be of interest to sociologists who study science for yet another reason. We shall not restrict our inquiry to an examination of the process of controversy—the refinement of the issues, the conduct of the disputants, and the achievement of a resolution; we shall also attempt to determine the impact upon that process of the social environment within which the dispute took place. In dealing with the influence on science of its social environment, this study treats a question of major concern in the sociology of science.

There is a fairly extensive literature on the impact of social factors on science.[25] There have been studies of the way in which science unfolds in relation to such external social factors as the economic, political, religious, and military institutions in a society.[26] And there have been studies of the impact upon the scientific enterprise of the internal social organization of science itself—its social structure and value system.[27]

In this work we will explore the impact on the controversy in rural studies of both sets of social factors—the social context within which the rural social scientists lived and the professional organization of their field of inquiry. Broadly speaking, the *social context* within which scientists conduct their research is composed of a number of aspects of the society in which they find themselves: its needs, its goals and commitments, and its socioeconomic structure, to name only a few. Without doubt, all of these features have some general bearing on the conduct of science, but the precise nature and extent of that bearing is often difficult to specify. There are, however, features of the social context that have been found to bear directly on scientific work. Of these, two in particular may be cited: the policy toward scholarship pursued by the agency (state or private) responsible for supporting science[28] and the state policy in the areas tangent to the subject matter of inquiry.[29] In the interests of precision, we have decided to resist the lure of broad interpretation and to limit our discussion of the social context of Soviet rural studies to a consideration of these two factors.

Similarly, the category *professional organization of science* can also be a broad one. It can refer to a wide variety of features of the environment within which scientists work: their patterns of communication and exchange of information, the reward system in their science, the structure of scientific publications, the stratification system of science, and the organization of research work.[30] In this instance as well, we shall be selective and consider under the rubric "professional organization" only the following features of Soviet rural studies in the 1920s: the structure of the community of scholars (the allocation of roles and the distribution of status and authority among scientists) and the structure and profile of the major research and teaching institutions in the field.

The examination of the impact of the social environment on the controversy in rural social studies will lead us to explore further a distinction that until now has only been implicit in the sociological literature—namely, the distinction between social influences and social pressures on science.[31] Social factors have been found to have an impact on almost every aspect of science: its foci of attention, its priorities, the allocation of its resources, and the behavior of its researchers. As a rule, the impact of these factors has been limited to the influencing or shaping of science; only rarely have such factors acted as a pressure on science, impeding its functioning. The limited experience we do have of pressure on science suggests that its major source in our age may be the state.[32] In the instances we know of, the state has sought to enforce a policy that requires of scientists their primary allegiance and demands that they set aside the canons of their profession whenever those canons conflict with the needs of the state. Such a policy come to constitute a political pressure on science in that it clashes with the scientists' conviction that the political preferences of the state should be irrelevant, both to the assessment of the validity of research and to the status of a researcher in the scientific community.[33] In their impact on science, political pressures differ in kind from social influences. In the short run such pressures may simply hinder the conduct of inquiry. Sustained over a period of time, they stand to transform an area of inquiry from a scholarly to a "politicized" field. In a politicized field of inquiry, scientists would be constrained to accept as true propositions imposed by a political authority, and the standing of a scientist in the community of researchers would be directly affected by his political beliefs and affiliations.[34]

In our study of Soviet rural inquiry, we expect to find evidence of the extensive influence of social factors on science. By virtue of its content, the field of rural studies was close to the core concerns of the state; indeed, for the Bolshevik leaders, who had taken power in an overwhelmingly rural country, the determination of rural policy was a major preoccupation. Consequently, it is to be anticipated that the scholars working in rural social studies would be influenced, to some degree at least, by the main lines of official policy toward the country-side. That influence would be the stronger in that rural social studies, like all fields of Soviet science, was totally supported by the state.

But evidence of the influence—even the extensive influence—of a social factor such as the policy commitments of the agency responsible for supporting a science says nothing in itself about the existence of social pressure on that science. We do know that at the end of the 1920s scholars working in rural social studies came to feel severe pressure from the state; indeed, political pressure on science was the single most important characteristic of the Cultural Revolution in rural social studies. The questions for research are the following. At what point did political pressure on rural studies begin? What new demands on science resulted from the presence of this pressure? What was the relationship between the social factors that constituted the pressure and those that had earlier acted only to influence the shape and direction of rural social science? In part at least, the present study will be devoted to answering these questions.

The book is divided into four parts. The first of these is introductory in nature. Chapter 1 has presented the problems to which the study is addressed and the case upon which it is based. Chapter 2 outlines the social and intellectual background of Soviet rural studies in the NEP period. The second part of the book, which is made up of four chapters, treats the controversy in its early phase (1923 to 1927). In this part, the position of each group is set forth separately. Chapters 3 and 4 examine respectively the theory and the research of the Organization-Production scholars. Chapters 5 and 6 explore respectively the theoretical orientation of the Agrarian-Marxists and their empirical work. The third part of the book, composed of three chapters, examines the controversy in its later phase (1927 to mid-1928). Chapter 7 describes a public meeting between the two groups, a meeting that triggered important changes in the issues around which the controversy centered. Chapter 8 canvasses the dispute strategies of the contending groups in this period, and chapter 9 chronicles the resolution of the controversy. The fourth part of the book concludes the study. Chapter 10 describes the denouement to our story—the onset of the Cultural Revolution in the field of rural inquiry—and chapter 11 draws out the implications of our case both for the study of certain questions in Soviet history and for problems in the sociology of science.

2. Rural Social Studies in the 1920s

Before tracing the course of the controversy itself, we shall examine the broader environment within which the dispute occurred. We begin with an exploration of the relevant social environment—specifically, the social context and the professional organization of the field of rural inquiry. We will then examine the intellectual content of the field in which the controversy took place.

The Social Context of Rural Studies

Two features of the social context of rural studies influenced the development of the field of inquiry in a demonstrable way: official policy toward the countryside and official policy toward social science.

The Russian countryside presented the Bolshevik leaders with a very delicate policy problem. They had inherited a rural sector whose basic unit of cultivation was the family household or *dvor*.[1] In most cases the *dvor* was a member of the repartitional commune, or *obshchina*,[2] and therefore had to submit to periodic redistribution of *dvor* land into strips often separated from one another by considerable distances. Moreover, because the *dvor* was a family unit, its holdings were subject to division when the family's children matured and left home or when disputes among family members could not be resolved.[3] The tiny size and disparate location of *dvor* holdings meant that cultivation could not be carried out with anything but the most rudimentary of equipment; indeed, the implements most often seen in the countryside in the 1920s were the wooden plough, the scythe, and the sickle.[4] To these tiny, inefficient *dvory* the Russian peasants showed themselves remarkably attached.[5] Though they did cooperate voluntarily with one another in the performance of a number of agricultural tasks, the peasants clung resolutely to their individual farms.[6] For much of the 1920s, the Soviet Union was predominantly a land of small peasant farms.[7]

Reared in the Russian Marxism of the twentieth century, the Bolshevik leaders were committed to the transformation of the rural sector they had inherited into one based on large-scale units of cultivation that would be farmed by the peasants on a collective basis with the aid of complex machinery.[8] But the bitter experiences of the period of War Communism (1918-1921) suggested that this commitment had to held in abeyance. The new regime had but scant support among the peasantry, upon whose goodwill depended the entire Soviet economy. Consequently, any action that might alienate the peasantry by flying in the face of custom or ingrained attitude had to be avoided. The New Economic Policy was an attempt by the Bolshevik leadership to forge a rural policy that would reflect these constraints.

Broadly speaking, the rural policy in force for much of the 1920s was based on a series of interrelated assumptions.[9] The most basic of these was that a country like the Soviet Union, whose economy was based primarily on a "petit bourgeois" agricultural sector, could not evolve to socialism without a transitional period devoted to raising agricultural productivity and fostering favorable (read "collectivist") attitudes among the peasantry. In this transition period the economy would be mixed: its "commanding heights" (heavy industry, mining, banking, transport, and foreign trade) would be in the hands of the state, but farming and crafts would continue to be conducted by the small commodity producer. This premise had two corollaries, each addressed to the problem of dealing with that difficult and enigmatic figure, the Russian peasant.[10] First, it was assumed that the best way to get the peasant to increase his grain production and delivery was through the use of market incentives; coercive measures would lead him to withhold his produce from the state. Second, it was assumed that no amount of force could alter the economic attitudes of the rural population; only prolonged participation in the voluntary cooperatives would condition the peasant to set aside his individualism in favor of a collectivist orientation.[11]

These assumptions were general in nature and, therefore, served only as the boundaries within which policy was formulated. Left open were such important questions as the duration of the transition period, the pattern of peasant evolution to socialism, the relation between economic growth and social change, and the link between the agricultural and industrial sectors of the economy. These questions became the subject of heated debates on several levels of Soviet society. They were focal points in the struggle for the leadership of the Communist Party that ensued after Lenin's death, and they were aired extensively within the bureaucracy, wherever agencies were charged with the task of planning economic development.

The debates over rural policy that took place among political leaders and bureaucrats will not be rehearsed here for several reasons. To begin with, they have received excellent treatment in a number of Western books published recently.[12] But more important, there is no evidence that the debate on either the levels mentioned above affected in a material way the dispute among scholars—the subject of this book. That is not to say that the rural scholars whose fortunes we shall follow were ivory-tower intellectuals with no interest in practical policy. As educated and involved citizens, they surely had preferences—even strong preferences—among the positions on the countryside expressed by the politicians contending for Lenin's mantle. Moreover, in the postrevolutionary period, many of these scholars came to serve as consultants to governmental agencies dealing with specific facets of rural policy.[13] The scholars probably prized their participation in these arenas; their roles as experts gave them added status and lent legitimacy to their scholarly activities.[14] But our reading of the events suggests that those who studied the Russian countryside identified themselves first and foremost as scholars. Their primary concern was the expansion of the frontiers of knowledge in their field. This concern was clearly reflected in the range of research they undertook, a range far greater than the net of peasant questions debated in either the political or the bureaucratic circles. In light of this reading, we cannot give credence to the suggestion that Soviet scholarly work was a subscript to the dramas being played out among politicians or bureaucrats. In our view, such a suggestion impoverishes—and therefore distorts—the meaning of what was occurring within the field of rural social studies during NEP; and it unfairly prejudges the degree of scholarly autonomy that prevailed in Soviet Russia prior to the advent of the Cultural Revolution. At most, we might accept as an hypothesis the statement by Shanin that the discord among politicians during the 1920s created a general atmosphere conducive to a heterogeneity of views among scholars.[15]

Though Soviet rural scholars seemed to have been little affected by the discussions among politicians and bureaucrats, they were both aware of and influenced by the palpable shifts of emphasis in official policy toward the countryside that occurred between 1923 and mid-1928.

In the first half of the decade, the primary aims of the Soviet regime were economic recovery and political stabilization. The Revolution and Civil War had left the regime with a severely depressed economy and a polity over which it had but tenuous control. So pressing were these problems that the determination to solve them took precedence over all other goals, even over the goal of the transition to socialism, in the name of which the October Revolution had been fought. Consequently, until 1926 the regime seemed bent on courting the individual peasant. A series of measures gave the peasant what he desired most—the right to market any grain that remained after he had paid the agricultural tax, the right to hire and lease both land and labor, and security of tenure in land.[16] In introducing these measures, the Party leaders admitted that they were entrenching individual farming and thus postponing the coming of socialism. However, they rationalized this course of action with the Leninist argument of 1921 that without the goodwill of the individual peasant, the Soviet economy, based as it was on small-scale agriculture, would never recover.[17] Even the long-range economic plans drafted during this period reflected the official preference for stability over change. The plan for agriculture drawn up by the RSFSR Commissariat for Agriculture (*Narkomzem* RSFSR) at the end of 1924 made no mention of any imminent conversion to large-scale socialist units of cultivation; in fact, the planners set their targets on the assumption that agriculture would continue to be conducted by a large, decentralized mass of individual farms.[18] At a meeting called the next year to review this plan, a lone voice was raised in support of socioeconomic change in the countryside, but it was silenced with the assertion that such change was out of tune with the Party line on the rural sector.[19]

By 1926 the Soviet economy had been restored to its 1913 level, and the Communist Party had secured hegemony over the political arena. These pressing tasks having been accomplished, the regime was now free to devote its energies to the building of socialism in Russia. The reordering of official priorities was mirrored in rural policy. The year 1925 proved to be the high point of the policy of conciliating the peasantry. Thereafter, the regime was increasingly less wedded to the individual peasant and his needs. In the course of 1927, as the difficulties with the individual farm sector began to multiply, decrees were passed calling for the strengthening of large-scale state and collective farms and urging tighter organization of the rural cooperatives.[20] Though in themselves innocuous, these decrees symbolized the Party's revived determination to restructure the countryside. As such they heralded a shift of emphasis in official policy toward the rural sector. Although the intent of these decrees differed from that underlying governmental measures before 1926, it did not in any way contravene what we have termed the "NEP assumptions." No mention was made of using force to effect the desired socioeconomic change. It would be another two years before such a suggestion would be voiced.

In the NEP period there were two prongs to official policy toward the social sciences. The Party's long-range objective was to foster the growth of a Marxist science of society. But in the short run, the Party strove simply to support existing social inquiry, whatever the ideological inclinations of the researchers.[21] The short-run aim may have been more than a stalling device; the Party may well have believed that, given time, it would win the allegiance of the non-Marxist social scientists.[22]

In the five-year period during which the field of rural social studies was enmeshed in controversy, there was a significant shift in the balance between these two goals. Before 1926 the long-range objective received very little attention. To be sure, the Communist (originally, the Socialist) Academy was established in 1918 as a teaching and research center for Marxist social science.[23] But in a variety of ways the Party encouraged the activity of the social science centers that had been established in universities and specialized institutions of higher learning before the Revolution. It left the administration of these centers largely free of its control[24] and permitted noncommunists and even non-Marxists who had been prominent before 1917 to continue their work here. Admittedly, neither the ideological diversity in the scientific community nor the administrative autonomy accorded the research centers was guaranteed in law,[25] but during the first half of NEP it was the Party's practice to accommodate existing social science. The logic behind this practice was sound. In the early 1920s the prerevolutionary social science centers were the main sources of creative inquiry; until the middle of the decade the Communist Academy concentrated primarily on pedagogy, as did the new communist universities created in the early 1920s.[26] And, until well into the NEP period, the pool of capable communist social scientists was woefully small. Thus, to withdraw support from the pre-Soviet centers or to exclude noncommunists from scientific activity would have effectively decimated social science in Russia—a consequence that the fledgling regime apparently did not wish to bring about. Finally, the disastrous state of the economy and the unstable political situation forced the Party to concentrate its energies upon controlling activity in the economic and political arenas;[27] in comparison with these pressing tasks, the regulation of social science was of secondary importance.[28]

The new emphasis on the building of socialism that came to the fore in 1926 altered the balance of goals in official policy toward social science scholarship. The long-term aim of creating a socialist science of society came to displace the short-term goal. Beginning in late 1925, there was a substantial expansion of Soviet social science institutions. New research centers were set up, and a concerted attempt was made to attract to those centers the most capable Marxist social scientists.[29] Moreover, the Party now began to assert some control over these centers.[30] It should be noted that the new efforts to develop socialist social inquiry were initially accompanied neither by serious restrictions on the activity of non-Marxist scholars nor by prescriptions about content issued by nonscientific authorities. Such limitations would begin only after the middle of 1928.

The shifts of emphasis in rural and in social science policy in the period 1923 to mid-1928 were considerable, yet they pale by comparison to those that took place after the middle of 1928. The latter shifts had their roots in two events in early 1928. The first of these occurred in the winter, when the regime sanctioned "measures of extreme severity" to ensure the collection of the needed amount of grain. These measures included the loosing of armed detachments against the peasants, the confiscation of grain stocks, the arrest of peasants who failed to deliver their promised quotas, and the closing of some free markets.[31] In giving its approval to these measures, the regime deviated sharply from its policy of using persuasion rather than coercion in dealing with the rural sector. Second, in the spring of that same year a group of engineers and technical specialists working in the coal industry in the Shakhty region of the Donbass were accused of industrial sabotage and brought to trial.[32] This event, known as the "Shakhty trial," was the first public attack by the Party upon the noncommunist intelligentsia whom it had been so careful to court since the Revolution.[33]

At the time these events occurred their meaning was not fully clear. Indeed, there was severe disagreement about their interpretation in the highest Party circles. Some segments of the leadership regarded the use of force against the peasantry as an exceptional device adopted solely to overcome the results of the disastrous harvest of 1927; others saw this measure as a test of a new path to rural development.[34] Again, some of the political leaders regarded the "sabotage" at Shakhty as an isolated occurrence, while others viewed it as but the first manifestation of pervasive treason by the "bourgeois specialists."[35] With the benefit of hindsight, it is clear that these two events were harbingers of a new period. In that period rural studies, like other fields of Soviet scholarship, would be profoundly changed.

Professional Organization of Rural Social Studies

For most of the 1920s, the major center for study and research on the Russian rural sector was the Timiriazev Agricultural Academy, situated just outside Moscow. Founded in 1865 as the Petrovskii Agricultural Academy,[36] this institution entered the Soviet period with a checkered history that was reflected in its frequent changes of name.[37] In the late nineteenth and early twentieth century, the Academy was well known for the political radicalism of its students, and consequently, for the first half-century of its existence, it was subjected to continual scrutiny—and occasional punitive action—by the Tsarist government.[38] In contrast to its early history, the decade of the 1920s was a bright period for the Academy.[39] Under the Bolshevik regime this institution, renamed the Timiriazev Agricultural Academy in 1923,[40] acquired a legitimacy it had never had before. It developed close relations with government agencies, in particular with the RSFSR Commissariat of Agriculture;[41] indeed, the Academy published one of its most important journals, *Puti sel'skogo khoziaistva* [Paths of Agriculture],[42] in conjunction with that Commissariat. At the same time, the Academy expanded its operations significantly. It undertook an extensive program of recruitment,[43] as a result of which it could by 1925 boast an enrollment of some three thousand students (undergraduate and graduate)—a figure that made it the largest such institution in all of Europe.[44]

During much of the period under study the Timiriazev Academy had only one developed area of social studies on the countryside—agricultural economics. The unique position of this social science was reflected in the organization of undergraduate instruction. In 1922, when the faculty structure was introduced into the Academy,[45] the faculty of "agricultural economics and policy" took its place alongside the faculties of agronomy, engineering, fisheries, and forestry.[46] The following year the faculties of fisheries and forestry were dissolved,[47] leaving the student to choose from among agronomy, engineering, and agricultural economics. This revised organization of instruction was retained until late 1928.[48] As a result, for most of the NEP period any student who wished to do social studies of agriculture in this prestigious institution had perforce to enroll in the faculty of agricultural economics.[49]

Research on agricultural economics also enjoyed special status in the Timiriazev Academy during this period. In 1923 the seminar on agricultural economics, which had been founded in the Petrovskii Academy in 1919,[50] was converted into a separate research institute known as the Scientific Research Institute on Agricultural Economics.[51] The members of this Institute regarded their center as the Soviet equivalent of the most important agricultural research centers of Western Europe—and not without reason.[52] The series of research reports (*trudy*) published by the Timiriazev Institute included some of the most creative social inquiry on the countryside published during NEP.[53] Nor did the Institute confine itself to research work. It carried out a full program of graduate instruction[54] and did extensive consultation (*nauchnoe obsluzhivanie*) for commissariats and economic agencies.[55] The research and pedagogic functions of the Institute were under the aegis of the Russian Association of Scientific Research Institutes for the Social Sciences (RANION); the administration of the Institute was under the jurisdiction of the Chief Administration of Scientific Institutes of the RSFSR Commissariat of Enlightenment (*Glavnauka Narkomprosa RSFSR*).[56]

So preeminent was the Timiriazev Academy that most of the important Russian scholars interested in the social study of the countryside in the NEP period were affiliated in some way with this institution. For example, in the years 1923 to 1926, the Academy housed the core of the two groups of scholars engaged in the controversy in rural social studies: the Organization-Production scholars and the Agrarian-Marxists. These groups were remarkably dissimilar; the members of one differed from those of the other in age, professional standing, attitudes toward scholarship, intellectual interests, and political sympathies. For most of the 1920s, the Organization-Production scholars were the undisputed leaders in the field of rural social studies in Russia. Well before 1917, these men had established reputations as agricultural economists[57] and occupied posts in the Timiriazev Academy (then the Moscow Agricultural Institute). Though committed primarily to studying Russian farming, these men took a "cosmopolitan" attitude toward scholarly work; they treated their foreign colleagues as an important reference group, exchanging research results with them on a regular basis.[58] For the first decade after 1917, the Organization-Production scholars retained their position of leadership, even though they were not Marxists by conviction and did not become members of the Communist Party.[59] They dominated the Timiriazev Academy's agricultural economics faculty, where they taught their courses; and the leader of the group, A. V. Chaianov, was the Director of the Academy's prestigious Institute on Agricultural Economics.[60] The Organization-Production scholars were among the principal contributors to the Academy's journal, *Puti sel'skogo khoziaistva*, and to the series of research reports published by the Institute on Agricultural Economics. By virtue of their positions and their activities, the members of this group played the leading role in training the first generation of Soviet specialists in rural social studies. By and large, the Organization-Production scholars' assumption of this role was accepted. There was some discontent expressed by undergraduates in the Academy, but these expressions were sporadic and directed less at the hegemony of the Chaianov group per se than at the absence of meaningful Marxist content in the Academy's curriculum.[61] The second set of scholars, the Agrarian-Marxists, were younger men.[62] With but a few exceptions, the members of this group came to maturity after the Revolution. In the first half of the 1920s they were still doing their graduate work in the Timiriazev Academy, where they were taught by and worked as research assistants to the Organization-Production scholars.[63] Only after the middle of the decade did the Agrarian-Marxists emerge as a force in the field of rural social studies.

The year 1925 proved to be a watershed in the professional organization of rural social studies. It ushered in important changes in the institutional structure of the field and in the distribution of status and authority within the community of scholars engaged in social research on the rural sector. The most significant of these changes stemmed from the creation in late 1925 of the Agrarian Section of the Communist Academy. The case for the founding of the new Section was presented to the June 1925 meeting of the Presidium of the Communist Academy by V. P. Miliutin, the Marxist agrarian expert. Miliutin made his proposal seem minimal. He claimed that in terms of the interest in subjects agrarian, there was justification for the creation of an institute, but that for reasons of prudence he was counseling only the founding of a section. For this section Miliutin predicted great success. He reminded his listeners that the special Agrarian Commission created in January 1925 to study the history of the Russian agrarian revolution had already attracted some fifteen scholars; a separate section with a broader mandate would undoubtedly bring together even more prominent Marxists interested in conducting social research on the countryside. Miliutin proved a persuasive advocate,[64] and the Agrarian Section was born.[65] The new Section, which was designed solely as a research unit, began its work with a staff of twenty-eight people.[66]

The Agrarian-Marxists working in the Timiriazev Academy were attracted to this newly created research unit. Affiliation with the Agrarian Section offered them a climate hospitable to their political views, the opportunity to devote all their efforts to studying the problem that interested them most—the social stratification of the peasantry—and the status of full-fledged researchers. Lured by these advantages, the Agrarian-Marxists joined the new Section soon after its creation.[67] Here they began to work on large collective projects under the intellectual and moral guidance of L. N. Kritsman.[68] The Agrarian-Marxists' work on rural social structure earned them the reputation in Russia of being the foremost Marxist social researchers studying the countryside. (Unlike their former teachers, these researchers were decidedly "local" in their attitude toward scholarship;[69] they evinced little interest in the opinions of their colleagues abroad, although some members of the group did visit research centers outside Russia.)[70] As their reputation grew, the interests of the Agrarian-Marxists came to dominate the Section as a whole. Indeed, the Agrarian Section soon became identified with the pursuit of rural sociology.[71] Working as they did under these auspicious conditions, the members of the Kritsman group developed a sense of cohesiveness and a deep institutional loyalty. These sentiments were reinforced by the fact that the Agrarian-Marxists served as the editors of and became some of the principal contributors to the Section's journal, *Na agrarnom fronte*.[72] Under the stewardship of the Agrarian-Marxists, the Agrarian Section prospered. It acquired more staff and took on new projects. In addition to its functions as a research unit, it began to do consulting work for government agencies.[73] In late 1928 it was elevated to the status of Institute within the Communist Academy.[74]

The founding of the Agrarian Section altered the professional organization of rural studies in two important ways. First, the Timiriazev Academy gradually lost its position of preeminence, since, once founded, the Agrarian Section became an alternative setting for social research on the rural sector. Indeed, before long the Agrarian Section was able to draw some of the best young students away from the Timiriazev Academy. Second, the hierarchical structure that had characterized the community of rural scholars prior to 1925 was leveled; now that community was composed of two groups of scholars equal to each other in status, if not in achievement.

Of less immediate, but of ultimately equal, importance in shaping the evolution of Soviet rural studies was the creation in 1926 of the International Agrarian Institute in Moscow.[75] Founded as the research center for the Peasant International, the Moscow Institute was envisaged as a counterweight to the venerable International Institute of Agriculture in Rome.[76] The new Institute had a broad mandate: the study of social relations in agriculture throughout the world.[77] In keeping with that mandate, the membership of the Institute included many specialists on foreign agriculture;[78] and every issue of its journal *Agrarnye problemy* [Agrarian Problems] carried articles and reviews about farming abroad. Initially, the Institute devoted comparatively little attention to Soviet agriculture.[79] As the decade wore on, however, led by its deputy director S. M. Dubrovskii,[80] it began to sponsor studies of Soviet farming and to make claims to speak authoritatively about the Soviet internal scene. By the end of the decade, the personnel of the Institute had become figures to be reckoned with in the community of Soviet social researchers on the rural sector.

Intellectual Content of Rural Social Studies

During the period of NEP, the substance of the Soviet field of rural social studies was broadened substantially. For the first half of the 1920s, as for the years immediately before the Revolution, the only developed area of social inquiry on the countryside was agricultural economics. The focus of attention in that specialty was the question of the internal dynamics of the individual peasant farm. In the mid-1920s, there arose a new object of interest in rural studies—the socioeconomic relations between farms. As this became an increasingly popular topic of inquiry, there was born in Russia a new specialty, which we will call "rural sociology." For most of the second half of the 1920s, the specialties of agricultural economics and rural sociology coexisted within the single field of rural social studies. Each had its own cognitive goals, but the fact that they were part of the same field—and were vying for primacy in that field—shaped the development of those goals.

From a methodological point of view, the rural social inquiry done in Russia in the 1920s was less sophisticated than that conducted at the same time in America or in certain countries of Western Europe, notable Germany. The Russian scholars certainly used the methods of field research (interviews and social surveys) so popular at the time. However, they were not pioneers in this area; one looks in vain in the Soviet rural research of the 1920s for novel ideas about survey sampling, the organization of field work, or data quality control.[81] Nor did the Soviet researchers always trouble to borrow the most advanced techniques in use elsewhere. For the problems confronting them were, in degree at least, different from those their foreign colleagues faced. To the Soviet rural researcher in the NEP period, the very collection of data was problematic. The Russian peasant was either too illiterate to keep records of the operation of his farm or too secretive to divulge accurate information about his well-being. Discussions of devices to obviate, or even minimize, these obstacles run like a red thread through the Russian rural scholarship of the day. These discussions reveal as much about conditions in the Soviet countryside as they do about the intellectual concerns of the researchers.

Agricultural Economics

Appearances would suggest that the Soviet brand of agricultural economics that predominated for most of the NEP period was a cross between the practical orientation of the American school of farm management developed between 1900 and 1920[82] and the theoretical approach characteristic of the German school of *landwirtschaftliche Betriebslehre* ("science of farm management") refined between 1905 and 1925 by such scholars as Aeroboe and Waterstradt.[83] Like the Americans, the Soviet agricultural economists were concerned to devise maxims that would assist the farmer in making decisions about cultivation patterns and farm organization; like their German counterparts, the Russians were interested in ferreting out the economic laws that governed farm activity.[84]

For all its external similarities to the German and American work, Soviet agricultural economics in the 1920s was highly distinctive, even idiosyncratic, in character. Its distinctiveness stemmed from the fact that its content was based on the study of the family farm, a commodity-producing economic unit that functioned without benefit of hired labor.[85] The family farm was not unique to Russia, but only there did its features shape the science of agricultural economics. That the Russian science was so closely linked to the study of the family farm should not be surprising. The years in which the field of agricultural economics was developed and institutionalized in agricultural academies and institutes (1910-1927) were those in which the family farm was the predominant form of agriculture in Russia.[86]

The credit (and the responsibility) for orienting the Russian field of agricultural economics in the direction described above belongs to the Organization-Production scholars, who dominated the field during its period of greatest development. The preoccupation of these men with the family farm can be traced to their early work experiences. During the first decade and a half of the twentieth century, many of the Organization-Production scholars were employed as agronomists by the *zemstva* (local governing councils).[87] Working as they did in the villages of Russia, these men witnessed at first hand the limited success of the Stolypin land reforms (1906-1910).[88] They became convinced that the redistribution of land would not in itself alleviate rural backwardness. What was needed was the thoroughgoing reorganization of agriculture—the intensification of production, the introduction of complex farm machinery, and the relegation of certain farm tasks to the rural cooperatives. Such reorganization, they came to believe, could not be legislated from above; it could only be effected through long and patient work with the peasantry. For these young men, agronomy, not politics, held the key to rural change.[89] They demanded of the agronomy in which they placed their faith that it be "scientific," founded on a precise understanding of the principles underlying the organization of agriculture and the behavior of the farmer. Their own observations of peasant life, coupled with the comments made by other agricultural officials,[90] persuaded them that the predominant form of farming in Russia, the family farm, was a distinctive economic unit whose springs of action had yet to be uncovered. To fill this important gap, the agronomists turned from a practical career to the full-time study of the family farm.

Over the course of a decade, the Organization-Production scholars formulated a theory of the internal dynamics of the family, or "noncapitalist," farm. To flesh out this theory, they examined every aspect of the farm they had described. They examined the principles underlying the farmer's calculation of optimal farm size and intensity of cultivation; with the help of data on the farm's resource budget, they analyzed farm organization; they charted the impact on the structure of a farm of its participation in cooperatives; and they traced the evolution of Russian farming by examining agriculture in various regions.[91]

The field of agricultural economics shaped by the Organization-Production scholars had two major characteristics. First, it was microeconomic in focus. Its major concern was the internal operation of the Russian family farm; little attention was paid to the relation of that farm to the rural sector, much less to the national economy as a whole.[92] This microeconomic focus was the result of a deliberate choice by the Chaianov group. Between 1890 and 1910 there had existed in Russia a fairly well developed tradition of studies in agricultural economics focusing on the problem of economic and social inequities among the peasantry. That tradition, whose leaders included some well-known Russian Marxists and populists, was never institutionalized in centers of learning and research.[93] In discussing their concentration on the internal structure of the individual farm, the Organization-Production scholars repeatedly underscored the extent to which they were breaking with the earlier tradition in their field.[94] Second, Soviet agricultural economics in the 1920s had a strong practical orientation. The Organization-Production scholars showed considerable talent as theorists, but they insisted on viewing themselves as applied social scientists whose task it was to provide sound guidance to agricultural officials working with the peasantry. The practical orientation of these men was reinforced by the fact that they were teaching and conducting research in specialized agricultural academies that prepared students for careers in agronomy or government service.[95] As the decade of NEP came to a close, both the microeconomic focus and the applied orientation of Soviet agricultural economics would come under attack.

Rural Sociology

In the middle of the NEP period, the boundaries of rural social studies were stretched to include the sort of inquiry that would subsequently become the core of rural sociology. The earliest Soviet studies in the new genre were conducted under the supervision of senior Organization-Production scholars working in the Timiriazev Academy's Institute on Agricultural Economics.[96] Formal arrangements notwithstanding, the supervision exercised by the agricultural economists was nominal. The research directors allowed their young assistants great scope for initiative and displayed little, if any, interest in the progress of the sociological work.[97] Indeed, one suspects that the Organization-Production scholars carried out their duties in this instance primarily because the sociological projects had been commissioned by a government agency that was one of the Institute's most important patrons.[98]

The agricultural economists' lack of interest in sociological work was more than offset by the enthusiasm of an emerging group of researchers. These researchers, who became known as the Agrarian-Marxists, soon claimed the new perspective as their province, stamping it with their own preoccupations and concerns.

The Agrarian-Marxists came to the study of the countryside without any background in general sociology,[99] but with a sound training in agricultural economics acquired during their graduate studies in the Timiriazev Academy. As a consequence, these young scholars defined the content of what was to be Russian rural sociology in terms of the lacunae in agricultural economics.

Although the Agrarian-Marxists referred to themselves not as sociologists, but as "agrarian experts" (*agrarniki*), the concerns of this group of scholars were clearly sociological (and are touted as such by present-day Soviet historians of sociological thought).[100] Indeed, the Agrarian-Marxists were interested almost exclusively in the study of rural stratification (or "differentiation," as they called it), a study that they believed crucial to an understanding of the evolution of the peasantry. As Marxists, they believed in both the desirability and the inevitability of the evolution of the peasantry to socialism; as researchers, they devoted all their energies to constructing maps of social stratification from which they could read the pattern of that evolution.

In the view of the Agrarian-Marxists, the salient form of stratification was social. These young researchers were concerned not with economic disparities as such, but with the relations of subordination and superordination that arose among peasants because of economic disparities in the possession of the necessary means of cultivation.[101] As a reliable indicator of the social relations they deemed significant, the Agrarian-Marxists chose the web of hire-and-lease transactions among peasants. To ferret out these transactions, the researchers used a variety of techniques—surveys, in-depth interviews of peasants, and budget inquiry—often in combination. To the data elicited by these various techniques, the Agrarian-Marxists applied complex systems of classification upon which they then based their maps of rural social structure.

Having devised what they believed was a successful methodology for the study of peasant stratification, the Agrarian-Marxists applied it with great energy to region after region in Russia. As a consequence of their efforts, between 1925 and 1929 there appeared in print a substantial corpus of rural stratification studies, all of which used variants of the same method. The energies expended by the young researchers were handsomely rewarded. The study of peasant social structure came to occupy a prominent place in Russian rural inquiry. Moreover, thanks to the Russian sociologist Pitirim Sorokin, who immigrated to the United States in 1923 and reshaped rural sociology there,[102] the examination of rural stratification was given pride of place in American rural sociology.[103]

The rural sociology that emerged under the stewardship of the Agrarian-Marxists had two central characteristics. First, it was very limited in its scope. The field did not progress beyond its original preoccupation with the single, albeit central, problem of rural stratification. The Agrarian-Marxist scholarship of the 1920s reflects none of the concern with rural life in its manifold dimensions that infused American sociology of the countryside in the same period;[104] one cannot even find in the Agrarian-Marxist work references to the rich literature in rural ethnography produced by Soviet scholars.[105] In short, Soviet rural sociology of the 1920s never transcended its origins as a scientific specialty born of revolt against an older discipline.

Second, Soviet rural sociology of the NEP period was almost entirely atheoretical. For the Agrarian-Marxists, the eschewing of theory was a conscious choice rather than the result of intellectual disinclination. In fact, the Agrarian-

Marxists began their work on rural stratification with an excursion into theory. As the first generation of Soviet Marxists to study the Russian rural sector, they were determined to demonstrate that the change of regime in 1917 had affected the evolution of the Russian peasantry. Hence they derided as "outmoded" the assumptions about rural evolution made by their prerevolutionary Marxist ancestors, and they refined a theory of rural development according to which the Russian peasantry in its transition to socialism could skip the stage of capitalism. However, the results of their early studies of rural stratification convinced the Agrarian-Marxists that the volume of hire-and-lease transactions in the countryside was on the rise and that the Russian peasantry was becoming increasingly capitalist. In response to the dissensus between their novel theory arrived at by assertion and their empirical findings, the Agrarian-Marxists set aside discussion of theory and concentrated on data collection. They structured their research projects around the hypothesis that capitalism was on the rise in the countryside, and the stratification maps they produced testified to the growing polarization of the peasantry into landless laborers and rural capitalists. Perhaps understandably, the Agrarian-Marxists never used their findings to modify their original theory; they simply made no reference to the postulates of that theory for the remainder of the decade.[106]

Had time and conditions permitted, Soviet rural sociology might have expanded in scope, and its practitioners might have gone beyond their exclusively empirical orientation. But the history of the field was a brief one. Indeed, so short was the period of gestation and development of Soviet rural sociology that it never became institutionalized as a social science in a university or agricultural academy. It remained a specialty in which expertise and skills were transmitted through on-the-job training.

Part 2
The First Stage of the Controversy, 1923 to 1927

Introduction

In the initial phase of the dispute, the two groups of scholars were engaged in a disagreement over the research goals for the field of rural social studies. Speaking as agricultural economists, the Organization-Production scholars claimed that their work on the internal structure of the family farm was the most important topic on the agenda of rural inquiry; as rural sociologists in the making, the Agrarian-Marxists countered with the declaration that the most urgent research task was the study of the social and economic stratification of the peasantry.

The disagreement over goals was conducted in moderate tones. To begin with, the controversy consumed very little of the energies of the contending groups. Each school devoted itself principally to enunciating its theory and conducting research on the problems it considered crucial. Serious intellectual criticism by one school of the other was sporadic; when criticisms were launched, they were benign in tone and more often than not directed at a particular omission rather than at the opponent's position as a whole. Moreover, in this period social relations between the disputants were cordial. Members of the two groups met frequently, since both were housed in the Timiriazev Academy. The teacher-student relationship that provided the occasion for many of their meetings made for a deferential tone, and the involvement of some members of the two groups in common research projects generated a spirit of cooperation. There is no record of hostile personal encounters between the two groups before 1927. Differences of opinion seem to have been confined to print, appearing in articles, book reviews, and the prefaces to monographs. To reflect the overriding concern of each school with its own program of inquiry, the views of the two groups will be presented separately in this section. Nevertheless, it will be abundantly clear that the two schools did interact in this period. Indeed, as we shall see, each school formulated and refined its position at least in part with the stand of its alterego in view.

3. Organization-Production Theory

Throughout their existence as a school of inquiry in rural studies, the Organization-Production scholars devoted their energies to examining the Russian family farm. Some of the distinctive features of this economic unit had been noted as early as the turn of the century by agricultural specialists working in the villages of Russia. However, it was the Organization-Production scholars who first examined this farm in detail and propounded an explanation of its internal dynamics.

The theory for which the Organization-Production group became known developed in three stages, which spanned a period of nearly fifteen years. Between 1912 and 1915 the theory unfolded as the Timiriazev professors articulated a set of concepts and a series of relationships that they knit together into a preliminary account of the family farm economy. In 1924, almost a decade later, on the basis of research done in the interim, these scholars presented the first full formulation of their theory. And in 1925, responding to criticisms leveled by their colleagues, the Organization-Production scholars reformulated their theory and faced squarely its implications for classical economic thought and for the evolution of the Soviet rural economy.

In this chapter we will examine the three stages of development of Organization-Production theory, tracing the ideas that culminated in the 1925 explanation of family farm dynamics. In the course of this examination, we will pay particular attention to the degree of intellectual consensus among the Timiriazev professors and to their relations with various reference groups.

The Unfolding of a Theory, 1912-1915

Concepts and Relationships

The account of the dynamics of the family farm put forth by the Organization-Production school was based on their conception of the psychology of the Russian peasant, a conception they derived by inferring a set of motives from observed behavior.[1] The observations crucial to the group's image of the peasant were first made in 1911 by A. V. Chaianov, who would become the school's leading theorist. Chaianov, working at the time as an agronomist, undertook a study of the organizational plan of the peasant farm in the flax-growing region. He focused his inquiry on the way in which the family farm used the manpower available to it from the pool of family members. Chaianov found that the head of the farm aimed at using all labor resources at his disposal but that he employed these solely for the purpose of satisfying the consumption demands of the family members. From this, Chaianov concluded that the family farmer was a nonacquisitive *homo economicus*.[2]

Having described the Russian peasant as disinterested in acquisition for its own sake, Chaianov turned to explore the way in which such a peasant calculated the amount of labor he would have to expend in order to meet the consumption demands made upon him. In *Ocherki po teorii trudovogo khoziaistva* [Essays on the Theory of the Labor Farm], an assiduously researched work published the following year, he sketched the economic reasoning of the family farmer. According to Chaianov, the family farmer invariably made two calculations. He estimated the drudgery of work involved in obtaining the last ruble of value (curve AB in figure 1),[3] and he calculated the marginal utility to him of that last ruble (curve CD). Where the two curves intersected (point X), the drudgery involved in securing the last ruble of value was exactly equal to the marginal utility of that ruble. At point X, the farmer ceased his work. Beyond that point, the family farmer's supply-curve of labor sloped backward.[4] Chaianov's figure illustrates a concept that was one of the cornerstones of the Organization-Production theory, namely, the labor-consumption balance (*trudovoi-potrebitel'nyi balans*) between the satisfaction of family needs and the drudgery of labor. In 1913, when he put it

FIGURE 1
Economic Calculation of the Family Farmer

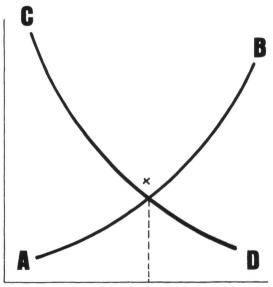

Source: Chaianov, *Ocherki* (1912-1913), p. 6.

forward, Chaianov did not dwell at great length on the balance itself. Instead, he concentrated on examining the consumption curve *CD*, about which he formulated a series of preliminary propositions:

1. The volume of consumption needs is a function of the number of mouths to feed.[5]
2. Some needs are more elastic than others. The head of the farm satisfies first those needs that are hardest to let go unsatisfied.[6]

3. The difference in the curves of satisfaction of two farms are the result of variances in the farms' lifestyle and cultural level.[7]

These propositions, refined through subsequent research, figured in the final version of the Organization-Production theory. Not long after the publication of *Ocherki*, Chaianov was presented with a unique opportunity to continue his exploration of the principles underlying the construction of the consumption curve. He was permitted to rework data collected in a 1910 *zemstvo* survey of the composition and activities of peasant farms in the Starobel'sk *uezd*[8] of Kharkov *guberniia*.[9] The fruits of Chaianov's labors appeared in 1915 under the title *Biudzhety krest'ian Starobel'skogo uezda* [Budgets of Peasants in the Starobel'sk District].[10]

For some time Chaianov had been intrigued by the idea that the shape of a peasant's consumption curve was related to the composition of the farming family; indeed, he had put forward a hypothesis to this effect in 1913. Provided now with a windfall of data, Chaianov made it the object of his Starobel'sk study to ascertain the precise role that family composition played in the farmer's assessment of the consumption demands made upon him. He began work on this question by analyzing the demography of the family. He related the size of the peasant family (number of members) to its age (number of years in existence); then he calculated the ratio of mouths-to-feed/workers for families of varying ages. In Chaianov's view, this consumer/worker ratio measured the intensity of the consumption pressure experienced by the family farm. He suspected that the intensity of this pressure influenced the farmer's expenditure of effort and hence the productivity of the farm itself. To verify his suspicions, Chaianov took a sample of farms varying in demographic composition and related their consumer/worker ratios to the volume of goods they produced. He found that while the consumption budget remained fairly standard,[11] farm production was adjusted to the intensity of consumption pressure.[12] Thus, for Chaianov, the ratio of consumers/workers on a farm became the variable that determined that farm's economic activity. That is, the farm became a form of biological organism whose growth and decay was governed by the composition of the farming family.[13] Differences in the level of activity between one farm and the other were attributed to variations in the family composition of those farms. In relying primarily on a demographic factor (family composition) to explain interfarm differences, Chaianov blunted the importance of the differential possession by farms of economic resources.

Chaianov's analysis of the dynamics of the family farm had interesting implications for classical economic theory. That theory had been modeled upon the capitalist economic unit, which relied for its operation upon hired labor, labor that had an objective valuation expressible in monetary terms. Work on the family farm, however, was performed by family members whose effort could only be valued subjectively, its worth varying in relation to the intensity of consumption pressure. Thus the Starobel'sk study raised the possibility that at least one of the concepts of classical economics—namely, wages— might not be applicable to the family farm in quite the same way that it applied to the capitalist farm. In 1915 Chaianov was reluctant to attack the structure of classical economics, and, consequently, he did not pursue the implications of his findings. He simply noted that the factor of wages functioned differently on the family and capitalist farms.[14] He went on the suggest a way to maintain the unity of economic thought. One might conceive of the peasant family as two entities, he submitted, the one hiring and the other hired labor. This bifurcation of the single family farm would allow wages on the family farm to be analyzed in the classical manner. The total expenses for labor could be divided by the number of days worked, yielding the wage or cost of labor.[15] Almost a decade later Chaianov would reject this conceptual expedient and would call for the development of a new noncapitalist theory of the peasant economy.[16]

The Range of the Theory

As former agronomists turned scholars, the Timiriazev professors were primarily concerned with the internal operation of the family farm. On the whole they were, as Chaianov expessed it in 1912, "disinterested" in studying questions of the national economy.[17] Nowhere did the Timiriazev scholars' microeconomic approach to rural studies come out as clearly as in the first history of the Organization-Production school, which appeared in print in 1920. Written by a prominent member of the school, N. P. Makarov, the history was part of a larger work devoted to the study of the Russian peasantry.[18] Makarov identified two main approaches to the study of the countryside and traced the history of each in Russian thought. The first approach, which he termed "socioeconomic," originated in 1857 with the work of N. Chernyshevskii and was later embraced by Marxists of all persuasions.[19] Scholars committed to this approach were primarily concerned with the distribution of wealth and the nature of class relations among the peasantry.[20] The second approach, which Makarov labeled "Organization-Production," was the newer one; it originated in 1875 with the work of A. Liudogorskii and was refined by a group of scholars writing in the second decade of the twentieth century. Scholars committed to this approach concentrated on the internal organization of the peasant farm. They investigated the optimal distribution of resources among the various farming activities, the interdependence of the different sectors of the farm, and the economic thinking of the head of the farm.[21]

Makarov's purpose in setting forth the two approaches to the study of the peasantry was clear. In the aftermath of the Bolshevik seizure of power in 1917, he wanted to argue for the legitimacy of the Organization-Production orientation. To do so, he traced the history of the approach, emphasizing how deeply embedded in Russian thought lay its roots. At the same time, he clearly delineated the range of the group's theory to underscore the fact that the Organization-Production approach did not and need not conflict with that of the Marxists.[22] Indeed, at the end of his historical presentation, Makarov made a plea for the coexistence of the two orientations; the socioeconomic approach would be applied to questions of macroeconomics, while the Organization-Production approach would be used in the analysis of microeconomic topics.[23]

Makarov's plea for coexistence made little impact on the academic community. At the time it was formulated, there was no group of Marxist scholars studying the Soviet countryside who could take up Makarov's suggestion of a division into spheres of influence. And by the time such a group had coalesced and was prepared to analyze systematically the theory of the Organization-Production school,[24] that theory had been extended into the arena of macroeconomics; its postulates had come to bear on the most urgent questions of the national economy.

The First Formulation, 1924

Although the rudiments of the Organization-Production theory had been set forth by 1915, it was almost a decade later before the first full formulation of that theory appeared in print. To a large extent, the hiatus may be explained by the political events in which the Organization-Production scholars, like many of their contemporaries, were caught up. The World War, the Revolutions of 1917, and the Civil War doubtless left little time for theorizing. However, mention must also be made of the differences of opinion *within* the Organization-Production school; these differences may well have contributed to the length of the hiatus between the publication of *Starobel'sk* and the codification of the group's theory.[25] One difference of opinion that was undeniably salient centered on the question of peasant psychology; here the protagonists were A. N. Chelintsev, G. A. Studenskii, and A. V. Chaianov. A second point of contention was the relation of the Organization-Production theory to classical economics; on this issue, the principal discussants were A. N. Chelintsev, N. P. Makarov, G. A. Studenskii, and A. V. Chaianov. These discussions show the limits of agreement within the Timiriazev group, and consequently they suggest the dimensions of Chaianov's task as leader of the group.

The Psychology of the Family Farmer

Chaianov's view of the psychology of the family farmer became the subject of a lively debate within the Organization-Production school. A. N. Chelintsev, the senior member of the school, adhered strictly to the view that the family farmer was a nonacquisitive economic being; according to him, the behavior of the family farmer was dictated solely by the consumption demands of the members of the farmer's family.[26] G. A. Studenskii, the young maverick of the group, rejected as primitive the notion that the family farmer responded to no stimulus other than that of consumption.[27] Arguing that only in a natural economy was production totally use-oriented, Studenskii urged that the Organization-Production theory be revised to include acquisitive behavior on the part of the peasant.[28]

In 1923 Chaianov entered the debate with a work written in German—*Die Lehre von der bauerlichen Wirtschaft; Versuch der Familienwirtschaft im Landbau.*[29] In this work he took a position halfway between those of Chelintsev and Studenskii. He began by admitting that the peasant might be acquisitive by nature:

> Of course our critics are free to understand the labor-consumer theory as a sweet little picture of the Russian peasantry in the likeness of the moral French peasants, satisfied with everything and living like birds of the air. We ourselves do not have such a conception and are inclined to believe that no peasant would refuse either good roast beef or a gramophone, or even a block of Shell Oil Company shares, if the chance occurred.[30]

However, he moderated this by an assessment of the opportunities for acquisition open to the peasant:

> Unfortunately, such changes do not present themselves in large numbers and the peasant family wins every kopeck by hard, intensive toil.[31]

In a less poetic vein, Chaianov explained that the tendency to expansion, which is characteristic of every economic unit, was limited on the family farm because of the fixed number of workers and the increasing drudgery of work. He concluded, "The labor-consumption balance we have analyzed is the expression of the mechanism for limiting the peasant family's consumer tendencies."[32] Chaianov's 1923 position represented a substantial modification of his earlier stand on peasant motivation. In 1912, he had attributed variations in the curves of satisfaction of different farms to differences in the level of culture of those farms. Now, a decade later, he explained that the level of culture itself depended upon a peasant's opportunity to expand production and acquire goods, an opportunity that, he cautioned, was extremely circumscribed.[33] The stand Chaianov took in 1923 would be reflected in the 1924 formulation of the theory.

The Family Farm and Classical Economic Theory

In addition to discussing the psychology of the family farmer, the members of the Organization-Production school gave extensive consideration to the implications of the family farm for classical economic theory. Their discussions of this second problem revolved around a single question: was the family farm they studied so unique an economic unit that its explanation required the construction of a new economic theory?

The discussion had its roots in 1915. In his Starobel'sk study Chaianov had shown that because the family farmer was both owner and worker at one and the same time, his labor could not be valued objectively; and he had therefore concluded that one of the core concepts of classical economics, wages, did not apply to the family farm in the same way that it did to capitalist agriculture.[34] Chaianov's conclusion was endorsed by other Organization-Production scholars, who repeated it with variations in their post-1915 works on the economics of peasant farming.[35] In the decade that followed the publication of *Starobel'sk*, these scholars went on to investigate the extent to which other concepts of classical economics could be applied to the family farm economy.

One of the concepts brought under scrutiny was that of profit. Members of the Organization-Production group generally agreed that the concept of profit as calculated for the capitalist enterprise (gross income minus both material expenses and wages) was inapplicable to the family farm, but the reasons for the inapplicability offered by these scholars differed widely. Makarov claimed that for the consumption-oriented family farm using its own capital, interest costs were impossible to calculate; only amortization could be assessed. In light of this, no objective assessment could be made of the farm's profit. To try to do so, he contended, would involve one in "logical nonsense."[36] Chaianov insisted that it was the problem of calculating the family farm's wage bill that made it impossible to determine pure profit for that farm. The inability to obtain an objective measure of profit had important ramifications, he alleged; it meant that the family farmer had to choose between alternative investments by determining which investment would yield the greatest gross (not net, as for the capitalist) income that could be used to satisfy the consumption demands of the family.[37] For Studenskii, it was the economic constraints under which the family farm operated that altered the meaning of "profit." Like all other economic units, the family farm sought the greatest possible net return,[38] he claimed, but the consumption needs of the family were so overriding that the head of the farm came to assess the profitability of a venture not in terms of the return per unit of effort but rather in terms of whether it would provide the volume of goods required to meet the family's needs.[39]

In addition to the concepts of wages and profit, the Timiriazev scholars examined the notion of differential rent as it applied to the family farm economy.[40] On this issue there was considerable disagreement within the group. The first to take a stand was Chelintsev, whose small monograph on this question was published in 1918. Chelintsev began from the premise that for the nonacquisitive family farm a surplus income above the consumption level would be most unusual. Indeed, such a surplus could be imagined only in one case, namely, when the construction of a new industrial center made agriculture profitable for farms on the urban-rural fringe.[41] However, Chelintsev hastened to add, even in such a case the advantage would only be temporary and would be eliminated because of the operation of two factors: first, if farming were to prove profitable, the nonacquisitive psychology of the family farm would lead to a reduction of the family's involvement in crafts to the point where total income just equaled consumption needs; and second, if a rent began to be earned by farms in a given area, the density of population in that region would rise, thus diminishing the advantage initially enjoyed by certain farms.[42] Therefore, conclued Chelintsev, "there is no need to talk about rent on the working farm."[43]

Chelintsev's position was shared by Makarov—with very slight modifications. While Makarov attributed differential rent to the superior quality of land rather than to advantageous location, like Chelintsev he maintained that any rent earned by the family farm was only temporary and would be eliminated by the migration of population.[44] Thus the two senior members of the Organization-Production school contended that the category of rent was meaningless when applied to the family farm economy.

This contention was strongly opposed by Studenskii, who claimed that the concept of rent was both applicable to the family farm and significant for the theory of its operation as an economic unit. Studenskii based his argument upon the view that the cause of the formation of rent was neither advantage of location nor quality of land, but the greater productivity of one farm as opposed to another. Because that superiority in productivity stemmed from the talent of the family farmer, it would not be eliminated by the migration of rural population.[45]

Among the members of the Organization-Production school, there were some differences of opinion about the extent to which the concepts of classical economics were meaningful when applied to the analysis of the family farm. Despite these differences, the Timiriazev scholars shared a belief that the family farm was a unique economic unit. Building upon this general feeling rather than upon any specific set of conclusions agreed upon by his colleagues, Chaianov moved to formulate a theory of the family farm.

The "Noncapitalist" Theory

In 1924 Chaianov set forth his new theory in an article written in German[46] entitled "Zur Frage einer Theorie der nicht-kapitalistischen Wirtschaftssysteme."[47] The article opened with the author's assessment of the hegemony of capitalist economic theory.

> In modern theory of the national economy, it has been customary to think about *all* economic phenomena exclusively in terms of a capitalist economy. All the principles of our theory—rent, capital, price and other categories— have been formed in the framework of an economy based on wage labor and seeking to maximize profits. . . . All other (noncapitalist) types of economic life are regarded as insignificant or dying out.[48]

Having taken stock of his prey, Chaianov proceeded to characterize the structure of capitalist theory. According to him, the hallmark of that theory was its integration into a systematic whole of the concepts of price, wages, profit, interest, and rent. This integration of concepts he regarded both as the source of classical economic theory's explanatory power and as its Achilles' heel. Chaianov put it rather dramatically:

> If one brick drops out of the system, the whole building collapses. In the absence of any one of these economic categories, all the others lose their specific character and conceptual content and cannot even be defined qualitatively.[49]

When classical theory was applied to the family farm, contended Chaianov, one of the most important conceptual bricks—wages—dropped out, distorting the meaning of all other classical concepts for the farm. Specifically, the concept of net profit became meaningless, for "the objective arithmetic calculation of highest possible net profit in a given market situation does not determine whether or not to accept any economic situation; this is done by the internal confrontation of subjective evaluations."[50] Moreover, when applied to the family farm, the concept of differential rent acquired a new connotation. It was no longer an unearned income but a temporary advantage enjoyed by certain well-situated farms. It would be nullified by the drudgery of labor, which would force the family farmer to reduce his effort to the point where the marginal utility of the last ruble gained was just equal to the sacrifice of leisure involved in obtaining that last ruble.[51]

Having characterized many of the core concepts of classical economic theory as either meaningless or distorted when applied to the family farm,[52] Chaianov declared categorically that the structure of the working farm "lies outside the conceptual system adapted to capitalist society."[53] He then proposed a theoretical framework that would be appropriate to the non-capitalist family farm.

The basis of Chaianov's new theory was the proposition that the return received by the family farm could not, like that of the capitalist farm, be differentiated into the traditional categories of net profit, rent, and interest. Rather, at the end of the year the family farm received a certain volume of produce, from which it was possible to deduct only the material expenses incurred. To the single sum that remained after this deduction had been made Chaianov gave the name "labor product."[54]

According to Chaianov, the undifferentiated return to the family farm had important ramifications for the behavior of the head of that farm as a *homo economicus*; it led the family farmer to follow rules different from those followed by the capitalist farmer. While the cultivator of a capitalist farm aimed at maximizing his profit, the family farmer strove to provide the highest possible level of well-being for his family— a goal that involved his so organizing production that the greatest yield per worker resulted. In practice, Chaianov admitted, the calculations of the capitalist and family farmers might coincide, for "the objects that yield the highest possible labor payment per unit invested and those that guarantee the highest net profit to a capitalist unit are roughly the same."[55] But there were exceptions that forced the family farmer to abandon the "conduct dictated by the customary formula for capitalist profit calculation."[56] For example, Chaianov pointed out, in a densely populated area the law of diminishing returns applied, dictating the point at which it was no longer profitable to continue work. While the capitalist farmer would cease his labor at that point, the head of the family farm might well continue his labor simply because his family's consumption needs had not yet been met. Or, confronted with a prospective investment, the head of the family farm would undertake a risk only if his family had not yet been fed; he would pay no attention to promised profits, only to the existing need. These examples, Chaianov insisted, underscored the "structural peculiarities" of the family farm. In adducing these instances, Chaianov was at one and the same time specifying some of the propositions of his theory and justifying its formulation.

The article of 1924 showed Chaianov to be an imaginative and sophisticated theorist. Having demonstrated that the family farm could not be successfully analyzed using the categories of classical economic theory, he proceeded to formulate a new, noncapitalist theory tailored to the peculiarities of the family farm.[57] Then, in the name of this new theory, he challenged the long-accepted hegemony of classical thought, suggesting that in place of a single overarching theory there be created a plurality of theories, each appropriate to a different form of economy. "We have no doubt that the future of economic thought lies not in constructing a single theory of economic life," he stated, "but in conceiving a number of theoretical systems. . . ."[58] Thus did Chaianov both make legitimate the theory he had set forth and revise the accepted notion of economic thought. His audacity did not go unchallenged.

Reformulation in Response to Criticism, 1925

The Organization-Production scholars had two intellectual reference groups. First, as agricultural economists, they were members of an international community of scholars, which included the great economists of Western Europe[59] as well as the American specialists on farm management.[60] The Timiriazev professors were very proud of their connections with foreign scholars. They took great care to keep abreast of foreign research, chronicling its development in their journals;[61] they made a practice of publicizing their own work abroad, often forwarding copies of their latest studies directly to foreign libraries and scholars;[62] and every so often they published articles and monographs outside Russia.[63]

Second, as researchers studying the Russian countryside, they were part of the Soviet community of rural scholars. Indeed, for most of the first decade after 1917, the Timiriazev professors were leaders of this community. Their preeminence derived both from their intellectual achievements and from the fact that they held the most important teaching and research positions in the major agricultural academy of the day.[64] Their status as leaders in this community made the Timiriazev professors feel both responsible for and accountable to the young agricultural specialists whom they were training.

The dual affiliation of the Organization-Production scholars proved to have disadvantages. Almost as soon as Chaianov's pioneering article of 1924 appeared in print, it was met by a storm of criticism from both reference groups. Chaianov was taken to task by foreign agricultural economists, who argued that the Russian case was exceptional and that therefore there was no cause to reject classical economic analysis. This charge was leveled primarily by A. Weber, K. Ritter, and A. Skalweit.[65] At the same time, Chaianov was castigated by his Soviet Marxist colleagues, who charged that his theory treated the family farm in isolation, divorced from its socioeconomic setting. This criticism was launched first by L. N. Kritsman and G. Meerson.[66]

To answer both sets of criticisms, Chaianov prepared for publication a work entitled *Organizatisiia krest'ianskogo khoziaistva* [Peasant Farm Organization].[67] The first five chapters of this work had appeared in 1923 as *Die Lehre*; to these Chaianov now added two new chapters, and the result appeared in print in 1925. The 1925 book became the most finished version of the Organization-Production theory.[68]

The Theory and Classical Economics

Chaianov's challenge to the hegemony of classical economic theory sparked an outcry by foreign agricultural scholars, who decried his attempt to destroy "the monism of economic thought."[69] To support their position, these foreign scholars advanced two arguments designed to discredit the noncapitalist theory of the family farm. First, they submitted, the Russian case was an exception, and therefore, in extrapolating from this single case, Chaianov had developed a theory with limited validity. In particular, the critics pointed to the fact that the demographic analysis that was so central to the Organization-Production theory had been developed using the repartitional commune as a model, and, consequently, the analysis would not be applicable to countries with laws against partible inheritance.[70] To this criticism Chaianov replied that where nonpartible inheritance was the rule, the land market might perform the redistributive function that the commune carried out in Russia.[71] Second, the foreign critics maintained, it was artificial to formulate a noncapitalist theory for the family farm, since by virtue of its activities that farm was involved in the capitalist economy. They declared that "*even purely family farms*, insofar as they become commodity producers and dispose of their produce on the capitalist market and are subject to the influence of its prices, should be called capitalist farms, since they form part of the capitalist system of the national economy."[72] In answer to this criticism, Chaianov admitted that the term "capitalist" might be technically correct for family farms for the reason cited, but, he explained, by using the term "noncapitalist" he had wanted to highlight the fact that the family farm hired no labor.[73]

In replying to the charges leveled by his colleagues abroad, Chaianov denied that he had violated the unity of economic thought capriciously. Rather, he insisted, he had had no alternative to formulating a new theory—short of continuing to make awkward modifications to traditional theory, modifications that hindered rather than aided comprehension. "We are out to accept either the concept of the fictive twofold nature of the peasant, uniting in his person both worker and entrepreneur, or the concept of the family farm, with work motivation analogous to that of the piece-rate system. No third possibility is offered."[74] At one point Chaianov even went so far as to suggest that since the properties of the family farm could be found in several economic systems, it was in fact the capitalist system that was the exception.[75] Thus, Chaianov came close to asserting that his theory of noncapitalist economics was more widely applicable than the traditional capitalist theory it had unseated.

Although he made no actual concession to his foreign colleagues, Chaianov did show some sensitivity to their criticism. After defending the utility of his theoretical innovation, he insisted that the Organization-Production school stood for more than the noncapitalist economic theory.

Recently, for some reason, it has been commonly considered that the scientific research work of the Organization and Production School amounts to the construction of a particular peasant farm theory. This is one of the deepest delusions. In answering the practical demands of agricultural officers and cooperative workers, our group has worked out a wide range of topics.[76]

Chaianov's answer to his foreign critics in 1925 was thus a mixture of audacity and submissiveness. He insisted that the theory he had developed was fully warranted and of great value, but he pleaded, somewhat disingenuously, that the theory not attract so much attention.

The Family Farm and the National Economy

Chaianov's account of the internal operation of the family farm was also attacked by the Agrarian-Marxists. These young scholars singled out two particular aspects of the 1924 formulation. First, they criticized the Organization-Production treatment of the family farm as a form of biological organism with its own, internally determined cycle of growth and decay. In the critics' view, the adherence to the biological analogy had led the Timiriazev professors to focus on the variable of demography and to miss the fact that the real cause of the differences between farms lay in the unequal distribution of resources among the peasantry.[77] In fact, the members of the Organization-Production school did acknowledge the existence of such inequalities, but they believed that any problems in distribution would eventually right themselves following changes in demography.

The Agrarian-Marxists also attacked the refusal by the Organization-Production scholars to accord to the market a major role in determining the activity of the family farm. They charged that the failure to consider the impact of the market had allowed the Timiriazev professors to insist that the family farm lay outside the sphere of the capitalist economy.[78] In truth, the Timiriazev professors had never treated the family farm as a natural economy; they had always insisted that it was an economic unit involved in commercial trade relations. But they had refused to follow the Agrarian-Marxists in their belief that the market exerted the decisive influence upon the activity of the family farm.[79]

In 1925 Chaianov took cognizance of the objections that had been raised by his Marxist colleagues and, in deference to these criticisms, extended his analysis to include a consideration of the interaction between the family farm and the national economy. He oriented this consideration around two related problems. To begin with, he explored the effect on the family farm of its participation in the larger economy. In his inquiry Chaianov admitted that some of the differentiation in the rural sector had stemmed from the involvement of the family farm in the national economy. But he insisted that the most important source of differentiation was biological or demographic. "There is nevertheless no doubt at all that demographic causes play the leading role in these movements."[80] As might have been expected, Chaianov's reassessment of the problem of differentiation failed to satisfy his critics.

Chaianov next inquired about the effect on the rural economy of the participation of a large sector of family farms. He found that, because of their unique properties, family farms in sufficient numbers could determine important aspects of the capitalist economy.[81] For example, the family farm could force up the price of land. "As farms increase and there is a relative shortage of land, ever growing numbers of buyers and hirers appear able to pay prices higher than capitalist ones."[82] This willingness on the part of the family farm to outbid its capitalist competitor had far-reaching implications; it would eventually lead to a redistribution of land from capitalist to peasant farmer.[83] Moreover, the family farm could influence the level of wages. In a good year the peasants could meet the consumption needs of their families through farming, and they would therefore not be inclined to hire themselves out as laborers;

thus the wages for agricultural workers would be relatively high. In a poor year the peasants would flood the labor market, thus depressing wages. In Chaianov's hands, the on-farm equilibrium determined the level of wages on the capitalist labor market.[84]

With the publication of "Peasant Farm Organization," it became clear that the Organization-Production scholars considered the family farm to be a determining, rather than a passive, force in the economy. As Chaianov put it most bluntly, if most of the production in a system called "capitalist" were carried out by family farms, that system itself could come to be determined by the noncapitalist sector. Not surprisingly, the 1925 extension of Organization-Production theory into the arena of macroeconomics distressed rather than satisfied the Agrarian-Marxists.

The School: Internal Consensus and External Relations

Our account of the evolution of Organization-Production theory has brought to light certain intriguing facts about the group of scholars who propounded it. First, among the members of the school there was intellectual agreement on fundamentals, but there were substantial differences on details. The Timiriazev professors agreed that the family farm was a unique economic unit whose dynamics could not be successfully explained using the concepts of classical economics; however, there was no unanimity on the ways in which and the extent to which that farm differed from the classical model. The limited consensus among the Organization-Production scholars makes clear the magnitude of Chaianov's contribution to the theory of the noncapitalist farm. Chaianov did much more than simply codify his colleagues' views; he provided the intellectual guidance for the creation of the theory for which the group became known.

Furthermore, the development of Organization-Production theory showed that the Timiriazev professors treated their foreign and domestic colleagues very differently. The works written by the members of the Chaianov group were studded with references to scholarship produced by colleagues outside of Russia. Yet, in reformulating their theory, the Organization-Production scholars ignored the criticism issued by their foreign colleagues and acceded to the demands issued by their Soviet counterparts.[85] The reasons for the difference in response are not hard to fathom. It was easier to comply with the demands made by the Agrarian-Marxists than to satisfy the German agricultural economists. The Agrarian-Marxists had challenged their former teachers to extend their work to include a discussion of the relation of the family farm to its capitalist environment. While the Organization-Production scholars were not generally interested in questions of macroeconomics, the content of their theory could readily serve as a basis for a treatment of the national economy. The German critics, however, had demanded nothing less than the abandonment of the challenge to classical economics, a demand that, if satisfied, would eliminate what the Organization-Production scholars believed to be their distinctive contribution. Social factors also made it likely that the Organization-Production scholars would respond more readily to their former students than to their colleagues abroad. The Timiriazev professors were the acknowledged leaders of the Soviet community of rural scholars. As men anxious to sustain their position, they could hardly have refused to enter into dialogue with young scholars who styled themselves as the representatives of the new period.

4. Organization-Production Research

In the fifteen years they dominated the study of agricultural economics, the Organization-Production scholars produced a dazzling array of research projects. Of the many types of projects conducted, we shall focus on four: the examination of farm budgets, the work on agricultural regionalization, the inquiries into rural cooperation, and the location studies. We choose these projects both because the members of the Chaianov group considered them to be among their major contributions to agricultural economics[1] and because they reveal most clearly two important preoccupations that ran throughout Organization-Production research on the the countryside. First, these projects show the Chaianov group making every effort to support the theory to which they had given birth. Whenever possible, they used their empirical findings to confirm and extend the propositions of the theory of noncapitalist economics. Second, these projects show the Organization-Production scholars arguing strenuously for the family farm as a viable economic unit in the new age. In many of their research reports, the Timiriazev professors compared the family farm favorably to both the capitalist and the socialist forms of agriculture. At the same time, they laced their empirical work with practical suggestions to agronomists engaged in rationalizing the operation of the family farms. On the whole, the Organization-Production scholars devoted little effort to making the case for the family farm to those who formulated rural policy.

Budget Research: The Study of Farm Structure

Of all their empirical work, the Organization-Production scholars were perhaps most proud of their research on farm budgets. To be sure, the study of economic budgets was not pioneered by these Russian scholars. As the Timiriazev professors themselves were quick to point out, budget research had a long and noble lineage. It began in England at the end of the eighteenth century and in the course of the next century spread to France and then to Russia.[2] In these early works, budget data were used to determine the level of well-being of some segment of the population. The originality of the Organization-Production scholars lay in their use of budget data to answer a new set of questions, questions about the internal organization of the family farm.

The idea of using the budget study to explore the intricacies of farm organization was first suggested in 1910 by K. A. Matseevich in a report delivered to the Ekaterinoslav Agronomical Congress.[3] Apparently Matseevich's proposal caught the imagination of his audience; in the following year, at a meeting of the Moscow Oblast Workers in Agronomy, Chaianov repeated the suggestion and called upon the assembled agronomists to conduct budget studies.[4] When he made the appeal, Chaianov was far from certain about the results such studies would yield. He knew that the budget method could provide data on consumption patterns, but it remained to be seen whether the same method could furnish independent information on the "soul" of the farm, its organizational plan.[5] Not only the utility, but also the practicability of the budget study was in question during this period. Hitherto, budget studies in Russia had been conducted on the basis of oral testimony taken from the peasants at the end of the year, a procedure that seriously diminished the reliability of the data collected. What was needed to make the budget study dependable was a system of registration that would be detailed enough to provide information on the farm's use of resources yet simple enough to be handled by the head of the farm himself at periodic intervals during the year. With these requirements in mind, in 1912 a group of Moscow economists (N. P. Makarov, S. Pervushin, A. Rybnikov, and A. V. Chaianov) devised a straightforward form based on the principles of double-entry bookkeeping, a form that allowed the family farmer to keep track of all incomes and expenditures in money and kind for each branch of the farm separately.[6] The design of this form proved to be a landmark in the study of peasant farm organization. For the first time, a budget study could provide information not only about the presence or absence of certain resources on the farm but also about the circulation or distribution of these resources within the various branches of the farm.[7] Thus at last the organizational plan of the family farm could be laid bare.

Not long after the bookkeeping form had been refined, a series of budget studies was undertaken with the express purpose of isolating the determinants of farm structure. The first was conducted by Chaianov in 1915 in the Starobel'sk region. That study, which we have described in part above, examined the effect of the rental of additional land upon the organization of the family farm.

Chaianov did not approach his inquiry without preconceptions. He began by defining land rental as a response by the family farmer to an increase in consumption pressure on the farm. Looking at the incidence of land rental in the Starobel'sk region, he found a high degree of correlation between the peasant's decision to acquire more land and an increase in the ratio of consumers to workers in the farming family.[8] From here, Chaianov went on to explore the effects of land rental upon certain key facets of farm structure. His research revealed that changes in farm size conditioned both the organization of labor and the use of inventory;[9] only the use of land, being dependent upon the economy and geography of the region, remained unresponsive to alterations in farm size.[10] His inquiry complete, Chaianov concluded that the organization of the farm was directly affected by the rental of additional land, which, in turn, was a function of changes in the demographic composition of the family unit. The research on the Starobel'sk budgets played an important part in the development of

Organization-Production theory. To the proposition that farm production varied in accordance with demography[11] Chaianov now felt able to add the hypothesis that farm structure was determined by family composition.

Chaianov and his colleagues were very proud of the Starobel'sk study; they regarded it as a model of the way in which budget data could be employed to shed light on the internal structure of the farm.[12] Scholars not affiliated with the Organization-Production group, however, were not nearly so persuaded of the merits of the 1915 study. They criticized the Starobel'sk research on the grounds that its author had not considered alternative explanations of the structure of the farm he examined. Specifically, they objected to Chaianov's failure to test for the influence of external factors (such as the market) upon the organization of the farm.[13] This objection was not unjustified; Chaianov, it will be remembered, began by "finding" that the recourse to land rental in Starobel'sk was the result of increased consumption pressure. He did not trouble to explore the relation between land rental and other factors, factors that might have cast doubt upon the view of the peasant as a nonacquisitive economic man, immune to the lure of profit. In this sense, Chaianov's study was an example of the way in which research can be used to confirm rather than to test a hypothesis.[14] When he carried out the study in 1915, Chaianov was unaware of its methodological deficiencies. In fact, even when he was led some twelve years later to criticize his earlier work, Chaianov faulted not his methodology, but the hypothesis he had attempted to confirm in this study.[15] Chaianov's mea culpa of 1927 would not have been sufficient for his earliest critics, for it lacked the methodological sophistication they demanded; nor was it sufficient for his final critics, for it came too late.

After Chaianov's Starobel'sk research of 1915, the next landmark in the study of farm organization by the Organization-Production scholars was the year 1919.[16] In that year two full-scale studies by Chelintsev appeared in print. The first, *Opyt izucheniia organizatsii krest'ianskogo sel'skogo khoziaistva* [An Attempt to Study the Organization of Peasant Farming], was a report on extensive research done in 1915 on the budgets of eighty-five farms in the Tambov region.[17] The second study, *Teoreticheskie obosnovaniia organizatsii krest'-ianskogo khoziaistva* [Theoretical Foundations of Peasant Farming], was based on the findings of a large budget inquiry undertaken by the Kharkov Society of Agriculture between 1914 and 1915, when Chelintsev was the head of its sector on farm organization.[18]

Unlike Chaianov, Chelintsev did raise the possibility that the organization of the peasant farm was influenced by certain factors external to it, namely the market and employment in crafts. Having paid lip service to this possibility, Chelintsev then made every effort to discount it. He challenged the view that the market determined the type and quantity of produce offered for sale by a given family farm.[19] According to him, the climate and the quality of the soil together conditioned the sort of crop grown in a given region,[20] and the head of the farm determined how much of his produce would be delivered for sale.[21] Further, Chelintsev attacked the widely held belief that craftwork exerted a decisive influence on farm structure by drawing labor away from the conduct of farming. He carried out research that showed that the extent to which the farmer engaged in craftwork was inversely related to the size of his landholding, and from this finding he concluded that crafts was a residual occupation, used only to supplement the income of a hard-pressed farmer.[22] Having to his own satisfaction discounted the influence of both the market and employment in crafts, Chelintsev turned to discuss the impact of consumption pressure upon farm structure. He focused on two major aspects of farm structure: the use of the means of production, and the use of labor. In each case, he found "proof" that the structure of farm activities was responsive to changes in demography.[23] On the basis of this evidence, he concluded triumphantly that farm structure was determined by the intensity of consumption pressure. In this none-too-subtle way, Chelintsev used budget research to bolster the portrait of the family farm as a biological, rather than an economic, organism.[24]

In the half decade that followed the publication of Chelintsev's two studies, the Organization-Production stand on the determinants of farm structure underwent some change. Responding to criticisms leveled by the Agrarian-Marxists, the Timiriazev professors came to reconsider the influence of external factors on farm structure.[25] The results of that reconsideration were reflected in Chaianov's 1925 study, "Peasant Farm Organization," which formally repudiated the proposition that demography alone defined the organization of farming activity. "We ought to stress that at any particular moment the family is not the sole determinant of a particular farm and determines its size only in a general way."[26] Backing away from his earlier stand, Chaianov broadened the circle of factors affecting farm structure to include the use of labor, the means of production, natural conditions, and, most important of all, the market. Chaianov allowed that the produce market influenced what a given farm offered for sale,[27] while the labor market played a role in the peasant's desicion to work in crafts or agriculture.[28] Anticipating surprised reactions from those who knew his former position, Chaianov hastened to deny that the market would violate the much-valued freedom of the peasant. According to him, the head of the family farm would welcome the growing role of the market, for his major concern would be the size of the return from sales.[29] Moreover, Chaianov added, the activity of the market would inevitably foster the growth of rational farming, for the family farm would come to produce only those items that could not be more easily obtained through exchange.[30]

Because it attributed to the market a substantial role in the determination of farm structure, Chaianov's 1925 study was a concession to the school's critics. Yet these men did not treat the work as such. For in "Peasant Farm Organization" Chaianov continued to insist on the uniqueness and durability of the family farm;[31] to the critics, that insistence vitiated any formal acknowledgment about the impact of the market upon noncapitalist agriculture. Consequently, the critics paid little attention to the 1925 study; they persisted in citing the Starobel'sk study of 1915 and the Tambov and Kharkov studies of 1919 as the archetypes of the budget study. They also continued to denounce the budget study as a research technique inextricably linked to the tenets of the Organization-Production theory.[32] Ironically, at a later date the critics themselves would come to use budget research to confirm the hypotheses of their own theory; at that point, they would swallow the words they had spoken and utter brave assurances about the separability of the budget method from the theory of the noncapitalist farm.[33]

Regionalization: Farm Organization in Historical Perspective

Having worked in the countryside for many years, the Timiriazev professors had firsthand knowledge of the staggering diversity of agricultural forms found in the Russian rural sector. To the agronomists-turned-scholars, this diversity constituted something of a problem. The country spanned so vast an area that generalizations made on the basis of farming in one locale were utterly inapplicable to agriculture elsewhere. To meet this problem, the Organization-Production scholars undertook the task of grouping farms into discrete regions.

The Chaianov group was not the first to carry out such work. Indeed, "regionalization" (*raionirovanie*) studies had been conducted by Russian researchers as early as the first quarter of the nineteenth century.[34] In these early studies, farms were invariably grouped into regions according to such natural indicators as the quality of the soil, fertility of the land, climate, and topography. Though nurtured in this tradition, the Organization-Production scholars broke with it. They instituted a new typology for grouping farms and, in so doing, substantially refocused scholarly interest.

The Organization-Production approach to regional studies dated from 1910, when A. N. Chelintsev first expressed dissatisfaction with the traditional basis of classifying peasant farms. According to Chelintsev, the reliance on natural indicators had two principal drawbacks. First, it implied that nature was the master of man. Such a suggestion was deplorable, Chelintsev contended, for if nothing else, agriculture was the result of man's mastery of nature.[35] Second, it led to a static analysis of agriculture. To Chelintsev, the hallmark of agriculture was its continual development, and therefore a nonevolutionary perspective on farming was unthinkable.[36]

To replace the widely accepted system of grouping farms,

Chelintsev aimed to design a typology that would present
farming as an economic activity in which the peasant was the
decisive actor and that, when applied, would lay bare the
development of agriculture. His first attempt at such a design
produced a typology composed of nine "economic" indicators:

1. density of population and percent of nonagricultural
   population
2. percent of long-fallow land in relation to total land sown
3. percent of fallow land in relation to total land sown
4. percent of grass grown in relation to total land sown
5. percent of cultivated crops in relation to total land sown
6. percent of fibrous crops in relation to total land sown
7. ratio of cattle to land sown
8. ratio of sheep to cattle
9. ratio of pigs to cattle[37]

Armed with his new typology, Chelintsev grouped all the farms
in European Russia, using data collected by *zemstvo* statisticians in the 1890s and 1900s.[38] The results were clearly satisfac-
tory to Chelintsev; although he was later to revise the number
of indicators[39] and to introduce a system for translating the
qualitative terms into numerical weights,[40] after 1911 he made
no important changes in the principles underlying his classification. Chelintsev's insistence on the primacy of economic over
natural indicators met with some resistance when first introduced.[41] But the virtues of the new typology were soon
recognized, and before long it had gained currency. Beginning
in 1919, a whole generation of agricultural researchers was
trained in Chelintsev's approach to regional analysis.

Chelintsev's colleagues in the Timiriazev Institute expressed
great pride in his work.[42] Their attitude was understandable.
Not only was Chelintsev clearly the leading figure in the field of
regional analysis, but his work was completely at one with the
principles underlying the Organization-Production approach
to rural inquiry. Chelintsev's typology, it will be remembered,
allowed a researcher to group farms without examining their
interrelations.[43] Equally important, by depicting agriculture as
the result of man's mastery over nature, Chelintsev reaffirmed

the utility of the scientific agronomy whose promise had led the Timiriazev professors to forsake their careers as agronomists for scholarly endeavors.

When he first began his work on regionalization Chelintsev touted his contribution as one that went well beyond the sphere of methodology. Not only did the indicators he had developed result in better groupings, but, he insisted, those indicators could also be used to shed light on agricultural history. In his seminal work of 1911, Chelintsev supported his assertion; he presented a portrait of the evolution of Russian agriculture, with the various regions representing different stages of development.[44] Had Chelintsev and his colleagues followed the philosophy underlying the 1911 history, they would have regarded the family farm they studied simply as the form of agriculture dominant at a particular stage of history. However, the Organization-Production scholars were advocates as well as men of learning. Convinced of the merits of the noncapitalist farm in the Russian setting, they did not treat that farm as a transitory economic unit but argued for its continued survival. For this "lack of historical perspective," the members of the Chaianov group would be taken to task by their critics at the end of the decade. Under fire, Chelintsev would moderate his claims, underscoring only the methodological aspects of his work on regionalization.

Cooperation: Toward the Rationalization of Agriculture

Like economists of all stripes during the first quarter of the twentieth century, the Organization-Production scholars were aware of the inefficiency of Russian agricuture. In the case of the Timiriazev professors, however, that awareness was heightened, for in their work as agronomists they had been repeatedly confronted by this inefficiency, which they came to attribute to the lack of coordination among farms. Each farm unit, no matter how tiny, performed all the tasks associated with the cultivation of the land. Such an arrangement resulted in a wasteful redundancy of function; moreover, the complex machinery that could have increased efficiency could hardly be profitably employed by a single farm.[45] To the members of the Chaianov group, this lack of coordination was the major obstacle to the modernization of the rural sector.

To remedy this situation, the Timiriazev professors recommended the voluntary integration of farms into vertically organized cooperatives.[46] These cooperatives would be limited in function. They would perform only those tasks that were most rationally executed by large-scale mechanized units; the remaining tasks would be carried out by the individual family farms. According to its supporters, this scheme of limited cooperation had several advantages over the horizontally organized integration that was usually advocated. While creating the preconditions for the introduction of advanced technology where it counted most, the scheme of vertical integration would preserve as the basic unit of cultivation the family farm, whose virtues for intensive cultivation and livestock breeding had been amply demonstrated. At the same time, the plan would have the effect of streamlining the activity of the individual farm by eliminating from its organizational plan all dysfunctional operations. To those who proposed it, vertical integration seemed the answer to the most pressing problems of Russian farming.

The virtues of vertical cooperation were first presented in a 1919 study by Chaianov entitled *Osnovnye idei i formy organizatsii krest'ianskoi kooperatsii* [Basic Ideas and Organizational Forms of Peasant Cooperation].[47] Drawing upon his experience in organizing cooperatives during World War I and upon his earlier studies of the problems of agricultural integration,[48] Chaianov produced a large monograph that canvassed the range of farming activities that could be advantageously performed by functionally defined cooperatives. Implicit in Chaianov's discussion were two tenets, or articles of faith: the belief that for each agricultural activity there was an optimum scale of operations; and the belief that in agriculture, as opposed to industry, there was no a priori reason to expect large-scale units to be more efficient than small-scale units of production. Upon these two beliefs Chaianov would later ground his assertion that for most of rural Russia, with its reliance on intensive cultivation, the family farm was a unit superior to either the large-scale capitalist or large-scale socialist form of agriculture. But in 1919 Chaianov trod gingerly. He made his case for the vertical cooperatives, arguing that these institutions would rationalize the activity of the family farm.

The Organization-Production scholars continued to advocate vertical integration until well into 1928. The reasons they offered for their stand, however, changed over time. In 1919 Chaianov recommended vertical cooperation primarily because of its advantages for the individual farm. In a series of writings on cooperation published in 1925, he repeated the original argument and added two new points in support of the scheme he favored.[49] In the short run, he claimed, vertical cooperation would be the most successful way of tying the family farm sector to the planned economy.[50] This linkage was vital, for as long as the mass of individual farms was independent of the control of state agencies, the stability of the whole economy was in jeopardy.[51] Chaianov's second argument was based on longer-term considerations. Ultimately, he declared, the vertical cooperatives would serve as conduits to socialism. To start with, the peasants would be exposed to cooperative marketing and processing, but eventually they would come to take part in cooperative production.[52]

Chaianov's reference to the coming of socialism in his 1925 discussion of cooperation is most intriguing. Here was a man who, like many of his colleagues in the Timiriazev Institute, had been openly skeptical about the effects of socialism on the Russian countryside. Not a year earlier, he had expressed a wait-and-see attitude toward socialist agriculture while proclaiming the virtues of the small-scale family farm.[53] The contradiction between Chaianov's 1924 and 1925 positions is more apparent than real, however. In the brief discussion of the coming of socialism which occurred on the final pages of "Peasant Farm Organization," Chaianov continued to champion the family farm. He claimed to expect "a gradual denial of the bases of the family farm economy,"[54] yet his image of socialism included the existence of private farming. As Chaianov defined it in 1925, the socialist economy (termed "social cooperative economy") of the future would be one "founded on socialized capital, that leaves in the private farms of its members the technical fulfillment of certain processes almost on the basis of a technical commission."[55] The reader is led to the conclusion that in using the term "socialism," Chaianov was employing the rhetoric of the day to argue in favor of the continued existence of the family farm.[56] The gap between Chaianov's terminology and the agricultural program it described did not go unnoticed by his critics, who charged him with an "unorthodox" view of socialism.[57]

Location Studies: Defining the Optimal Farm

Committed as they were to the reorganization of Russian agriculture, the Timiriazev professors were interested in isolating principles for determining the optimal farm unit, its size, and its pattern of cultivation. These important questions had been treated by European agricultural economists in their work on location theory.[58] Consequently it was to this corpus of research that the Organization-Production scholars turned for inspiration.

In approaching the question of cultivation patterns, the Timiriazev professors turned to the classic work *The Isolated State*, written by the German Heinrich von Thunen in 1826.[59] Von Thunen, himself a farmer as well as an economist, had noticed that the same crop was often cultivated under different systems of intensity and set about to discover the factors responsible for the choice of one pattern of cultivation as opposed to another. He elaborated an economic model of an isolated state, uniform in fertility, at the center of which was a large market town; and he held constant all the factors commonly believed to determine intensity (climate, fertility of the soil, native ability of the farmer) except one: distance from the market. Von Thunen found that a farmer's decision about agricultural intensity was a function of the price he received for his produce and that that price, in turn, was determined by the distance of the farm from the market.

Not surprisingly, the Timiriazev professors judged the conclusions drawn in *The Isolated State* inapplicable to Russian agriculture. With the economy of the family farm in mind, they insisted that it was not the market but the pressure of consumption demands that was the most important factor in determining agricultural intensity.[60] Although they rejected von Thunen's conclusions, the Timiriazev professors were clearly impressed by his work.[61] Therefore, they decided to replicate his approach in order to ascertain the way in which the family farmer calculated the intensity optimal for his farm. The work of replication was undertaken by Chaianov, who published his results in 1921 under the title *Opyty izucheniia izolirovannogo gosudarstva* [Attempts to Study the Isolated State].[62] The purpose of Chaianov's study, as he himself admitted, was to construct an economic model that would capture the unique features of the family farm in much the same way that von Thunen had laid bare the mainsprings of capitalist agriculture.[63] In keeping with this aim, Chaianov formulated a model of an isolated state in which there was no private landowning; the entire island was composed only of family farms.[64] At its center was a single market town, around which were five concentric circles, each containing six different degrees of intensive cultivation.[65] Into this model Chaianov then introduced capitalist farms, whose method of determining optimal intensity he compared to that of the family farm. He discovered that the family farmer calculated intensity following rules different from those that the capitalist farmer followed. The head of the family farm, motivated by the desire to satisfy the consumption needs of his dependents, determined the optimal intensity for his economic unit in relation to consumption pressure; the capitalist farmer, motivated by the quest for gain, calculated the intensity optimal for his farm by taking into account the potential for profit.[66] The conclusions Chaianov drew from his study provided confirmation of one of the central tenets of Organization-Production theory, namely, that because of his psychological orientation, the family farmer differed significantly from the *homo economicus* upon whom classical theory had been modeled. Thus the 1921 study reinforced the growing conviction among the Timiriazev professors that a new "noncapitalist" economic theory was warranted.

As a complement to their interest in agricultural intensity, the Organization-Production scholars were concerned with the question of farm size. In itself, this concern is hardly startling, for discussions of the optimal size of an agricultural enterprise had been commonplace in Russia for decades.[67] It is significant, however, that when the Timiriazev professors turned to study the question in 1922, they deliberately dissociated themselves from the work of their Russian predecessors and stressed instead their debt to the work of two German economists, K. Werner and V. Stebel, who had explored the same problem.[68] As the head of the Timiriazev Institute's project on farm size, Chaianov had to explain his group's choice of roots. This he did without mincing any words. Russian economists, contended Chaianov, had traditionally treated the question of farm size from a quantitative point of view, fusing the issue of optimal size with that of the relative merits of large- as opposed to small-scale cultivation.[69] To the Organization-Production scholars this approach was an anathema, for they believed that the most important differences between the two types of farming were qualitative in nature and hence were not susceptible of numerical measurement.[70]

Although Chaianov took pains to link his group's work to the research of the German economists, he was careful to point out that his approach differed substantially from that of his foreign colleagues. The German scholars, following von Thunen, had calculated optimal size by referring to the distance of the farmstead from the fields; he, on the other hand, believed that the form of cultivation determined the optimal size for any farm. To support his point, Chaianov applied a general method of calculating farm optima refined by his colleagues in the Timiriazev Institute[71] to a series of farms whose cultivation patterns differed. He found that for each system of agriculture, there was a distinct optimum size.[72] In correlating farm structure and size, Chaianov was working on the frontiers of location theory; at the same time, he was extending the range of Organization-Production theory by moving it into uncharted areas.

The Timiriazev project on optimum size came in for much criticism. Kritsman, for one, faulted Chaianov for having failed to declare himself categorically on the issue of large- as opposed to small-scale farming.[73] On the face of it, Kritsman's criticism seems grossly unfair, for at the outset of his work Chaianov had made it clear that he did not intend to discuss this thorny issue and that his current research on optimum size was meant to apply only to large-scale capitalist farms.[74] Upon second glance, however, Kritsman's riposte becomes most understandable. Despite his disclaimers, Chaianov did not really shy away from the debate over farm scale. On the contrary, he dropped hints to the effect that agriculture, unlike industry, was not governed by any firm laws of scale.[75] This suggested that he was championing the cause of the small-scale family farm. In a small but explosive paragraph, Chaianov was explicit.

> According to our deepest belief, the ideal vehicle for agricultural production is not at all the large-scale latifundia, nor the individual peasant farm, but a new type of economic organization in which the organizational plan would be distributed into various links, each of which would be organized in a size optimal to it. In other words, the ideal for us would be the peasant family farm, which would have deleted from its organizational plan all those branches of farming in which large-scale production is superior to small-scale production and which would have organized these in varying degrees of scale in cooperatives.[76]

Thus, Chaianov used the study of optimal farm size to underscore the Organization-Production belief in the viability and superiority of the family farm economy.

Although their research focused on Russian farming, the Timiriazev professors hoped that their studies would be of interest to agricultural economists working beyond the frontiers of Russia. Their hopes for recognition proved largely vain. The scholarship of the Timiriazev Institute during the 1920s, though known to economists outside Russia, proved to have little lasting impact upon the field of agricultural economics. More likely than not, this was due to the fact that the research of the Organization-Production scholars was so closely tied to their theory. To their critics—both hostile and friendly—that theory was of limited utility, for it was based on the peculiar realities of a form of agriculture destined to pass into oblivion.

5. Agrarian-Marxist Theory

The Agrarian-Marxists devoted most of their energies to sociological research; and it was this research that earned these young men a place in the community of Soviet rural scholars. Yet they were no crude empiricists. They began their work on the countryside with a discussion of theory.

The theoretical interests of the Kritsman group centered on the transition to socialism of the Soviet peasantry. In approaching this question, the young scholars were much influenced by the fact that they were the first generation of Soviet Marxists to study the Russian countryside. Underscoring their unique position in history, the Agrarian-Marxists declared that the thinking of their Russian Marxist ancestors about the transition to socialism was inapplicable under Soviet conditions. In place of the "outmoded" thought of the past, they refined a new theory, which they claimed would explain the evolution of the agricultural sector in a country that had experienced a proletarian revolution.[1]

For many reasons, adherence to their novel theory proved problematic for the Agrarian-Marxists. First of all, they came to see that their theory provided little guidance in the study of certain salient questions. Moreover, their proclamations of originality coupled with their youth hindered the Agrarian-Marxists in their efforts to secure a place for themselves in the Soviet community of rural scholars, in which they were of course newcomers. In light of these intellectual and professional considerations, the Agrarian-Marxists came to reassess their relationship to the Russian Marxism of the past.

In this chapter, we will examine the theory developed by the Agrarian-Marxists, focusing first on the heritage they denied and later on the tradition they embraced. We will then examine the way in which these young scholars reaffirmed their roots and suggest some of the long-range implications for the group of this concession to tradition.

The Rejected Tradition: Russian Marxism in the 1880s and 1890s

On the question of the evolution to socialism of a primarily small-peasant society, the position of the Russian Marxists was crystallized in the course of their debate with the populists (narodniks) in the last two decades of the nineteenth century.[2] The disagreement between these two groups of intellectuals, each of which claimed to be the authentic interpreter for Russia of the thought of Karl Marx, broke out over the issue of the development of the Russian economy. As followers of Marx, both groups agreed that the final goal of development should and would be socialism, although each defined that goal in its own way. Moreover, on the basis of their analysis of the Russian economy at the end of the nineteenth century, both groups agreed that capitalism had made and was continuing to make substantial inroads into the industrial sector.[3] The populists and Marxists differed only on a single point, namely, whether the continued spread of capitalism would lead to the goal of socialism to which they were committed.

Of the two groups, the populists had the more negative appraisal of the effects of capitalism.[4] According to them, in subsidizing and protecting industrial capitalism for some thirty years, the Russian government had been propping up an artificial, "hothouse" plant, whose continued growth would lead to distress in agricultural and industrial sectors alike. As evidence for this dire prediction, the populists advanced two arguments. First, they submitted, there would be no market for the goods the hyperactive industrial sector was pumping out. The pressure of expanding capitalism, so ran the argument, was gradually dissolving the self-sufficient peasant economy, thus destroying the only viable domestic market for industrial goods.[5] Moreover, foreign markets were virtually closed to Russian products, for those markets had been captured by countries producing goods far superior to those made in Russia. Deprived of both internal and external outlets for its goods, Russian industry could not but atrophy. Second, the populists argued, the stagnation of industry would result in the ruin of agriculture. The towns, limited perforce in size, would be able to provide neither employment nor refuge for the surplus rural population. Consequently, the countryside would continue to be burdened with a surfeit of mouths to feed and would be unable to accommodate new and more efficient techniques of farming. Distressed by the specter of a stagnating industry and an impoverished agriculture, the populists called upon the government to cease its support of industrial capitalism, arguing that the continuation of the old policy would lead to the collapse of the Russian economy. Genuine economic progress, they submitted, could only come about if Russia were to skip the stage of capitalism and move to create within her borders a socialist economy.

The recommendation that Russia bypass the stage of capitalism involved the populists in both logical and ideological difficulties. To begin with, by advocating a noncapitalist path, the populists were implying that economic developments already in motion could be undone. To be sure, they did not perceive the problems inherent in this position because they maintained that Russian capitalism was an artificial import, which, if denied government support, would wither of its own accord. To the populists, a noncapitalist path represented not a reversal of economic developments, but a return to natural, as opposed to artificial, economic growth. Even more important than the logical puzzles were the ideological questions raised by the populist position. In suggesting that Russia skip the stage of capitalism on its road to socialism, the populists were in effect recommending for Russia a path of development different from that envisaged by Marx for the nations of Europe. Defending themselves against the accusation that their suggestion was "un-Marxist," the populists pointed out that Marx himself had been sympathetic to the notion that Russia follow a unique path and build socialism on the foundations of the rural commune.[6] Pursuing this strand in Marx's thought, the populists envisaged a socialist Russia whose core would be the traditional rural institutions (the *artel'* and the *obshchina*) and whose economy would be primarily agricultural, with industry playing the role of an appendage.[7]

The Russian Marxists objected strenuously to the populist vision of a rural-based socialism.[8] They were committed to a socialist Russia that would be primarily industrial, a Russia in which agriculture would act as the handmaiden of industry, adapting itself to the demands of the industrial sector.[9] Even more strongly than they objected to the populists' goal, the Marxists rejected the populist claim that Russia could pursue a noncapitalist path to socialism. To them such a transition was inconceivable in the light of two facts. First, capitalism was already firmly entrenched in both industrial and agricultural sectors. The populists, it will be remembered, had never denied that capitalism had penetrated the industrial sector, but they had always insisted that the rural sector was free of capitalism, that the dominant form of production in the countryside was noncapitalist ("popular production"). In order to refute the populist contention, in 1899 Lenin published his study of the social structure of the Russian countryside. In this work, entitled *The Development of Capitalism in Russia*, Lenin showed that the rural sector was characterized by the type of social stratification symptomatic of the presence of capitalism.[10] The implications of Lenin's study were clear: no area of the economy could be said to be free of capitalism. Second, the Marxists argued, the capitalism that had taken hold in the industrial and agricultural sectors was not an imported, but an indigenous, plant. In making this point, they were taking issue directly with the populists, who had contended that there was a difference in kind between the noncapitalist ("popular") production that prevailed in agriculture and the capitalist production that had been grafted onto industry. The Marxists maintained that the difference between these two forms of production was one of degree rather than one of kind; indeed, they submitted, industrial capitalism had developed out of popular production.[11] Upon this argument the Marxists based their belief that Russian capitalism was a plant with native roots and, as such, was a plant that would continue to grow in Russian soil irrespective of government support.

On the strength of these two arguments, the Marxists declared that a noncapitalist path to socialism was unthinkable. The path, as Lenin put it, "had already been chosen."[12] Consequently, the Marxists urged that the process of development be allowed to run its course and warned against the government's placing any impediments in the path of expanding capitalism.[13] In making these recommendations, the Marxists were by no means unaware of the ills that would accompany the further growth of capitalism.[14] However, they believed that capitalism could best be fought by speeding up its development and thereby hastening the coming of socialism.

As is well known, the Russian Marxists emerged victorious from their debate with the populists.[15] Their victory left an indelible stamp upon the content of Russian Marxism. From the turn of the century, most Russian socialists were committed to the view that for the agricultural as well as the industrial sector, a period of capitalist development was inevitable.[16] As they saw it, the unequal distribution of resources and talents would produce a peasantry stratified into various gradations of well-being. Economic advantages and disadvantages being cumulative, the peasantry would eventually be polarized into two groups of unequal size. At one end of the spectrum would be a tiny group of large-scale landowners, who were in effect agricultural capitalists; at the other pole would be the vast majority of the rural population, small-scale landowners, who were more often than not landless laborers working the land of the rural capitalists. The middle independent peasants, who were the backbone of traditional peasant society, would be absorbed into one or the other—usually the latter—of these two groups.[17] Thus for almost all those who tilled the land, capitalism meant proletarianization. Painful though this process might be, the Russian Marxists welcomed it. They were convinced that, by dissolving the traditional peasant society, capitalism would pave the way for the coming of socialism. In their view, the polarization of rural society would breed hostile relations between the exploiting capitalists and the exploited landless laborers. That hostility would issue in a social conflict that would be resolved only when the expropriators had been expropriated and when large-scale production organized on socialist lines had become the dominant form of agricultural production. Belief in this pattern of rural development was an integral feature of Russian Marxism for several decades after the populists had been vanquished. Indeed, not until almost five years after the Bolshevik Revolution was the legacy of the 1890s reassessed.

The Accepted Tradition: Lenin on Cooperation (1923)

The Bolshevik seizure of power in 1917 provided the impetus for a reevaluation of the view that in the transition to socialism the Russian peasantry had of necessity to pass through the stage of capitalism. In the turbulent years between 1917 and 1923, Lenin reversed his stand on this issue several times, leading his followers through a maze of theoretical distinctions and refinements that were often little more than ad hoc responses to the press of circumstance. In 1923, in what was to be his last word on the subject, the ailing leader declared that a primarily petit bourgeois economy could evolve to socialism through the cooperatives. This statement implied that the Russian peasantry might avoid the agonies of the capitalist stage of development. It was this final dictum of Lenin that provoked the Agrarian-Marxists to formulate a new theory of the transition to socialism.

The real significance of Lenin's 1923 position for the subsequent evolution of Soviet Marxism cannot be appreciated without an analysis of its historical roots. In March 1921 Lenin inaugurated the New Economic Policy with a proposal to substitute a tax in kind for the forced requisitioning of grain that had been the rule under War Communism.[18] Once passed, the decree on the tax in kind triggered the adoption of a series of measures which stimulated the revival of free trade and market relations between the agricultural and industrial sectors of the economy. Within a short time, these measures wrought substantial changes in the social and economic life of Russia. When he introduced the tax in kind, Lenin could not foresee the full extent of the changes that would occur, but he did anticipate that the measure would foster the growth of capitalism.

Free exchange and freedom of trade means circulation of commodities among petty proprietors. All of us who have studied at least the elements of Marxism know that this exchange and freedom of trade inevitably lead to a division of commodity producers into owners of capital and owners of labour-power, . . . i.e., a revival of capitalist wage-slavery, which . . . springs the world over precisely from the agricultural commodity economy.[19]

To forestall criticism of his new program, Lenin declared that the stimulation of capitalism in post-1917 Russia was necessary for the fulfillment of both immediate and long-term goals. The Civil War had left the country in such an impoverished condition, he asserted, that the most urgent task was to repair the economy and increase the production of goods. The accomplishment of this task in an agricultural country was dependent on the goodwill of the central figure in the countryside, the "industrious" middle peasant, who wanted nothing more than to trade freely and to be able to obtain commodities. Refusal to allow him to do so would doom the economy and threaten the very stability of the new regime.[20]

A period of capitalist development was as indispensable for long-term aims as it was for short-term aims, Lenin insisted. The attainment of socialism depended on the existence of certain preconditions that capitalism would supply.

Socialism is inconceivable without large-scale capitalist engineering based on the latest discoveries of modern science. It is inconceivable without planned state organization which keeps tens of millions of people to the strictest observance of a unified standard of production and distribution.[21]

Had the proletarian revolution taken place in an advanced capitalist country, so ran the argument, the transition to socialism could have been effected directly. But Russia, being a primarily petit-bourgeois country whose economy was based on agriculture, required a long period of capitalism, during which the necessary capital would be accumulated and important skills assimilated by those who would administer the future society.[22]

In answer to members of the Party who might consider NEP a "retreat," Lenin termed his new program "state capitalism" and asserted that it was a continuation of the policy he had pursued before the adoption of War Communism in June 1918.[23] The analogy between NEP and the policies of the first half of 1918 was strained;[24] however, in drawing the connection Lenin was speaking primarily as a politician whose purpose was to secure support for the new policy by minimizing its novelty.

Lenin used the term "state capitalism" not only to give NEP the legitimacy that derived from precedent, but also to define the nature of the transition period upon which he was setting Russia. As he envisaged it, during the period of state capitalism, the proletarian state would ally itself with capital. If successful, such a policy stood to enhance the Soviet state.

> If we were able to obtain even a small quantity of goods and hold them in the hand of the state—the proletariat exercising political power—and if we could release these goods into circulation, we, as the state, would add economic power to our political power.[25]

At the same time, the policy of state capitalism was fraught with risks. "The whole problem," Lenin remarked soberly, "is to find the correct method of directing the development of capitalism (which is to some extent and for some time inevitable) into the channels of state capitalism, and to determine how we are to hedge it about with guarantees to ensure its transformation into socialism in the near future."[26]

Lenin's understanding of the dangers inherent in setting Russia on the capitalist path was clearly reflected in his comparison of the two main forms of state capitalism: concessions to large-scale capitalist industry and the extension of freedom and rights to the small commodity producers' cooperatives. Although he included them under the same rubric, Lenin admitted that these two forms of state capitalism differed substantially in form, in purpose, and in relation to socialism. Concessions to capitalist industry were to be granted for specified periods of time on the basis of a written agreement between the Soviet state and "the most civilized advanced Western European capitalism."[27] Foreign capitalists would be invited to construct a number of large-scale industries, which would eventually "revert" to the Soviet state.[28] From here, to socialism, Lenin explained, the transition would be fairly direct; what was involved was simply the evolution of one form of large-scale production to another.[29] The extension of rights to the cooperatives was a less simple case. To be sure, important benefits could flow from such a policy. Millions of small commodity producers could be brought together in associations that would simplify "accounting, control, supervision and the establishment of contractual relations between the state . . . and the capitalist."[30] But cooperative capitalism was a risky venture. It was difficult to keep an eye on the cooperators because agreements with the cooperative societies could be bounded neither by time nor by specific conditions.[31] Most important, the transition from cooperative capitalism to socialism would be complex. The cooperatives were based on small proprietor production, and their conversion to socialist institutions would therefore require the transition from small-scale to large-scale production, an evolution that could only be effected, Lenin warned, after "an indefinite period."[32]

Lenin was conscious not only of the practical problems but also of the ideological difficulties inherent in a proletarian state's encouraging the development of capitalism. There were those in the Party who were given to repeating the litany "capitalism is a bane and socialism is a boon." To them Lenin explained that the simple formula was meaningless in the Soviet case. For Russia in 1921, the choice did not lie between "capitalism" and "socialism." The Russian economy was still dominated by small commodity production, from which no direct transition to socialism could be made. Consequently, the route to change lay through state capitalism,[33] which, he insisted, represented a "gigantic step forward" from the existing "medievalism."[34]

At many points in his 1921 discussions of state capitalism, Lenin made it clear that he considered the foremost enemy of socialism to be not the capitalist, but the petit bourgeois element in Soviet society.[35] Indeed, it was to defeat this element that Lenin urged an alliance of the proletarian state and capitalism. Yet in the very same speeches and writings Lenin stressed the need to preserve the alliance with the middle peasantry. "We know," he reminded his listeners at the Tenth Party Congress, "that so long as there is no revolution in other countries, only agreement with the peasantry can save the socialist revolution in Russia."[36] Lenin's ambivalent attitude toward the small commodity producer was as characteristic of his thought as his shifting attitude toward the role of capitalism in a proletarian state.[37]

Not long after he had argued so vehemently in its behalf, Lenin was to have second thoughts about the policy of state capitalism. At the Eleventh Party Congress in March 1922, he announced that he was halting the retreat to capitalism begun only a year earlier.[38] The reasons for his reassessment were not difficult to fathom. Essentially, the attempt to derive economic benefits from foreign concessions had failed.[39] Foreign capitalists had not been attracted by Lenin's terms and had shied away from investing in the Soviet economy. Nor was there any immediate prospect of a world revolution that could rescue the Soviet economy from its dire straits. Therefore, as Lenin recognized, the only recourse was for the Soviet regime to turn inward and rely upon the peasantry for both accumulation and support.[40] As the grim realization of the necessity for self-sufficiency took hold, the policy of state capitalism based primarily on foreign concessions was abandoned.

To replace state capitalism as the intermediary stage between the petit bourgeois economy and socialism, Lenin turned to the rural cooperatives. In January 1923 he wrote two articles, in which he argued that the incorporation of the peasantry into cooperatives would place the Soviet Union "with both feet on the soil of socialism."[41] He admitted that such incorporation would constitute nothing short of a cultural revolution and would require an entire historical epoch to bring into being.[42] But once accomplished, he insisted, the prerequisites for socialism would have been secured.

Lenin's 1923 writings on cooperation revealed important changes in his thinking. First, over the two-year period since the inauguration of NEP, Lenin revised his rank ordering of the obstacles to socialism. In 1921 he had focused primarily on the economic and political barriers to change in Russia; two years later, he was almost exclusively preoccupied with the cultural obstacles to socialism. Lenin himself drew attention to this shift in emphasis, which he explained as a function of the fact that the economic and political problems had been solved.[43] Second, Lenin's articles on cooperation reflected a change in his attitude toward the rural cooperatives. In 1921 Lenin had treated these institutions as forms of state capitalism, whose sole contribution would be the improvement of small-scale agricultural production. In 1923 he was treating the cooperatives as institutions whose growth was identical with that of socialism.[44] "Under our present system," he said, "cooperative enterprises . . . do not differ from socialist enterprises if the land on which they are situated and the means of production belong to the state, i.e., the working class."[45] In redefining the cooperatives, Lenin redefined socialism. In his final articles, socialism became "the system of civilized cooperators."[46]

Illness prevented Lenin from addressing himself again to the question of Russia's transition to socialism. As a result, the 1923 articles on cooperation became Lenin's final bequest to the Russian people. As such these two pieces proved problematic. They raised a host of questions that Lenin's heirs were left to puzzle out. The task of interpretation was not accomplished without difficulty or altercation. In 1925, as is well known, there erupted a debate among Party leaders over whether Lenin was referring to consumers' or producers' cooperatives.[47] That he had consumers' cooperatives in mind seems abundantly clear from the drift of his articles; however, both sides in the debate were able to cite the original text in support of their positions. A less cited, but equally important, problem of interpretation arose because of Lenin's failure to detail the relationship between the capitalism he had declared to be on the rise in 1921 and the cooperatives whose development he discussed in 1923. This issue was particularly bedeviling to the Agrarian-Marxists, for, following Lenin, they subscribed to a theory that pointed to the possibility in the Soviet setting of a cooperative path to socialism; yet their research findings showed the increasing spread of capitalism among the Russian peasantry. This contradiction was to haunt the Agrarian-Marxists throughout the 1920s.

Agrarian-Marxist Theory: The Original Statement

Most of the work involved in elaborating a theoretical framework was performed for the Agrarian-Marxists by the group's senior scholar, L. N. Kritsman. Kritsman's younger colleagues, who had been trained as researchers in the Timiriazev Academy, seemed quite content to leave the concerns of theory to their leader.[48]

Kritsman himself did not begin to tackle the problem of formulating a theory of rural development appropriate to Soviet conditions until 1925. Before then he devoted his energies to criticizing what he considered the most important omissions in the work of the Organization-Production school. The brunt of his attack was directed against the failure of the Timiriazev professors to take into account the economic and technological backwardness of the precapitalist farm they championed.[49] To Kritsman, this omission was particularly glaring, for, as a Marxist, he subscribed to the premise that small-scale cultivation was inferior to, and would therefore be superseded by, large-scale units of production.

At mid-decade, Kritsman set aside his criticism of the Chaianov group[50] and began constructing a theory of the transition of the Soviet small-scale peasantry to socialism. In January 1925 he presented the outline of his theory for the first time in an address delivered to the Communist Academy on the first anniversary of Lenin's death.[51] In the same month he published a long article in which he supplied the underlying logic of his theory and spelled out some of its implications.[52]

Kritsman approached the question of rural development to socialism with the conviction that the particulars of the Soviet situation were such as to constitute a pressure for the revision of conventional wisdom. His principal target was the theory, espoused by both Western and late nineteenth-century Russian Marxists alike, that the only route to socialism for the petit bourgeois peasant was *via* capitalism. While he admitted the validity of this line of thinking for the countries of Western Europe and even for his native Russia before the October Revolution, Kritsman declared it inapplicable under Soviet conditions.[53] When political power was in the hands of the proletariat, he insisted, the ironclad rules of the past no longer held sway.

For guidance in the new situation, Kritsman turned to Lenin's 1923 articles on cooperation. These articles provided several important insights. First, the peasant had a dual nature; he was inclined not only to large-scale individual cultivation but also toward cooperative farming. Second, under the dictatorship of the proletariat the cooperative inclinations of the peasantry, which in a capitalist system were invariably channeled in a private direction, could be so molded as to forge among the peasantry a genuinely collectivist spirit. And third, under the dictatorship of the proletariat the cooperatives would cease to be capitalist institutions and would become institutions whose growth was identical with that of socialism.[54] In the light of these insights, Kritsman declared, the countryside was "outmoded." Lenin had revealed the possibility of a second path—the cooperative route. Under the hegemony of the proletariat, the middle independent peasant could avoid the agonies of a contest with the rural capitalist and the almost-certain proletarianization that would result from that struggle; instead he could join the cooperatives, as a member of which he could engage in a struggle that pitted one against the other two forms of large-scale agricultural production: capitalist and cooperative farming. Out of this more equal struggle would emerge socialist cultivation.[55]

Although Kritsman insisted that both the capitalist and the cooperative paths would lead the peasant to socialism, he greatly preferred the cooperative route. To begin with, the new path would promote the development of a homogeneous Soviet economy. Instead of industry evolving directly to socialism and agriculture evolving first to capitalism and then to socialism, the cooperative option would permit both sectors of the economy to develop in tandem.[56] Moreover, the cooperative path would accomplish the important task of dissolving the precapitalist peasantry at a smaller social cost that would the capitalist route.[57] Last but not least, the pursuit by the peasantry of the capitalist path would provide concrete evidence of the novelty (and greatness) of the Soviet achievement.[58]

Although he favored the cooperative path to socialism, Kritsman was aware that not all the peasantry would find the prospect of being incorporated into the rural cooperatives appealing. Some, to be sure, would flock to these institutions; but others, influenced by their attachment to individual farming, would cling to their tiny parcels of land and thus play their roles in bringing capitalism to the countryside. Convinced that a fundamental change in peasant attitudes would be required before the cooperative path could be successful,[59] Kritsman predicted that during the initial phase of the dictatorship of the proletariat both the cooperative and the capitalist paths would be pursued.[60] Over time, however, as it became abundantly clear that the vast majority of the peasantry could no longer sustain themselves as individual farmers, increasing numbers of peasants would join the cooperatives, and the new route would come to eclipse the old.[61] Thus did Kritsman add to his preference for the cooperative route a prediction of its eventual success.

In championing the cooperative route, Kritsman continually underscored his role as an innovator. Indeed, throughout his theoretical discussions, the reader finds Kritsman proclaiming, not altogether modestly, the revisionist nature of his thinking on the question of rural social change. In point of fact, his work as a theorist was more that of a codifier than that of a pathbreaker. Essentially, Kritsman took a series of propositions found in Lenin's 1923 articles on cooperation, refined them, and cast them into a theoretical framework.

In Search of Old Roots: Agrarian-Marxism after 1925

The novel aspects of Kritsman's theory, of which he was so proud, fell into desuetude after 1925. The factor primarily responsible for this development was an intellectual one. The data collected by the Agrarian-Marxists revealed that in the Soviet Union of the mid-1920s the cooperative route was losing rather than gaining ground. As Kritsman himself recorded, the poor and middle peasants were continuing to display individualistic attitudes, holding on to the illusion that they could sustain themselves on their own land.[62] Moreover, the cooperatives that did exist were not fulfilling the function anticipated by Lenin; they were being used by the rich peasants for their own purposes.[63]

The contradiction between the postulates of his theory arrived at by assertion and the research findings was striking. Confronted by this, Kritsman adopted what seemed at the time to be an optimal solution. He did not disclaim those propositions of his theory that pointed to the eventual ascendance of the cooperative over the capitalist path to socialism. However, he framed the research projects he directed around the proposition that the Russian peasantry was pursuing the capitalist path.[64] He also refined a set of indicators of capitalism, which, when applied to the study of the Soviet countryside, showed that the Russian peasantry was becoming increasingly polarized into rural capitalists and agricultural wage workers.[65] In this way, Kritsman led the Agrarian-Marxists to rejoin the tradition of Russian Marxism.

The Kritsman group set aside its disavowal of the past not only for intellectual, but also for professional, reasons. From 1923, the young Agrarian-Marxists were embroiled in a controversy with the members of the Organization-Production school. This was a David-and-Goliath contest in which the young researchers felt themselves at an enormous disadvantage. They were pitted against their former teachers, the acknowledged leaders of the Soviet community of rural scholars. Feeling their youth and lack of experience keenly, the Agrarian-Marxists looked for any device to increase their stature. With this goal in mind, they applied the epithet "neo-narodnik" (neo-populist) to the members of the Organization-Production school.[66] This epithet recalled the debate of the 1880s and 1890s between the Marxists and the populists, a debate that had ended in the victory of the Marxist group. In thus labeling their rivals of the 1920s "neo-narodniks," the Kritsman group was laying claim to an ancestry they hoped would add luster to their position. Although they used the evocative label freely, the Agrarian-Marxists drew few concrete connections between their own work and that of their supposed predecessors.

History records that the Agrarian-Marxists' reaffirmation of their roots failed to fulfill either of the purposes for which it had been designed. The modifications that the group undertook for cognitive reasons proved to have liabilities as well as advantages. There developed a tension between the Kritsman group's adherence to the belief in the eventual success of the cooperative path and their professional commitment to demonstrating the ascendancy of the capitalist route. To minimize the strain, the Agrarian-Marxists took to avoiding any discussion of the cooperatives. By the end of the decade, they would find themselves under attack by a rival group of Marxist scholars because of their "neglect" of these rural institutions. Similarly, the Russian roots the Agrarian-Marxists "discovered" for professional reasons did not prove to be an asset in the way they had imagined. The reference to the debates of the 1880s and 1890s did not raise the stature of the Kritsman group in the scholarly community; it only incurred the wrath of the Organization-Production scholars. Moreover, the homage paid by the group to Lenin's work of 1899 did not sit well with their critics, who insisted that the Lenin of 1923 was more relevant to NEP Russia than was the Lenin of the turn of the century.

Despite the problems associated with the theory they had formulated, the Agrarian-Marxists were able to do significant scholarship on the rural sector. They refined a methodology for measuring differences between peasant households and, using it, studied social structure in large parts of Russia's countryside. This empirical work earned the Kritsman group a distinctive place in the Soviet community of rural scholars.

6. Agrarian-Marxist Research

In contrast to their mentors, the Agrarian-Marxists confined their research in rural sociology to the study of a single problem—the social structure of the Soviet peasantry. Under the leadership of L. N. Kritsman, the group in the Agrarian Section conducted study after study of social stratification in the countryside, using a methodology they had designed especially for this purpose. The methodology reflected the Agrarian-Marxists' preconceptions about the evolution of the Russian peasantry in the Soviet period. With Lenin's forebodings of 1921 fresh in their minds, the young researchers assumed that under NEP the rural sector would become increasingly enmeshed in capitalism. Consequently, they anticipated that the peasantry would be polarized into two large groups, rural capitalists and agricultural wage workers, with the middle independent peasant being absorbed into one or the other (usually the latter) of the two groups. The new system of measurement, with which the Kritsman group soon became identified, had the particular merit of being sensitive to the pattern of rural social development that the Agrarian-Marxists anticipated.

The New Methodology

The Agrarian-Marxists devoted a great deal of time and energy to the formulation of their research methodology. Indeed, so intensely were these young men preoccupied with the nuances of measurement that they drew criticism from Marxist scholars not affiliated with the Kritsman group.[1] On the one hand, S. M. Dubrovskii, always more concerned with policy than with scholarship, claimed that the group in the Agrarian Section was spending too much time refining a method for study and too little time devising solutions for the problems that beset the rural sector.[2] On the other hand, the statistician A. I. Khriashcheva, who herself worked on problems of rural stratification, contended that the efforts of the Agrarian-Marxists were superfluous, since in her view the methods traditionally used to study the class structure of the peasantry were perfectly applicable under NEP.[3]

Speaking as the leader of the Agrarian-Marxists, Kritsman rationalized the group's concentration on methodology with the argument that the capitalism fostered by the New Economic Policy differed so fundamentally from the capitalism that had prevailed before the Revolution that its nature could not be laid bare using the old tools of measurement.[4] Before 1917, Kritsman explained, peasant households had differed primarily in the amount of arable land possessed, and, consequently, there developed the practice of measuring rural differentiation by charting the distribution of land among the peasantry. Eight months after the October Revolution, the Soviet regime undertook a program of land redistribution, a program that continued throughout War Communism. This redistribution changed the face of the Soviet countryside; differences in the size of peasant holdings were leveled, and by 1920 the middle peasant had emerged as the dominant figure in the countryside.[5] The leveling of differences, complained Kritsman, had created the impression among some observers that all significant variations among peasant farms had been eliminated and that therefore the period of socialism was at hand. In Kritsman's opinion, these impressions were erroneous and, worse, prejudicial to the proper study of the peasantry under NEP. The period of socialism was still to come, he insisted. The leveling of 1917-1920 had been petit bourgeois in nature, for the land had been distributed for private, not communal, use, and the redistribution had been effected by peasants whose chief aim was to become petit bourgeois farmers.[6] Moreover, he stressed, the redistribution of land under War Communism had not ended rural differences. The elimination of glaring inequalities in the possession of land had simply made other inequities more obvious, specifically the unequal possession by the peasantry of livestock and inventory. Unlike the land, these means of cultivation had not been redivided after the Revolution,[7] and consequently, after 1920, they became the foundation of class structure in the countryside. The emergence of new determinants of class structure made it impossible to continue using the traditional system of measuring differentiation;[8] a new method would have to be devised, Kritsman submitted.

Convinced that he had made a forceful case for the elaboration of a new methodology, Kritsman turned to the task of devising the system of measurement for which he had argued. The methodology was presented in two stages. First, the core concepts were defined, and significant relationships were isolated. Then appropriate indicators were selected, and a method of measurement was proposed. The newly designed methodology was then tested in a series of research studies on the Soviet peasantry.

Concepts and Relations

Kritsman treated rural differentiation as a socioeconomic phenomenon. Consequently, his interest was not in the inequities in the distribution of resources in the countryside, but in the unequal social relations generated by those economic inequities. In Kritsman's view the primary task of researchers studying rural differentiation was to ferret out the relations of subordination and superordination among the peasantry. To facilitate the identification of these relations, Kritsman began with the concept of the independent peasant.[9] He defined this peasant as one who was able to farm his own land using only his own livestock and inventory. The peasant who relied on others for these means of cultivation was termed a "false" (*mnimy*) cultivator; the peasant upon whom others relied for these resources was termed an "entrepreneur" (*predprinimatel'*). The criteria of independence that Kritsman laid down were so demanding that they guaranteed that few, if any, peasants would qualify as "independent." This bias in the typology was not unintentional. Indeed, Kritsman declared that he expected to find few independent peasants in the NEP countryside; as the rural sector became capitalist, he explained, most of the self-sufficient peasants would disappear.

Though easily defined, independence was difficult to measure, Kritsman admitted. The peasants, wary of the new regime, had developed a complex set of ruses by which they could hide their economic activities and thus mask their social relations.[10] Consequently, the rural sector under NEP was characterized by a series of inverted relations that made it uncommonly difficult to determine who was dependent upon whom. For example, a man might not work on his own land but instead might hire a worker equipped with horse and inventory. At first view, it would appear that the hirer was an entrepreneur, perhaps even a nascent capitalist (depending on the scale of the farm). But, as Kritsman pointed out, the relation was often inverted; it was the "worker" who was the entrepreneur, for he was in fact renting the land from the "hirer."[11] Or a peasant might do part of the work on his farm and in addition employ a worker equipped with horse and plough to do the remainder of the work. On the surface it would appear that the hiring peasant was the entrepreneur.[12] However, the relationship could be deceptive, for often such a "worker" left his hirer only the equivalent of a salary and took for himself the surplus value. In such a case the "worker" was actually the lessor of farm implements and a covert entrepreneur, and the "hirer" was in fact the proprietor of a "false" farm.[13]

To disentangle the complicated web of social relations in the countryside, Kritsman proposed a simple procedure. He recommended that the size of a peasant's own plot of land be compared with his means of production (inventory and livestock). If the means of production were more than were required to farm the plot, then it was reasonable to assume that the excess resources were being utilized on other farms and that the farmer was in fact a "covert capitalist." If, on the other hand, the landholding was too large to be serviced by the peasant's own resources, then it was reasonable to assume that the farmer would be forced to rent additional means of cultivation and that he was in fact a "covert proletarian."[14] If there was a one-to-one correspondence between the size of the plot and the means of cultivation, then one of three situations might obtain.[15] The farm might belong to a capitalist (if labor were hired), to a proletarian (if the plot were minuscule), or to a petit bourgeois cultivator (if neither of the above seemed appropriate).

Although Kritsman set forth the concepts and relations that were to be the building blocks of Agrarian-Marxist methodology, he was not the first to attempt to convert these into a workable system of measurement. That important task was carried out by the statistician V. S. Nemchinov.[16] This was not a case of one scholar "scooping" another's discovery, but rather a unique example of cooperation between statisticians and social researchers.[17]

Toward Measurement

Nemchinov began his work on methodology by frankly acknowledging Kritsman's work as the source of his inspiration. He singled out two facets of that work for special praise: the treatment of differentiation as a socioeconomic phenomenon, and the development of the procedure of comparing the size of a peasant's plot to his means of production.[18]

Having paid his intellectual debt, Nemchinov turned his attention to elaborating a workable methodology. He began by conceiving of the farm as an agricultural enterprise with four basic resources at its disposal: land, fixed capital (cattle, inventory, and buildings), circulating capital (seeds, fodder, fertilizer), and labor. Following Kritsman, Nemchinov explained that these resources could be used either by the peasant to farm his own land or could be rented out to another farm. The allocation of the resources, contended Nemchinov, determined the socioeconomic significance of the farming activity. To illustrate this point, Nemchinov produced a chart, shown here as table 1.

The chart, as originally set forth, described qualitative relations, but Nemchinov assured the reader that these rela-

TABLE 1

Use of Means of Production by Farm Type

Conditions and Means of Production	On Own Farm		On Other's Farm Own Means of Production
	Other's	Own	
1. Land	Entrepreneurship	Independence	Dependence
2. Fixed Capital	Dependence	Independence	Entrepreneurship
3. Circulating capital	Dependence	Independence	Entrepreneurship
4. Labor	Entrepreneurship	Independence	Dependence

Source: Nemchinov, "O statisticheskom izuchenii klassovogo rassloeniia derevni," p. 27.

tions could easily be quantified by setting a monetary value on all the means of production.[19] Once the valuation had been accomplished, the nature of the farm could be analyzed. To illustrate the operation of his method of calculation, Nemchinov composed two different examples.

For the farm described in table 2, the indicators of entrepreneurship were: the employment of another's labor on one's own farm (351.00 rubles), the rental of land (27.25 rubles), and the leasing of livestock and inventory (11.00 rubles). These indicators totalled 389.25 rubles, which was 37.2 percent of the total value of the peasant's own means of production used on his own farm (1046.18 rubles).

For the farm described in table 3, the indicators of dependence were: the sale of labor to another farm (266.77 rubles), the use of another's means of production on the peasant's own farm (20.99 + 8.24 rubles), and the leasing of land (17.99 rubles). These indicators totalled 313.89 rubles, which was 123.3 percent of the total value of the peasant's own means of production that he used on his own land (247.88 rubles).

Nemchinov proposed seven groupings into which the peasant farms might be classified on the basis of the percentage of dependence or entrepreneurship obtained by calculation:[20]

Dependent Farms —with indicators of dependence of
50+ %
—with indicators of dependence of
15-50%
Independent Farms—with indicators of dependence of
2.5-25%
—with indicators of dependence of
less than 2.5% and indicators of
entrepreneurship of less than 2.5%
—with indicators of entrepreneurship of 2.5 to 15%
Exploiting Farms —with indicators of entrepreneurship of 15-30%
—with indicators of entrepreneurship of 30+%

Using these groupings, the first farm analyzed by Nemchinov
was classified as an entrepreneurial farm of the most extreme
type, whereas the second farm was classified as a dependent
farm of the most extreme type.

Nemchinov advanced two claims for this methodology and
system of classification. First, he maintained that his approach
was much more sensitive to the social relationships among the
peasantry than was the traditional methodology; compared to
either of the well-worn methods of studying peasant farms
(classification by the amount of sown land or grouping by the
size of herds), the new methodology brought to light many of
the inverted relations the traditional methods overlooked.[21]
Second, Nemchinov claimed that his approach could be easily
supplemented by grouping peasant farms according to their
economic strength (that is, according to their income). In other
words, Nemchinov made it clear that this approach to the
study of the peasantry was not all-inclusive; rather, it aimed
only at exposing social relations and would be enhanced rather
than diminished by the addition of a grouping based on
quantitative or economic indicators.[22]

Nemchinov's article was warmly received by Kritsman, who

TABLE 2
Use of Means of Production on an Exploiting Farm (in rubles)

Conditions and Means of Production	On Own Farm		On Other's Farm Own Means of Production	Total
	Others	Own		
1. Arable land and haymowing	27.25	76.84	-	104.09
2. Inventory and livestock	-	104.58	11.0	115.58
3. Seed and fodder	-	499.66	-	499.66
4. Labor	351-00	365.00	-	716.00
Total	378.25	1046.18	11.0	1435.33

Source: Nemchinov, "O statisticheskom izuchenii klassovogo rassloeniia derevni," p. 32.

TABLE 3
Use of Means of Production on a Dependent Farm (in rubles)

Conditions and Means of Production	On Own Farm		On Other's Farm Own Means of Production	Total
	Others	Own		
1. Arable land and haymowing	-	23.88	17.99	41.87
2. Inventory and livestock	20.99	0.38	-	21.37
3. Seed and fodder	8.24	10.29	-	18.53
4. Labor	-	213.33	266.67	480.00
Total	29.23	247.88	284.66	561.77

Source: Nemchinov, "O statisticheskom izuchenii klassovogo rassloeniia derevni," p. 33.

was particularly delighted over the change in outlook among statisticians reflected in Nemchinov's work. For the first time in the statistical literature, crowed Kritsman, the peasant farm was being examined not as an isolated unit but as an economic entity whose nature was defined by its links to similar entities.[23] To Kritsman, Nemchinov's article represented a conceptual breakthrough.

Kritsman was somewhat less ecstatic about the details of Nemchinov's methodology. He claimed that Nemchinov had viewed labor and the means of production separately, which had led him to assert that a peasant's labor on his own farm was an indicator of independence. But, argued Kritsman, such work could be considered a manifestation of independence (or petit bourgeois farming) only *if*, at the same time, the peasant labored with his own means of production. The peasant who used his own means of production but not his own labor was a capitalist, and the peasant who applied his own labor but not his own means of production was a proletarian.[24] In his critique Kritsman made two important modifications of Nemchinov's scheme: first, instead of the ambiguous terms "dependent" and "entrepreneur," Kritsman substituted economic categories (capitalist, proletarian, and petit bourgeois); second, he provided more rigorous criteria of independence than had Nemchinov. He enunciated these criteria in the form of two rules of calculation.

1. For a capitalist or semicapitalist farm, one must calculate the ratio of the peasant's own labor to all the labor used on the farm, and the ratio of the peasant's means of production applied on his own farm to his means of production as a whole. These two ratios should then be multiplied and converted into a percentage.

2. For a proletarian or semiproletarian farm, one must calculate the ratio of the peasant's own labor applied on his own farm to the total of his labor expended, and the ratio of his means of production used on his own farm to the total means of production used on that farm. These

two ratios should then be multiplied and converted into a percentage.[25]

Using these two new rules, Kritsman reworked Nemchinov's two cases. He discovered. that Nemchinov's calculations severely underplayed entrepreneurship in case 1 and overplayed dependence in case 2.[26] In putting forward his own methodology, Kritsman claimed that it would yield a truer approximation of rural socioeconomic relations.

Kritsman's two rules became the core of the Agrarian-Marxist methodology for the study of differentiation in the rural sector.[27] Around this core grew a series of research studies, and, in the process of carrying out these studies, the researchers refined the rules.

Research on Rural Stratification

In the short space of two years (1927 through 1928), the Agrarian-Marxists produced an impressive series of empirical studies on rural social structure. These studies form a coherent body of work. Their authors explored a single problem, shared a common conceptual apparatus, and employed the same procedures of measurement. This coherence in the output of the group was not the result of chance; it was deliberately fostered by Kritsman, who favored team research and called frequent symposia at which researchers thrashed out common difficulties.

Here we shall focus on three large-scale studies of rural social structure produced by the Agrarian-Marxists. These works, in which Kritsman expressed particular pride, are of interest less because of their concrete findings than because of the passion for methodology they reflect. That passion was particularly notable because the research we shall review was commissioned by a variety of government agencies, some of which were involved in the formulation of rural policy. Yet the Agrarian-Marxists rarely, if ever, drew out the policy implications of their work; instead, they drew attention to the methods of inquiry they employed. This concentration on measurement need not be interpreted as the refuge of reluctant experts. Instead, it reflected the attitude of scholars determined to distinguish themselves by being "scientific" about their work and by refraining from making policy recommendations on the basis of insufficient evidence.

The first study to emerge from the Agrarian-Marxist camp appeared in print in 1927 under the title *Proizvodstvennaia kharakteristika krest'ianskich khoziaistv razlichnykh sotsial-nykh grupp* [Production Characteristics of Peasants' Farms of Different Social Groups]. It was a piece of research on rural stratification in the Volokolamsk region conducted by three young researchers: Anisimov, Vermenichev, and Naumov.[28] The Volokolamsk project occupies an unique place in the corpus of Agrarian-Marxist studies in rural sociology. The study had its origins in 1924, when the Presidium of the planning division of the Commissariat of Agriculture (*Zemplan Narkomzem RSFSR*) commissioned the Timiriazev Institute to study the productive significance of different social groups and to examine the economic and organizational differences that characterized farms in those groups.[29] When the work was first commissioned, the Institute scholars thought that these questions could be studied through secondary analysis of existing data. However, since the available data had been grouped and analyzed according to the traditional indexes (arable land and the size of herds), a decision was made to launch a new project, which would address itself directly to the problem of socioeconomic grouping of peasant farms in the NEP period.[30] So in 1925 the collegium of the Timiriazev Institute sent out an expedition under the direction of Chelintsev to the flax-growing region of Volokolamsk.[31] (At the same time a second group under Studenskii went to the grain region of Penza.)[32] The Volokolamsk study received very little supervision from the Institute staff, for the Organization-Production scholars were interested in studying the farm as an organizational, not as a socioeconomic, unit.[33] Left to their own devices, the young researchers came to work under the spiritual, if not the actual, guidance of Kritsman. This is apparent not only from the authors' application of the principles of Kritsman's methodology but also from the restrained way in which they thanked the Director of the Timiriazev Institute in the preface to their study.[34] (After 1927 such public expressions of gratitude by the Agrarian-Marxists to their teachers would cease altogether.)

The young researchers approached their work with the expectation of finding rather extensive differentiation among the peasantry, for as they explained, the area chosen for study—Volokolamsk—was characterized by a high degree of commercial relations, and the peasants in that region produced primarily for the market. To ascertain the extent of this differentiation, the authors used two methods. First, they employed statistical surveys to obtain a composite picture of 648 farms in the Volokolamsk region and to determine the questions that should be put to the peasants.[35] Then, true to their training in the Timiriazev Academy, they did budget analyses of 60 farms,[36] taking care to purify themselves ideologically by pointing out that the budget method was not logically related to populist (read "Organization-Production") positions.[37] To analyze the budgets, the researchers established valuations for the means of production and labor of each farm and then recorded the extent to which the peasant used these resources on his own farm as opposed to the farms of others. To farms that generally rented out their inventory or sold their labor, the authors applied Kritsman's first rule; to farms that generally hired labor or leased inventory, they applied Kritsman's second rule.

The farms that had been analyzed were then classified into five groups:[38]

Proletarian—1. with signs of dependence of 50+%
　　　　　　 2. with signs of dependence 20.1-50%
　　　　　　 3. with signs of dependence 0-20%
Capitalist—4. with signs of entrepreneurship from
　　　　　　　　 0-20%
　　　　　　 5. with signs of entrepreneurship 20.1-50%

The grouping of peasant farms in this study clearly showed the stamp of Kritsman's outlook. The polar categories (proletarian and capitalist) encompassed the entire field, leaving no room for the truly independent peasant. This was no accident. Early in the study the authors mentioned the possibility of so grouping the peasantry that the middle category would be "the farm of the small commodity-producing *seredniak* [middle peasant], who could develop in either direction";[39] but, in setting up their final categories, the authors subsumed that category under the rubric "proletarian." They rationalized their decision as follows: "In reality our *seredniak* group according to budgets hardly has any representatives who do not exhibit, in some measure or other, elements of dependence."[40]

Not surprisingly, the authors had little difficulty distributing the farms into their categories in such a way as to confirm the preconceptions that underlay their categorization. And when the fit was imperfect, they did not cavil. Confronted by the fact that the statistical survey revealed less peasant polarization than did the budget research, the three authors voiced their confidence in the budget inquiry, since it had been the more detailed.[41]

The next study published by Agrarian-Marxist researchers was based on an expedition to Samara. Entitled *710 khoziaistv Samarskoi derevni* [710 Farmsteads in the Samara Countryside], it was the work of three members of Kritsman's group: I. Vermenichev, A. Gaister, and G. Raevich. The study appeared in late 1927 with a preface by L. N. Kritsman.[42] The expedition to Samara had been part of an ongoing project set up by the Central Statistical Administration (TsSU) to explore the processes of class stratification in the countryside.[43] According to the authors, the Samara expedition was of short duration; in March 1927 the team spent ten to twelve days doing a massive statistical survey of 710 farms (15 percent of the total number) in the Aksakov *volost'* of Samara *guberniia*.

From their preliminary reading on the area, the authors expected to find extensive class differentiation among the peasantry. They also looked forward to the opportunity to test the Kritsman methodology, which had been refined as a result of the Volokolamsk research.

Following the by now traditional Agrarian-Marxist approach, the young researchers began by isolating three socioeconomic relations they considered salient: the rent and hire of livestock and inventory, the hire and sale of labor power, and the renting and leasing of land. Like other members of the Kritsman group, the authors of the Samara study were convinced that the mere presence or absence of these relations on a given farm was, in itself, insufficient to categorize that farm; what was needed was to ascertain the context (economic need or the desire for gain) and the extent (frequency and amount) of these relationships.[44] To capture the nuances of context and extent, the authors envisaged each of the three important relations as a continuum and assigned values to various points on those continua:[45]

Hire of labor		*Sale of labor* [46]	
up to 10 days	+1	up to 10 days	−1
11-50 days	+3	11-30 days	−3
51-90 days	+4	31-50 days	−4
90+ days	+5	over 50 days	−5

Leasing inventory, livestock		*Hiring inventory, livestock*
receiving up to 10 rubles	+1	Hire of simple inventory and not more than two implements of complex inventory −1
receiving 11-50 rubles	+2	
receiving 50+ rubles	+3	
		Hire of working livestock and complex inventory of 3+ implements −2

Renting of land		*Leasing of land*	
up to 2 *desiatins*	+1	up to 30% of sown land	−1
2+ *desiatins*	+2	30+% sown land	−2

The farm's social relations were examined through budget analysis, and, on the basis of the results, a composite score was assigned to each farm. The composite was derived in one of two ways: if the points accorded a given farm were all preceded either by negative or positive signs, the team simply summed the points attaching the relevant sign; if the signs were mixed, the researchers balanced the points.[47]

After each farm had been assigned a composite score, it was

classified into one of five social groups:[48]

1. *Agricultural Proletariat and Semiproletariat*
   This group was characterized by the maximal sale of their labor power.
   Score required: –5 and lower

2. *Small-Scale Producers*
   a. *with signs of dependence*
   This group was characterized by an average amount of labor sale, or the renting of working herds, or the renting of a significant amoung of complex equipment.
   Score required: –4 to –2

   b. *with no appreciable sign of dependence or entrepreneurship*
   This group was characterized by the minimal sale of labor power, or by the hire of up to ten days of labor, or by the renting of a small quantity of equipment, or by the lease of a small quantity of inventory, or by the absence of these relations.
   Score required: –1 to +1

   c. *with signs of entrepreneurship*
   This group was characterized by average hire of workers, leasing of inventory and livestock that yielded a relatively large income.
   Score required: 2 to +4

3. *Semicapitalist and Entrepreneur*
   This group was characterized by the hire of workers in the greatest quantities.
   Score required: +5 and above

The farms in the Samara sample turned out to be distributed as follows: 1—10.3 percent; 2a—22.4 percent; 2b—40.4 percent; 2c—18.9 percent; and 3—2.8 percent.[49]

The concentration of the farms in the Samara sample toward the middle groups (and especially toward the group with no appreciable signs of dependence or entrepreneurship) drew Kritsman's fire. Committed as he was to the hypothesis of the growing polarization of the peasantry, Kritsman criticized the Samara results as a "distortion" that stemmed from the authors' faulty method of arriving at a composite score. Confronted by a farm that hired labor for 560 days and sold labor for 60 days, the authors of the study had calculated as follows: 560 days of hire is worth +5 points; 60 days of sale is worth –5 points; the total for the farm is 0. To Kritsman, such a farm was nothing if not entrepreneurial in nature.[50] Despite the thrust of his criticism, Kritsman was not willing to see the middle independent farm read out of the picture entirely. In the preface to the Samara volume, he faulted the team's image of a certain region as a battleground between the forces of capitalism and socialism. He argued that the tendency to view the rural sector in polar terms had gone too far, and he counseled his followers to focus attention on the petit bourgeois elements in both the capitalist and proletarian groups.[51]

The Samara study was significant for two reasons. First, it established a methodology for grouping peasant farms, a methodology that was replicated with little variation in study after study conducted by the Agrarian-Marxists; and second, the young agrarianists considered the study's findings typical of social structure in the Soviet Union and treated the Samara data as a base line against which the results of subsequent studies were compared.[52] In particular, the Kritsman group made repeated reference to the Samara finding that most farms were enmeshed in capitalist relations of one sort or another.[53] Implicit in the Samara results was a more dramatic finding— namely, that the majority of the economic transactions occurred between peasants belonging to the highest and lowest groups, while peasants of the middle group tended to deal exclusively with one another.[54] But the authors did not draw out this latter finding, for, in combination with the first result, it suggested that while capitalist relations in the countryside were bringing an ever greater number of peasants into contact—albeit hostile contact—the middle independent peasantry remained both economically and socially insulated from the rest of the peasantry and continued to constitute an impenetrable force.

In 1928 the output of the Agrarian-Marxist group was further enlarged by the publication of *Rassloenie Sovetskoi derevni* [Stratification of the Soviet Countryside]. Unlike the Volokolamsk and Samara projects, it was not a collective effort; it was written by a single author, A. I. Gaister.[55] Gaister's book, which included a long and thoughtful foreword by Kritsman,[56] was the fruit of a large project on social stratification organized by the Agrarian Section of the Communist Academy in 1926. The project was financed by the USSR Commissariat of Worker-Peasant Inspection (*Narkom-RKI SSSR*).[57]

Gaister's study was very ambitious; indeed, on two counts it was the most ambitious of the Agrarian-Marxist studies examined thus far. The research covered an enormous territory: farms in the central agricultural region, the west, the Urals, Siberia, the North Caucasus, and the Ukrainian plains and forest region were examined.[58] Gaister did not collect the data for this study himself; rather, he reworked the 1924-1925 budget studies that had been done in the areas he selected. To ensure the validity of his results, Gaister used data collected by two separate methods: budget analysis and statistical survey. This was a Herculean feat, in the execution of which Gaister's material sometimes suffered. But his attempt was praised by many, not the least among whom was his exacting teacher, L. N. Kritsman.[59]

Gaister used a separate system of classification to deal with each type of data. He grouped the farms in the statistical survey according to the value of their means of production. This grouping, he claimed, satisfied the urge to classify farms according to their economic strength (*moshchnost'*) but avoided the pitfalls that invariably occurred when natural indicators (arable land, herds) were used.[60] Gaister then distributed the farms so studied into five categories.[61]

1. smallest farms—value of means of production, up to 200 rubles

2. small farms—value of means of production, 200-500 rubles

3. average farms—value of means of production, 500-800 rubles

4. above-average farms—value of means of production, 800-1400 rubles

5. large-scale farms—value of means of production, 1400 rubles

As a complement, Gaister grouped the farms studied by budget analysis according to their social relations. Then he enumerated five social types and distributed the farms analyzed into the appropriate categories.[62]

1. Proletarian farm—with sale of labor over 50 days

2. Semiproletarian—with sale of labor of 20-50 days, or with rent of inventory over 20 days, or with rent of inventory over 10 days

3. *Seredniak* farm—with sale or hire of labor up to 20 days, or with rental or leasing of livestock up to 10 days, or with rental or leasing inventory up to 10 days

4. *Seredniak* with entrepreneurial elements—with rent of labor of 20-50 days, or with leasing of working herd over 20 days, or with leasing of inventory of 10+ days, or
   —with renting out land under crops of 2+*desiatins*, or with rental of meadow land of 5+ *desiatins*

5. Small capitalist—with hire of labor for more than 50 days

Gaister's desire to combine these two types of data did not stem solely from a methodological motive. Evidence points to the existence of a "political" motive. Apparently the Agrarian-Marxist group that had gathered in the Communist Academy's

Agrarian Section was being attacked by the agricultural spokesman of Gosplan, M. Vol'f. Vol'f claimed that Kritsman's group was using a crude social typology.[63] To defend himself and his group against this accusation, Gaister checked the results he obtained using his classification by social type against those he obtained using his classification into economic type. He was able to report that in no case was there a significant divergence. For the time being, it appeared that Gaister's defense was adequate.

In arguing for the validity of the social typology, however, Gaister went beyond a purely defensive position. Not only did he claim that the social typology did not distort reality, but he also asserted that the social groupings reflected the actual weights of the various peasant groups in the rural sector.[64] At this suggestion Kristman was aghast; according to him, the social groupings indicated only the direction in which farms were moving. To postulate, as Gaister had done, an identity between the social groupings and the class composition of the countryside was naïve and, worse, pernicious, for it obscured the fact that in both the capitalist and proletarian groups there were petit bourgeois farmers.[65]

Kritsman's vehemence on this point is of considerable interest. In 1925 the leader of the Agrarian-Marxist group began his excursion into methodology with the statement that under NEP he expected to find almost no examples of the petit bourgeois, independent peasant farmer. Only three years later we find the same Kritsman arguing against a certain application of methodology, in part because it tended to obscure the presence of the middle peasant. The intervening factor, of course, was the refusal of the independent peasant to disappear. The Agrarian-Marxists would have to deal more directly with that factor in the next phase of the controversy.

With the publication of Gaister's study, Agrarian-Marxist work in rural sociology attained a certain maturity. The sense of coming of age was reflected most clearly in the preface Kritsman wrote to the work. There the leader of the group praised the research done by his young colleagues and opposed with vigor the Organization-Production scholars' approach to the study of the countryside. Despite the confidence Kritsman radiated, the work of the Agrarian-Marxists had serious limitations. It was addressed to a single problem—albeit a central one—and that problem was approached with certain assumptions to which a methodology was tailored. Oddly enough, it was not these specific defects of its approach, but rather the obsolescence of its central concern, that was to become the Achilles' heel of the Kritsman group.

Part 3
The Second Stage of the Controversy, 1927 to mid-1928

Introduction

The second stage of the controversy in rural social studies saw striking changes, both in the issues dividing the contending schools and in the behavior of the scholars. The two groups were no longer engaged in a disagreement over the goals of inquiry in their field. They were now involved in a dispute over a single point of substance—the nature of the family farm. As the disputed point became the focus of the controversy, all other differences between the Organization-Production and Agrarian-Marxist scholars were relegated to the background. The shift from a disagreement over goals to a substantive dispute was accompanied by fundamental alterations in the intellectual and social conduct of the contending social scientists. Whereas earlier the scholars had paid only minimal attention to the work of their rivals, for each school the position of its alter ego now became a consuming interest. Indeed, for both groups the scrutiny of the opponent's work assumed priority over the continuation of research in progress. Moreover, whereas once social contacts between the contending schools had been cordial in tone and marked by some degree of cooperation, now interchanges were conducted in polemical accents, and collaboration of all types between representatives of the two schools came to an end.

These changes in issues and conduct during the second phase of the controversy had their origins in early 1927, when the two groups of scholars met to debate the question of differentiation in the Soviet countryside. As a consequence of that debate, the stakes in the rural studies controversy increased significantly. No longer was the controversy simply a battle of ideas; it became a struggle for the leadership of the community of rural scholars, a struggle that would not be resolved definitively until 1931.

7. The Differentiation Debate

Early in 1927, at a plenary session of the Timiriazev Academy's Institute on Agricultural Economics, the Organization-Production and Agrarian-Marxists scholars came together to discuss the question of differentiation in the Soviet rural sector.[1] This meeting broke precedent on several counts. Throughout the early phase of the controversy, the exchange of views between the two schools had been conducted in print; the opposing groups had set forth their views in articles, monographs, and research reports. The plenary session was the first time the contending scholars aired their differences in public. No less important, before 1927 the two schools had disagreed primarily over the priorities for their field of study. At the Timiriazev debate the contending scholars argued for the first time over a single question, the stratification of the Soviet peasantry.

The subject of the Timiriazev meeting was a topical one. The problem of peasant stratification had been under discussion within the Party leadership since 1925. The disagreement among the contending politicians was primarily one of policy.[2] Representatives of the left and right wings of the Party leadership, while concurring about the nature and extent of rural differentiation, differed over the advisability of a socialist regime's allowing the process of stratification to proceed unchecked.[3] Despite the similarity of subject, the debate over rural differentiation held in the Timiriazev Institute bore little resemblance to the debate that had divided the Party. Unlike the politicians, the social scientists could not agree on a definition of stratification. Consequently, the discussion at the plenary session turned not on matters of policy, but on the logically prior problems of conceptualizing, measuring, and assessing the differences among peasant farms. In this chapter we will examine the arguments offered by the two groups of scholars at the Timiriazev meeting and also assess some of the long-term effects of the differentiation debate upon the controversy between the Organization-Production and Agrarian-Marxist groups.

Structure of the Meeting

Although there is a full stenographic report of the proceedings of the 1927 meeting, certain aspects of the differentiation debate remain shrouded in mystery. It is unclear, for example, at whose initiative the debate was organized. It may well have been that the Organization-Production scholars decided to sponsor a discussion of rural stratification in order to demonstrate their responsiveness to the concerns of the regime. It is equally likely, however, that the Timiriazev professors were prodded to arrange the meeting by their Marxist students, who considered the examination of peasant social structure to be the most important topic in rural inquiry. Whatever the origins of the debate, it is clear that as the hosts of the meeting the Organization-Production scholars structured the session to their own advantage. The meeting opened with four keynote addresses, three of which were delivered by members of the Organization-Production school.[4] These addresses were followed by comments from the floor; most of the commentators were members of the Agrarian-Marxist group, which, it will be recalled, was well known for its original research on peasant stratification.[5] As we shall see, the structure of the 1927 meeting played no small part in its outcome.

Argumentation

The two groups of scholars came to the 1927 debate with widely varying views of differentiation in Soviet Russia, its nature, its causes, and its effect upon peasant society. The

Agrarian-Marxists considered the most important differences among the peasantry to be social in nature and economic in origin. These researchers began from the fact that the means of cultivation were in short supply and were unevenly distributed in the rural sector. The existence of these inequalities, so ran the argument, generated webs of hire-and-lease transactions whose objects ranged from inventory and livestock to the land itself. By virtue of these transactions, some peasants became dependent upon others for the means of their existence. Thus arose the social relations of subordination and superordination, which, to the Agrarian-Marxists, constituted the essence of rural differentiation. According to these young researchers, the process of differentiation would end by transforming rural society. The peasantry would become increasingly stratified until the rural population was polarized into two groups: rural capitalists and agricultural wage workers. The middle precapitalist peasant would be absorbed into one or the other— usually the latter—of the two groups; and with him would disappear traditional peasant society.

The Organization-Production scholars approached the question from another perspective. They considered the salient differences among peasant households to be demographic in origin. The head of each farm, according to their analysis, adjusted his expenditure of effort to the pressure of the consumption demands made by the members of his family. The intensity of that pressure was defined as a function of family composition, specifically, or the ratio of consumers/workers in the farming family; and this ratio was held to vary with the age (number of years in existence) of the family unit. Thus, the Timiriazev professors attributed differences in the economic productivity of farms to the forces of demography.

The Organization-Production scholars' analysis led logically to an equilibrium model of rural development.[6] Assuming that the cycle of growth and decay of each farm was determined by the composition of its family, for every farm that expanded its activities there would be another in the process of contracting its operation. Thus, any *net* change in the social structure of the peasantry was highly unlikely. Although the Timiriazev professors never spelled out this equilibrium model, they did predict that traditional peasant society would endure in Russia for some time to come.

The discussion of differentiation in the Timiriazev Institute was a disorderly mix of theoretical pronouncements, references to empirical research, and ad hominem attacks. Nevertheless, in the course of the debate the substance and implications of the two divergent positions came to the fore.

The Keynote Addresses (Makarov, Chelintsev, and Chaianov)

The Organization-Production speakers were at a considerable disadvantage at the 1927 meeting. Unlike their former students, they had devoted relatively little attention to the problem of differentiation. They had never conducted any first-hand research on rural social structure;[7] moreover, except to counter criticisms leveled by their Marxist colleagues, the members of the Chaianov group had never addressed themselves to the problem of interfarm differences.

The Organization-Production speakers obviated this handicap by means of a clever strategem. They preempted the role of critics, forcing the Agrarian-Marxists into a defensive posture. The keynote speakers began by admitting that differentiation as defined by their former students was a real problem in the Soviet countryside and consequently was worthy of study. For scholars who had heretofore paid scant heed to interfarm variations, this was something of a concession. However, having doffed their hats to their opponents, the keynote speakers then went on the raise serious questions about the analysis of rural stratification presented by the Kritsman group.

The Organization-Production speakers focused their critique on two particular aspects of the work that was emanating from the Agrarian Section of the Communist Academy. First, they voiced doubts about the Kritsman group's reliance on social relations as the sole indicator of differentiation. Makarov, who delivered the opening address, claimed to be sympathetic to the Agrarian-Marxists' desire to develop qualitative (social) rather than strictly quantitative (economic) indicators of stratification[8]—a claim he buttressed with extensive references to the research studies conducted by his former students.[9]

Having declared his sympathies, Makarov went on to point out that statistical studies rarely provided the kind of data on the basis of which social relations could be accurately mapped.[10] The tone of Makarov's criticism was gentle, but the implications of his remarks were clear. Maps of rural social structure constructed solely on the basis of social indicators would have to be considered arbitrary.

A more direct challenge was issued by Chelintsev, who addressed himself to the question of the desirability, rather than the feasability, of using qualitative indicators to study differentiation. Chelintsev contended that the dependence upon social relations to the exclusion of all other indexes of stratification produced an exaggerated portrait of interfarm differences. To avoid distortion, he insisted, a combination of qualitative and quantitative indicators should be adopted.[11] Later in the same speech, Chelintsev dropped all pretensions of evenhandedness and came out directly in favor of quantitative indicators, on the grounds that they provided "almost all" the information required to make an assessment of differentiation.[12]

An even more critical stand was taken by Chaianov. Unlike his colleagues, Chaianov made no reference to the studies done by the Agrarian-Marxists. Using the excuse that he was not a researcher but a methodologist, he ignored the Kritsman group's work and posed, as though anew, four questions around which he claimed the study of rural differentiation ought to revolve. He asked, first, was a new capitalist ("farmer") type of agriculture arising in Russia, and, if so, how widespread was this capitalist type of farming? Second, to what extent was rural differentiation a function of the exodus into industry? Third, how and why did exploitative relations develop? Finally, how did productive differentiation arise?[13] In order to answer each of these questions, Chaianov asserted, the researcher had to examine the process of demographic differentiation.[14] The declaration that the demographic explanation of interfarm differences took precedence over other accounts carried with it more than a trace of the suggestion that the biological (read "Organization-Production") account was superior to any of its competitors. It may well have been easier for Chaianov to adopt this uncompromising position because he was absent from the meeting and forwarded his address in written form.[15] Whatever the case, the thrust of Chaianov's challenge was not ignored by those who heard his speech read. The keynote speakers also criticized the Agrarian-Marxists' interpretation of the research results. The group working in the Agrarian Section had charted the increase of hire-and-lease transactions and on this basis had concluded that capitalism was on the rise in the Soviet countryside. True to their Leninist heritage, they had greeted the prospect of rural capitalization with a mixture of relief and apprehension.[16] Reviewing this work publicly for the first time, the keynote speakers now charged that the Kritsman group had misinterpreted its findings and added that, if correctly understood, the research results gave no cause for concern. Thus, the Organization-Production speakers attempted to reassure their former students by faulting their analytic acumen.

The "reassurance" offered by the keynote speakers was based on the contention that the mere increase of hire-and-lease transactions did not constitute evidence of the spread of capitalism; if the rural sector were to become capitalist, so ran the critics' argument, a fundamental social change would be required—the transformation of the working family farm based on the balance between labor and consumption into the "farmer"-type agricultural unit operated with hired labor and run in order to maximize profit.[17] In the Soviet case, submitted the keynote speakers, such a transformation was improbable. For one thing, the growth of capitalism in agriculture would be inhibited by the growth of capitalism in industry. Available capital and labor would invariably be attracted to the industrial sector, which promised a faster and better return on investment.[18] Moreover, within the rural sector itself, capitalist farming would be checked by the survival of the family farm economy. According to the Timiriazev professors, the family farm enjoyed certain important advantages over its capitalist rival. While the capitalist farm had to vie for labor with capitalist industry, the noncapitalist farm always had a ready supply of labor from among the members of the family.[19] Furthermore, the family farmer, following his own definition of profitability, was invariably willing to pay more for land and equipment than his capitalist rival and, consequently, would best his competitor in the race to acquire these means of cultivation.[20] Thus, it was argued, the distinctive properties of the family farm would ensure its survival and forestall the spread of capitalism in the countryside.[21]

To the Agrarian-Marxists, the reassurances offered by the Organization-Production scholars were cold comfort indeed. The members of the Kritsman group were at least as troubled by the prospect of the survival of the family farmer with his individualistic psychology as they were by evidence of the spread of capitalist relations in the rural sector.

Agrarian-Marxist Commentary

A cursory reading of the comments made by the respondents suggests that the Agrarian-Marxists who attended the plenary session were primarily distressed by the Organization-Production contention that differentiation was a demographically determined process. Most of the respondents directed comments against Chaianov, who, alone of the keynote speakers, had articulated the group's traditional view of peasant farm differences.[22] Of all the comments on Chaianov's speech, the most noteworthy was that made by Anisimov, who declared that the socioeconomic and demographic accounts of differentiation could not logically be employed in tandem, for each purported to explain the same range of phenomena.[23] Anisimov's contention was incorrect; in fact, the Chaianov group had undertaken to explain cyclical mobility in the countryside, while the Kritsman group had attempted to account for unidirectional change in rural social structure. Even more important, Anisimov's argument was nefarious. It polarized the participants in the 1927 debate into two groups, each of which supported a monocausal explanation of peasant stratification, and it thus worked against the development of a more sophisticated multifactorial account of the differences among peasant farms.[24]

Upon closer examination, it becomes clear that the Agrarian-Marxists were less troubled by the Organization-Production definition of differentiation than they were by the keynote speakers' prediction that the family farm would survive for some time to come. In an effort to counter this view of the future, the respondents tried several tactics. Some commentators attacked the premise that underlay the Organization-Production scholars' case, namely, the belief that industrial capitalism would draw both labor and capital away from capitalist agriculture.[25] They derided this belief, using the argument that there was no shortage of labor in Russia and that, therefore, the growth of capitalism in industry would not preclude its spread in agriculture.[26] Curiously, no mention was made of the availability of the other factor whose scarcity was discussed by the keynote speakers—capital. Other speakers accused the Organization-Production scholars of having analyzed the family farm in isolation from its environment. The family farm was linked to the market, the critics submitted, and thus was subject to the laws of the market, which so operated that large-scale farms survived and small-scale farms died off.[27] Finally one speaker, clearly in desperation, revived the old argument about the cooperatives. Citing Lenin, he reminded his listeners that the capitalist route was not the only one that would lead to the disappearance of the family farm economy. The same objective could be accomplished by the absorption of the precapitalist farm into the rural cooperatives.[28]

The structure of the meeting did not provide an opportunity for rebuttal by the Organization-Production scholars. However, the weakness and disorganization of the Agrarian-Marxists' response effectively gave the keynote speakers the last word.

Outcome

There was little dispassionate discussion at the plenary session. Almost immediately after it opened, the meeting became the scene of a heated confrontation between the representatives of the contending schools. The responsibility for this turn of events must be equally distributed. Both among the keynote speakers and among the respondents there were those who viewed the session as an opportunity to score points for their own approach by denigrating the work of their opponents. Regrettably, these "fighters for truth" set the tone of the meeting.[29] When Chaianov came out with a declaration of the superiority of the demographic account of stratification, Anisimov retorted with the assertion that a choice would have to be made between the demographic and socioeconomic explanations. The more tractable positions taken by Makarov and Chelintsev were swept aside as the participants at the meeting were polarized into supporters of one or the other monocausal theory, neither of which captured the complex reality of peasant differentiation.

The turn to confrontation may in part have been due to the fact that the Timiriazev meeting was not only a battle of ideas but also a struggle for the leadership of the community of rural scholars. Before 1927 the Organization-Production scholars had exercised undisputed power and authority over those working in rural inquiry. The Timiriazev session offered the Agrarian-Marxists the opportunity to use their expertise on peasant social structure to challenge the leadership of their former teachers.

In the contest of ideas there was no clear winner at the Timiriazev session. The meeting had been called to debate the relative utility of rival explanations of rural differentiation. However, the discussion did not long revolve around empirical questions; it quickly became an argument over the future of the Soviet countryside. The Agrarian-Marxists predicted that with increasing capitalism in the rural sector, the peasant way of life would disappear, and with it would go the small family farm. The Timiriazev professors predicted that the family farm would not only withstand but also inhibit the spread of capitalism in the countryside. In this contest of rival predictions, no winner could be declared in 1927; only time would tell which of the two schools was correct in its selection of the dominant trends in the countryside. As is well known, subsequent developments proved both schools to have been wide of the mark.

In the struggle for the leadership of the community of rural scholars, there was a winner. The Agrarian-Marxists, deprived of the services of L. N. Kritsman,[30] did not manage to capitalize on their superior knowledge. The Organization-Production scholars more than held their own, and the potential challenge to their leadership was turned back. In this sense, the Timiriazev debate must be accounted a triumph for the Chaianov group.

By virtue of their role as keynote speakers the Chaianov group was able to define the terms of the discussion. This prerogative proved to be a considerable advantage, for the content of the opening speeches caught the Agrarian-Marxists off guard and scattered their forces. The young researchers had come prepared to handle the old canard about demographic differentiation, but they seemed somewhat taken aback by the insistence of the Chaianov group that the family farm would dominate the rural scene for the foreseeable future. The respondents tried to handle this assertion with a barrage of arguments, which they put forward in a hit-or-miss fashion. Their best efforts notwithstanding, they were unable to win their point. Not having studied the family farm in any depth, they were unable to say anything definitive either about its principles of operation or about the behavior of its head—both of which points bore directly on the question of the future of the noncapitalist farm. Thus, the Agrarian-Marxists missed a genuine opportunity to best their rivals. Ultimately, however, the differentiation debate would turn out to be something of a Pyrrhic victory for the Timiriazev professors. From this time on the members of the Kritsman group, embarrassed by their failure at the 1927 meeting, redoubled their efforts to displace their opponents as leaders of the rural studies community.

Impact of the Debate

The Timiriazev session had an important and lasting effect upon the controversy in rural studies. It brought to the fore certain substantive differences in the positions taken by the Chaianov and Kritsman groups, differences that had previously been muted because the two groups were engaged in a disagreement over the goals for their field of study. During the debate over peasant stratification, the Organization-Production and Agrarian-Marxists groups voiced conflicting predictions of the future of the Soviet countryside. The discussion that followed revealed that the two groups of scholars were divided over a prior question—the nature of the family farm.

The Chaianov group considered the family farm to be a form of biological organism with its own internally determined cycle of growth and decay; these scholars regarded the farm as influenced only indirectly by the socioeconomic environment within which it existed. The Kritsman group treated the family farm as an economic unit, which, like other such units, was determined by its socioeconomic setting. In the course of the year 1927 the differences between the two schools on this point became increasingly important. Indeed, before long, they became the center of the controversy in rural studies, eclipsing all other divergences of opinion between the two groups. Thus did the controversy in rural studies become a substantive dispute over a single issue.

The emergence of the issue of the family farm as the center of the rural studies controversy was by no means unrelated to developments in society as a whole. It was hardly coincidental that during 1927, as the substantive dispute was taking form, the Party began to devote increased attention to the problem of the family farm. Soviet agriculture, reliant as it was on the individual small-scale farmer, had been perennially plagued by low productivity, inefficiency, and peasant recalcitrance. When, however, the pace of Soviet industrial development began to accelerate, the difficulties with the rural sector became both more apparent and less tolerable to the regime. By December 1927, when the Fifteenth Party Congress convened, there was concrete evidence of the Party's disenchantment with the family farm; there were repeated calls for the "collectivization" of agriculture, although, of course, no thought was given to the use of force to effect such a change.[31] The official discontent with precapitalist farming colored the issues and the conduct of rural studies controversy in its second phase.

8. Controversy in a New Key

As the controversy in rural studies changed from a disagreement over goals into a substantive dispute over the family farm, the disputants made important modifications in the strategies they used to press their cases. The first of these modifications related to the focus of inquiry. Before 1927 each group had prided itself on the breadth of its work and had attempted to show that its approach could explain a wider range of significant phenomena than that of its opponent. During 1927, as attention became riveted on the question of the family farm, each set of scholars reshaped its research program; ongoing promising projects were discontinued in favor of new, hastily conceived inquiries. The second area of modification was the behavior, both intellectual and social, of the participants in the controversy. Beginning in 1927, the disputants began to examine one another's work with care; indeed, the scrutiny of the rival's work became a—perhaps even *the*— major intellectual activity in the dispute. In reviewing its opponents' research, each school took pains to delineate precisely the similarities and differences between that research and its own scholarly work. At the same time social contacts between contending schools became strained. Some strain was evident in the ad hominem attacks that took place during the differentiation debate, but thereafter the tension deepened considerably. As a result, in the course of 1927 collaborative research between the two schools ceased, and the exchange of recognition between schools came to a virtual end, as each group used the payment of intellectual debts as an occasion to vindicate its own position and press its case. In altering their strategies, the two schools were influenced not only by the requirements of conducting a substantive dispute. They were also affected, in varying degrees and in different ways, by the facets of the social context within which they carried out their work: the disenchantment with the family farm sector, which was becoming increasingly evident in official rural policy; and the change in the professional organization of rural studies, as a result of which each group of scholars was housed in a separate institution.

In this chapter we will examine the modifications in strategy made by each set of scholars in the course of 1927. From this examination will emerge a portrait of the dispute in its second phase. The chapter will close with an assessment of the state of the dispute at the beginning of 1928.

The Agrarian-Marxist Group: Scholarship on the Offensive

Before 1927 the Agrarian-Marxists concentrated almost entirely on designing and executing studies that would support their hypothesis that the Soviet peasantry was pursuing the capitalist path to socialism. Preoccupied with their own research, they paid little attention to that of their opponents. When they did turn to criticize the work of the Organization-Production scholars, the members of the Kritsman group usually focused on those points at which their former teachers had deviated from a "Marxist"[1] position. These young men were newcomers to the field of rural social studies, and this form of critique was a useful exercise, for it helped them to forge a distinctive cognitive identity. Despite its advantages, though, the focus on "omissions" seriously diminished the force of Agrarian-Marxist criticism. Even the most vitriolic attack by the Kritsman group read as if it were a proposal for further research addressed to its opponents. More important, in concentrating as they did on the lacunae in Organization-Production scholarship, the Agrarian-Marxists did not develop the facility of discussing their opponents' work on its own terms.

The limitations of their approach became painfully clear to the Agrarian-Marxists in the course of the differentiation debate, when they were unable to counter effectively their teachers' contentions about the nature and prospects of the family farm.[2] Their palpable failure at the 1927 meeting convinced the young researchers of the need to develop a new strategy. Clearly it was no longer enough to deal with the omissions in the work of the Chaianov group; the content of Organization-Production scholarship would have to be approached directly. Specifically, some of the fundamental propositions of the theory of noncapitalist economics would have to be invalidated and the hegemony of the Timiriazev professors over certain fields of inquiry would have to be challenged. To implement this strategy, the Agrarian-Marxists undertook to study topics traditionally regarded as the province of the Timiriazev professors, and they pursued these studies with vigor. By shifting the focus of their research program,[3] the Kritsman group hoped to displace their former teachers from their positions as leaders of the rural studies community. The fact that the Organization-Production position contravened current Party thinking on the family farm likely strengthened the resolve of the Agrarian-Marxists.

The Attack on Theory

With an eye for the jugular, the Agrarian-Marxists launched an attack upon the "biological analogy" that lay at the heart of the theory of the family farm. The Timiriazev professors, it will be remembered, had treated the family farm as a form of biological organism, with a cycle of expansion and contraction that was internally determined, governed by the composition of the farming family. The Agrarian-Marxist implicitly rejected the biological analogy as early as 1923. Regarding the farm as a socioeconomic unit, they repeatedly castigated the Organization-Production scholars for having examined this unit of cultivation in isolation from its environment. Before 1927, however, they did not directly assess the validity of the analogy. Evidently the traditional line of attack on the biological analogy was jettisoned sometime during 1927. For during the next twelve months there appeared a series of articles by the

Agrarian-Marxist, M. Kubanin, which were hailed by his colleagues as having shown that the celebrated analogy was invalid.[4]

The subject of Kubanin's work was the splintering, or division (*droblenie*), of peasant households.[5] According to the theory of the family farm espoused by the Organization-Production scholars, splintering was the result of a natural, biological process in which the farmer's offspring attained sufficient maturity to be able to leave home and establish new agricultural units of their own. To counter this analysis on its own terms, Kubanin employed a research technique novel for a member of the Kritsman school: he undertook an examination of the internal dynamics of the family farm. Using data collected in 1926, Kubanin constructed a portrait of the family farm strikingly different from that presented by the Timiriazev professors.[6] According to Kubanin, the family farm was not a harmonious unit composed of individuals striving for a common cause. Rather, the farm was rent by strife, the basic cause of which was the fact that the head of the farm had undisputed control over the distribution of the farm's income.[7] Allegedly this control aroused a double resentment among the members of the farming family. They felt inadequately rewarded for their contribution to the income of the farm,[8] and they railed against the refusal by the head of the farm to share his authority with them. Thus friction was inherent in both the economic and social relations within a farming family. The typical outcome of such friction, Kubanin found, was the departure of the disgruntled family members and the splintering of the original farm unit. In this interpretation, splintering was the resolution of a power struggle within the farming family.

According to Kubanin, the political tensions that led to splintering were unique to the capitalist stage of development. In the precapitalist stage, he explained, the farm was run in an egalitarian manner, each member having an equal voice in the distribution of the farm's income and in decisions about cultivation. All this changed, however, when the farm was drawn into the orbit of the market.[9] At that point the head of the farm began to act like a capitalist, assuming all the prerogatives of ownership and treating his kin as if they were workers. Despite the strain produced by this high-handed behavior, the farm remained intact so long as the "proletarians" found no other form of employment. However, Kubanin explained, when the exploited family members discovered that the market could absorb the sale of their labor power, they departed, splintering the original farm unit as they left. For Kubanin, then, splintering was a by-product of proletarianization. As he put it, "the systematic conversion of a portion of the working family into a commodity is the reason for the dissolution of the peasant family."[10] According to Kubanin, class antagonisms did not end with the act of splintering itself. Rather, when the farm was divided, the conflicts that had rent the peasant household were simply transferred to the interfarm arena. As in intrafarm tensions, the source of this conflict was also economic. When the farm was splintered, the "mother" farms kept the lion's share of the land and inventory, leaving the "daughter" farms with the remainder. The unequal division eventually resulted in a polarization between agricultural proletarians (formerly equal members of the farming family) and agricultural capitalists (former heads of family farms).[11] Regrettably, Kubanin added in an aside, the process of proletarianization did not go far enough, for the daughter farms clung to their miserable allotments and only rarely sent any of their members out to work in industry. Such was the fascination of the small holding for the Soviet peasant.[12]

Kubanin's study was, to say the least, contrived. The analysis of intrafarm friction as a struggle between representatives of various socioeconomic classes led to certain absurd conclusions—for example, the notion that a capitalist would grant a portion of his resources to proletarians leaving his employ.[13] Moreover, Kubanin's insistence that the division of Russian peasant households was an aspect of proletarianization led him to ignore the fact it had been going on well before the advent of capitalism.[14] So distorted were some of his findings that A. I. Khriashcheva, the Marxist statistician who had done solid research on the splintering of peasant households, expressed doubts as to whether he had properly worked through his material.[15]

Flawed though it was, Kubanin's study received the endorsement of the head of the Agrarian Institute, L. N. Kritsman.[16] Kritsman was quite candid about the reasons for his approval. In the controversy with the Organization-Production scholars, Kubanin's work performed two important functions. First, it demonstrated that the family farm was amenable to analysis from a Marxist perspective. Before 1928 the investigation of the internal dynamics of the peasant household, like the budget study, had been regarded as the province of the Timiriazev professors. Not having studied the operation of the small-scale farm themselves, the members of the Kritsman group were not able to counter effectively their teachers' contentions about this form of agriculture. But Kubanin's microeconomic study removed this impediment to refutation—an achievement of which Kubanin was suitably proud.[17]

Second, Kubanin's study showed the family farm enmeshed in the process of rural stratification. In so doing it cast doubt on the assertion by the Timiriazev professors that because its growth and decay were internally determined, the family farm would withstand capitalism. To the Agrarian-Marxists, this was an estimable accomplishment, for it made more realistic their prediction that the family farm would be dissolved as the rural sector became polarized into capitalist and proletarian farmers. Thus, Kubanin's research removed the last *theoretical* obstacle to the supersession of the family farm economy.

The Attack on Research

To challenge effectively the hegemony of the Timiriazev professors over certain areas of research, the Kritsman group had to redefine the subject of inquiry so that the work of the Chaianov group became peripheral and to offer a Marxist approach to the newly defined problem areas. One of the first attempts by the Kritsman group to do so took place in the area of farm organization. The assignment was a difficult one, for this area of study had been pioneered by the Organization-Production scholars and virtually ignored by the Agrarian-Marxists. Despite these obstacles, at the end of 1927 the Agrarian-Marxists sought to wrest control of the area from their former teachers. It is likely that the Kritsman group was emboldened to choose this subject because the Chaianov group's study of farm organization had been based on the dynamics of the family farm, a form of agriculture with which the Party was manifesting growing disenchantment.

The Agrarian-Marxists' effort to end that monopoly began at the end of 1927, with an article by Lubiako and Naumov on the formulation of organizational plans for sovkhozy.[18] The authors were writing on a complex subject in which they had no expertise, and they consequently produced a short article devoid of substantial insight. Its deficiencies were no doubt apparent to the other members of the Kritsman group, for there was no further attempt to forge out of whole cloth a Marxist approach to the study of farm structure. Rather, the Agrarian-Marxists who followed Lubiako and Naumov invariably began with a detailed critique of the Chianaov group's work on farm organization and then proceeded to generate certain principles upon which a Marxist approach might be constructed.

An excellent example of this approach to the problem can be found in the work of Ia. A. Anisimov, a young Agrarian-Marxist who had been trained in the Timiriazev Academy. In the first half of 1928 Anisimov produced a series of three articles that were apparently part of a larger work in progress on the subject of farm structure. The first article, which appeared in the January issue of the Timiriazev Academy's journal, was devoted to a review of the history of the study of farm organization.[19] As he traced the development of the field from 1762 through 1925, the author emphasized the congruence between the form of inquiry prevalent at a given point and the form of agriculture that predominated. Anisimov's point was obvious: the Organization-Production approach to the study of farm structure was appropriate to the first quarter of the twentieth century, when it was formulated and refined, but as the Soviet regime moved forward to restructure agriculture, the old approach became outmoded. Not content with showing the irrelevance of the Timiriazev professors' work, Anismov went on the refute its theoretical underpinnings. In a second article published the following month, the young critic contended that the Organization-Production scholars' study of farm structure had been based on the labor-consumption theory, which, he reminded his readers, had been called into serious question by the findings of the Marxist, S. N. Prokopovich.[20] Having to his satisfaction discredited the work of his former teachers, Anisimov turned to elaborate guidelines for a Marxist science of farm structure. That this task was not easy is clear both from the fact that Anisimov's third article did not appear until May and from the fairly slim content of the final piece. Essentially, the May article was a plea for a "normative" approach to the study of farm organization. In using the term "normative," the author was inveighing against what he termed the "technical" approach adopted by Chelintsev and Makarov, who had allegedly treated the construction of a farm plan simply as a question of finding the optimal combination of the vital factors of production (land, labor, and capital).[21] Anisimov's distinction between a "technical" and a "normative" approach was unsound from a linguistic point of view, but his point was plain. At a time when the Soviet regime was engaged in altering the structure of farming, it was inappropriate to confine the science of farm organization to an extrapolation from the status quo; the researcher ought instead to adopt a "creative," or teleological, approach to the analysis of farm structure.[22]

Anisimov's articles were carefully researched and relatively free of invective—features not always found in the work of his Agrarian-Marxist colleagues.[23] But the three pieces on the science of farm structure accomplished only part of their purpose. Anisimov was able to redefine the subject of inquiry so that the members of the Chaianov group would no longer necessarily be the key researchers in the field, but he was unable to provide a Marxist approach to the field he had redefined. The problem was not unique to Anisimov nor peculiar to the area of farm organization.[24] Having come to maturity by reacting against their teachers, the Agrarian-Marxists were accustomed to defining their approach by negation—as non-Organization-Production, non–petit bourgeois, nondeviationist. It would require time before they would be able to put forward a constructive Marxist approach to the full range of subjects in the field of rural social studies. Unfortunately, time was a commodity they would not have in plenty.

The Organization-Production Group: Scholarship on the Defensive

Before 1927 the Timiriazev professors were given to boasting about the importance of their contribution to the field of rural studies. As they saw it, the Organization-Production school had performed the invaluable and unique service of laying bare the internal dynamics of the prevalent form of agriculture in Russia, the family farm. Without such work, these scholars insisted, the field of rural inquiry would have been barren indeed. The Timiriazev professors did not deny that other research on the rural sector (specifically the Marxists' examination of interfarm relations) had its place, but, convinced of the overriding importance of their own work, they devoted only passing attention to that of their younger Soviet colleagues.

During 1927, as the family farm sector began to pose serious problems for the regime, it became the topic of frequent discussions within Party circles. The publicity given this question probably suggested to the Organization-Production scholars that their group's association with the study of the family farm had now become a liability, which, if continued, could end by undermining their position of leadership within the community of scholars. So, in the wake of their victory at the differentiation debate, the Organization-Production scholars adopted a new strategy. For the first time, they minimized the uniqueness of their work and drew attention to the links between the research they had conducted and that carried out by their opponents. In addition, wherever possible, they presented their old research as relevant to the current concerns of the regime. This change in strategy was most apparent in the work of the Chaianov group on farm budgets and agricultural regionalization.

The Denial of Novelty

The Organization-Production scholars regarded themselves as pioneers in the use of budget research, and with justification. They had taken the budget method that had traditionally been used to detail consumption patterns and, making certain modifications, had applied it to the analysis of farm structure. Then, using the results of their analysis, they had presented a new theory of noncapitalist economics. So impressive was this innovation that, in Russia, the budget method was invariably associated with the theory of the family farm. The Organization-Production scholars denied that there was any logical status to this link; in fact, they repeatedly insisted that the budget method was a tool that could be applied in a variety of research projects. These disclaimers notwithstanding, the connection between the method and substance persisted for some time, reinforced by the fact that it was Chaianov who wrote the history of budget work in Russia.

Initially the Agrarian-Marxists treated the budget method as the preserve of their former teachers. However, they gradually became persuaded that the method might be employed with profit in their own research on rural social structure. Taking care to dissociate themselves publicly from those who had pioneered the method, the Kritsman group used the technique freely. Indeed, every major stratification study conducted by the group after 1925 relied to some extent on information culled from peasant budgets.

During the first phase of the controversy, there was no public assessment by the Organization-Production scholars of their students' use of budget research. However, in the third edition (November 1927) of the history of budget research, Chaianov presented an extensive discussion of "Marxist innovations" in the field.[25] With accuracy and nuance he traced the development of the Agrarian-Marxist work, giving great weight to the contributions of Nemchinov and Kritsman. This history was followed by a detailed account of the research results obtained by the Volokolamsk and Samara teams and by Gaister. Chaianov's treatment of his rivals' work was laced with compliments. He described the Kritsman group as being "at the height of its powers" and included the group's use of budget data among the three most important applications of the method, the other two being the study of consumption patterns and, not surprisingly, the analysis of farm structure.[26]

In subsuming his group's budget research under the same

rubric as that conducted by his rivals, Chaianov was minimizing the uniqueness of the studies he and Chelintsev had carried out. He did so quite deliberately, in order to deflect attention from the fact that the Organization-Production studies had been based on the now-problematic family farm. This strategy, while eminently rational, produced a somewhat biased history. For example, Chaianov played up the importance of the Volokolamsk study executed by three young Agrarian-Marxists, yet he devoted but four lines to its sister project, the Penza study, which had been carried out by G. A. Studenskii. (Studenskii, whose relations with the Organization-Production school had never been easy, had included in the Penza study questions on socioeconomic differentiation in the attempt to become part of the Agrarian-Marxist group.)[27] Moreover, indulging in clear hyperbole, Chaianov claimed that the Marxist use of budget research was the most profitable application of the technique.[28]

Not content with making positive comments about the work of his rivals, Chaianov denigrated his own budget research. He criticized the Starobel'sk study of 1915, once his pride and joy, because its purpose had been to verify the hypothesis that farm structure was a function of family composition. Writing at the end of 1927, Chaianov did not say that this hypothesis was incorrect. He simply declared that it was not the most important object of study and should not, therefore, have been allowed to draw energies away from other, more vital, topics of study.[29]

Though willing for strategic reasons to accord priority to the Marxist use of budget data, Chaianov was clearly not prepared to have his own group's budget work cast aside as useless. To forestall such a development, he attempted to demonstrate that the Organization-Production and the Agrarian-Marxist uses of budget research could coexist. The result of his efforts was a study of beet cultivation published in 1927.[30] In introducing the new work, Chaianov explained that he now understood that a study of rural dynamics required not only an analysis of farm organization, but also an examination of peasant social structure.[31] Having said this, Chaianov presented a list of research questions which was clearly divisible into queries that touched on the concerns of the Timiriazev professors and queries that related to the interests of the researchers working in the Agrarian Section.[32] The questions were bound together only by the fact that all were to be answered using budget data. Ultimately, then, the unifying force in Chaianov's study was method. Within a short time, as we shall see, the emphasis on method or technique over substance would be deemed unacceptable.

The Quest for Relevance

In their work on the family farm, the Organization-Production scholars repeatedly stressed the fact that the form of agriculture they were studying constituted 90 percent of Russian farming. Without doubt the Timiriazev professors made this statement in order to claim for themselves the role of experts on the Russian rural sector. In the second half of the 1920s, as official dissatisfaction with the family farm began to mount, the future of that form of agriculture became an open question. In this new context, the Timiriazev professors were understandably concerned lest the agricultural unit about which they knew so much become outmoded and they themselves be declared obsolete. To avoid just such a fate, they began to cast about for ways to make themselves indispensable in the new age.

Strangely, it was Chelintsev, the oldest member of the Organization-Production school, who was most successful in this endeavor. In 1927 Chelintsev took the method of regional analysis he had pioneered sixteen years earlier and presented it as directly relevant to one of the most important endeavors of the Soviet regime—economic planning. Chelintsev began the task of putting old wine in new bottles with the observation that early attempts at economic planning had been unsuccessful largely because the planners had lacked adequate knowledge of the particulars of the various regions.[33] What was needed, he contended, was a form of regional analysis that would define the correct unit for planning[34] and at the same time lay bare its particular features. With the aim of filling these requirements, Chelintsev wrote a series of articles that appeared in the last quarter of 1927. Here he elaborated a set of maxims for regional analysis and tested his prescriptions with data on the economic regions of Russia.[35] In presenting his new work, Chelintsev was careful to emphasize the continuity with his original studies. Thus he reminded his readers that he had always been interested in the problem of rural change; indeed, his very first study of Russia's economic regions had been in effect a history of agriculture, with the various regions representing different stages of development.[36]

Apparently Chelintsev's attempt was successful; as he recorded with pride, his set of indicators was adopted by the Zemplan Commission.[37] If nothing else, the success of Chelintsev's efforts reveals that in 1927 it was still possible for an expert to be consulted regardless of his ideological orientation. Over the next few years that permissiveness would diminish, with the result that the quest by the Organization-Production scholars for a continuing role as experts would become increasingly difficult.

The Controversy at the Beginning of 1928

In the course of 1927 the advantages in the rural studies controversy had shifted noticeably. The Agrarian-Marxists, once the underdogs in status, experience, and expertise, were now clearly on the rise. They were making substantial strides in their own research projects and were moving forward with confidence to attack the position of their former teachers. The Organization-Production scholars, once the leaders in rural studies, were now deliberately keeping a low profile. They were minimizing their distinctiveness and trying to make their work relevant to the new age. But they were neither retracting their basic propositions nor disowning their original value commitments. In the first quarter of 1928, the third edition of Chaianov's study of optimal farm size was published under the title *Optimalnye razmery sel'skokhoziais-tvennykh predpriiatii* [Optimal Sizes of Agricultural Enterprises].[38] Because the subject matter of this work lay at the heart of the substantive disagreement in rural studies, it is reasonable to assume that any retreat by the members of the Chaianov group would have been reflected here. But in the 1928 edition, the reader finds the familiar championship of varying optima for farms of different descriptions, a championship on which Chaianov had based his case for vertical, rather than horizontal, cooperation. Moreover, the optimal sizes presented in the 1928 version were substantially the same as they had been in the first edition, which had appeared in print in 1922. To be sure, the third edition was probably prepared for press some time before the winter of 1928, yet Chaianov clearly did not feel it necessary to make any last-minute deletions or alterations, a prerogative of which he would avail himself in years to come.[39] Thus, although the advantages in the rural studies controversy may have shifted substantially in the course of 1927, one may infer that in early 1928 the precise outcome of the debate still remained to be determined.

9. The Resolution of the Controversy

In the middle of 1928 the controversy that had divided the rural studies community for over half a decade was resolved. The end came quietly, with no fanfare. The Organization-Production scholars conceded their position on the future of the family farm. Perforce, this made the Agrarian-Marxists the victors in the rural studies debate. In this chapter we examine the resolution of the controversy in detail: the forces that induced the Timiriazev professors to concede, the form of the concession, and its meaning within the framework of the dispute between the two groups of scholars. The chapter concludes with a portrait of the victorious Kritsman group and an assessment of the state of rural inquiry after the controversy had been resolved.

The Demand for Utility in Scholarship

When the third edition of Chaianov's study of optimal farm size appeared in print in early 1928, it met with stringent criticism from the opponents of the Organization-Production school. Reviewing *Optimal'nye razmery*, the young Agrarian-Marxist M. Sulkovskii began by labeling Chaianov a champion of small-scale agriculture.[1] Not content merely to brand the author, Sulkovskii went on to insist that Chaianov had disguised his sympathies and, under the guise of objective research, had produced biased scholarship. For example, he contended, Chaianov had played up the problems of large-scale farming while minimizing the deficiencies of small-scale cultivation. Moreover, Chaianov's handling of the data had been faulty. Chaianov had interpreted his findings as showing that where cultivation was intensive, the advantages that normally accrued to large-scale farming decreased greatly. But, averred Sulkovskii, if Chaianov's findings were reworked properly, they would demonstrate that even when cultivation was intensive, large-scale farming was superior to small-scale agriculture.[2] Then, adding insult to injury, Sulkovskii declared that Chaianov's attitude to farming was "pretechnological."[3] The implications of this remark were clear, but the reviewer went on to spell them out. Chaianov's study might have some theoretical value, but it had no practical use, for the optima it presented were too low to be of any utility in the construction of either state or collective farms.[4]

Sulkovskii's review was most revealing on several points. To begin with, it demonstrated that by early 1928 criticism of an opponent was becoming a vehicle for attack and vilification. The 1928 review contrasted strikingly with a review of the first edition of Chaianov's *Optimal'nye razmery*, a review written in 1923 by none other than L. N. Kritsman.[5] In his review Kritsman did point out certain "flaws" in Chaianov's study—principally the author's refusal to declare categorically the superiority of large- over small-scale farming—but he treated the points he raised as minor defects that marred an otherwise excellent work rather than as major faults that vitiated the value of Chaianov's research. Moreover, Kritsman termed valuable the method of calculating optima that had been pioneered by the group working in the Timiriazev Institute under the direction of Chaianov.[6] In the review published by Sulkovskii only five years later, there were no traces of such generosity.

Second, and much more important, Sulkovskii's review showed how the demand for "useful" research could serve as a weapon in controversies between contending schools. At the Fifteenth Party Congress in December 1927, the Soviet regime put new teeth in its commitment to construct large-scale socialist farms;[7] and, in the wake of that Congress, the optimal size of a farm unit became a practical as well as a theoretical question.[8] In advocating differential optima for farms of varying sizes, Chaianov's *Optimal'nye razmery* went against the preference for gigantism which was rapidly becoming the bias of the age. Bent on scoring points against his rivals, Sulkovskii did not trouble to make reasoned arguments; he simply denounced the work of his onetime teacher as "irrelevant."

In itself, the demand for useful scholarship was not anathema to the Organization-Production scholars. Quite the contrary; they always presented themselves as applied social scientists and pointed with pride to the fact that their scholarship was of use to agronomists working in the countryside. Now, however, for the first time, the demand for useful research was being used to undermine the position of the Chaianov group.

Concession

The implications of the call for useful rural scholarship in the new conditions were not lost on the members of the Chaianov group. They picked up the appropriate cues and altered their research program accordingly. In the months between the late winter and the early autumn of 1928, the Organization-Production scholars ceased to study the family farm economy and began instead to examine large-scale socialist cultivation. This was no simple shift in research program. In abandoning their traditional interests for new concerns, the Timiriazev professors were effectively conceding that the small, noncapitalist farm would not play the role in Soviet agriculture that they had envisaged for it. This concession brought the rural studies debate to an end.

The first sign of the Organization-Production scholars' new interest in socialist cultivation occurred in a speech delivered by A. V. Chaianov on March 16, 1928, to the Plenum of the Timiriazev Academy's Institute on Agricultural Economics. Chaianov's address, which was published almost immediately in the Institute's Bulletin, centered on the problem of constructing organizational plans for state farms.[9] In itself the speech was unexceptional;[10] but coming as it did from Chaianov, the 1928 address was a *volte-face*. The Director of the

Timiriazev Institute had been one of the most consistent champions of the family farm. Moreover, he had been profoundly skeptical of large-scale socialist units of cultivation.[11] Therefore the very topic of his address to the Plenum signaled Chaianov's surrender of a long-held position. When he delivered his address in March, Chaianov did not give reasons for his new interest. However, from comments he made subsequently, it seems clear that Chaianov wanted his contemporaries to believe that his favorable attitude toward socialist farming stemmed from his recent awareness that the use of sophisticated farm machinery in Soviet agriculture would eliminate many of the problems he had identified as stumbling blocks.[12] Some Western commentators have been persuaded by Chaianov's account.[13] The explanation seems somewhat suspect, however, for it glosses over the fact that as early as 1921, Makarov was writing about the use of tractors and other complex farm machines in American agriculture.[14] In view of the close relationship between Chaianov and Makarov, it hardly seems likely that Chaianov only became aware of the potential benefits of technology seven years after Makarov's work was published. What does seem plausible is that Chaianov became interested in state farms in 1928 because he sensed that Soviet agricultural policy was animated as never before by the determination to create large-scale socialist farms. He probably realized that to retain his credentials as a scholar relevant to the new age, he would have to prove himself an expert on the new farms. In this spirit, Chaianov composed his 1928 address. By reporting on the problem of constructing state farm plans, he drew attention to the need for qualified advice; in offering a set of guidelines for plan construction, Chaianov subtly reminded his audience that by virtue of his earlier work he was uniquely suited to tender such advice.

Although a shift in official rural policy had motivated Chaianov's new work, his March address made no mention of this factor. Rather, by drawing a link between his new and his previous work on farm organization, Chaianov implied that the ability to formulate sound organizational plans was a technical skill that could be applied to a variety of agricultural forms in any sociopolitical context. Thus, by bracketing out the factor of politics, Chaianov attempted to present himself as a man of the new age.

Chaianov reinforced his image as a technical expert with a chapter on agriculture he contributed to a collection of essays published in 1928 under the title *Zhizn'i tekhnika budushchego* [Life and Technology in the Future].[15] The editor of the volume referred to the contributors as "theoreticians of scientific socialism," but Chaianov made no reference in his article to any sociopolitical system. He concentrated strictly on examining the ways in which technological innovations in farming could revolutionize Russian agriculture. His discussion, which included references to such advances as soilless agriculture and grain factories, was a leap into the future—so much to that the editor felt constrained to add a note at the end of the article cautioning that some of the advances discussed by the author were so novel as to be more appropriately included in dreams and utopias.[16] Chaianov's piece, which showed him a prophet of the future, contrasted sharply with a utopia he himself had written but eight years earlier. In 1920 he had spoken out against rapid, wholesale change in the countryside, warning that such change might enrage the peasantry and lead to the overthrow of proletarian power.[17] Eight years later, avoiding all mention of political considerations, Chaianov became the champion of progress.

The attempt to divorce technical expertise from politics was not unique to Chaianov; the same approach was taken by Chelintsev in his work on socialist agriculture. In the final months of 1928 Chelintsev published two articles on the organization of collective farms.[18] He suggested that the task of kolkhoz construction would be best accomplished if guided by the principles of regional analysis—an area of study that he himself had pioneered some fifteen years earlier. To illustrate his point, Chelintsev did a region-by-region survey of the factors that in his opinion ought to dictate the organization of collective farms.[19]

In terms of their subject matter, the two articles by Chelintsev were very much in the spirit of the concession begun by Chaianov in March of the same year. The pieces would therefore have been of little interest had they not been preceded by a "theoretical" article written by Chelintsev in August.[20] The purpose of the August article was to sever the study of farm organization from the labor-consumption theory. In his determination to accomplish this purpose, Chelintsev made a torturous argument. Historically, he explained, the Organization-Production approach to the study of farm structure had often been used by scholars who espoused the labor-consumption theory. (As examples, Chelintsev cited some of his close colleagues, taking care to exclude himself from their number.) But, he continued, the connection between the Organization-Production approach and the "anachronistic" theory[21] was neither logical nor necessary.[22] The study of farm structure was a technical enterprise, which could—and should—be conducted free of any theoretical underpinnings.

Chelintsev's August article marked the beginning of the intellectual and social disintegration of the Organization-Production group as a school in rural inquiry. Men of established reputation before they had coalesced as a group, the Timiriazev professors had been bound together by their common belief in the labor-consumption theory. The jettisoning of that theory in the latter half of 1928 left little basis for agreement on cognitive matters. Moreover, for more than a decade, the Chaianov group had worked together in an institution they had helped to make famous. Chelintsev's attempt to dissociate himself from his colleagues strained the social solidarity that had been built up.

The Agrarian-Marxists later declared that the Organization-Production school had disintegrated from within, its forces scattered because of the internal inconsistencies in the intellectual stand of its members.[23] This interpretation must be viewed as self-serving. In fact, the Chaianov group dissolved because a shift in Party policy toward the countryside made its theory anachronistic and forced its members to look for ways of making themselves relevant to the new context. That search ended with each of the founding members of the Organization-Production school working in that area of applied knowledge in which he was expert. It was the attempt to ward off obsolescence that led to the scattering of the group's forces.

When the Organization-Production school disintegrated, the Kritsman group found itself cast in the role of victor in the rural studies controversy. As the Agrarian-Marxists were to discover, that role brought with it a new set of problems. Far from indemnifying the Kritsman group against criticism, its "triumph" seemed to make it the more vulnerable to attack.

Portrait of the Victors

Just as the Agrarian-Marxists were moving within sight of a victory over the Timiriazev professors, they found their position as the foremost Marxist students of the countryside coming under challenge. The setting in which the challenge was issued was as bizarre as the challenge itself. On January 16, 1928, a meeting of the Agrarian Section of the Communist Academy brought together most of the members of the Kritsman school and a few invited guests.[24] The audience had been assembled to hear Kritsman deliver a report on the study of rural differentiation.[25] The leader of the Agrarian-Marxists began his report by justifying his group's concentration upon the study of peasant stratification. Differentiation was the most important process at work in the Soviet countryside, he averred, and consequently its study was a matter of priority.[26] From there Kritsman went on to review the approach to differentiation adopted by his research group. It had been traditional, Kritsman reminded his listeners, to study differentiation using the index of amount of arable land[27] or the size of the herd possessed.[28] This seasoned approach, while useful in ascertaining the differences in economic strength among peasant farms,[29] could not be the basis for the construction of a stratification map, for the most fundamental inequalities in the Soviet rural sector were social in nature. It was with this consideration in mind, Kritsman recounted, that he had led the move away from an economic classification of farms to a social typology of the peasantry.

With appropriate modesty, the leader of the Agrarian-Marxists acknowledged that the methodology he had pioneered had yet to be perfected. However, he added, definite progress had been made in refining the method of calculation and the groupings themselves. With the pride of an innovator and teacher, Kritsman pointed to three milestones in the development of approach associated with the Agrarian Section: the Volokolamsk study by Anisimov, Vermenichev, and Naumov; the Samara study by Vermenichev, Gaister, and Raevich; and Gaister's study of seven regions.[30]

Kritsman's obvious pride in his research group did not strike a responsive chord in every member of his audience. After the report had ended, one of the assembled Marxist scholars, S. M. Dubrovskii, rose to launch a critique of the Agrarian-Marxists.[31] Dubrovskii focused his attack on three points. First, he expressed skepticism about the Kritsman approach to the study of rural social structure because it did not result in the grouping of peasants into the traditional categories of *bedniak* ("poor peasant"), *seredniak* ("middle peasant"), and *zazhitochnyi* ("better-off peasant").[32] The absence of the well-known labels, he insisted, prevented the layman from judging whether capitalism was increasing at the expense of socialism. Second, Dubrovskii attacked the findings reported by the Kritsman group. There were too many capitalists and poor peasants and too few middle peasants, he insisted.[33] Such a distribution implied that the government's policy of encouraging the middle peasants may have misfired, an implication that Dubrovskii was not prepared to consider, regardless of whether it was true.[34] Finally, Dubrovskii challenged Kritsman's contention that the land redistribution of 1917-1920 was petit bourgeois in spirit and results;[35] in the critic's view, that redistribution had been nothing if not proletarian in character. The point at issue here was not a small one. Upon the appraisal of the redistribution depended the scholar's assessment of the state of development of the Soviet countryside and, consequently, his recommendations for future policy toward the peasantry.

Dubrovskii's attack was interesting—it revealed that by early 1928 Marxist scholars were being subjected to the demand for "useful" scholarship and that they, no less than their non-Marxist colleagues, were vulnerable to the charge of producing irrelevant work. Kritsman was defended against this charge by the members of his group. The young researchers accepted the appropriateness of judging scholarship according to the criterion of utility and attempted to show that the work done in the Agrarian Section was relevant to the current concerns of the regime. They began by explaining that it had been Kritsman's purpose to study systematically the hiring and leasing of land and inventory by peasants.[36] For such a study, they insisted, the traditional categories (*bedniak, seredniak, kulak*) were useless; what was required was a quantitative measure of qualitative relations.[37] Having made the argument for utility, the Agrarian-Marxists went on to attack Dubrovskii's credibility by comparing his position to that of the leader of the Organization-Production school, A. V. Chaianov.[38] As evidence, the young researchers pointed to Dubrovskii's assertion that, for the most part, the social relations that Kritsman had included under the rubric "capitalist" were in fact precapitalist in nature. The Agrarian-Marxists had little difficulty in showing that Chaianov had espoused a similar position.

At the January meeting Dubrovskii stood alone. Kritsman, on the other hand, was loyally defended by his coterie of students. One after another, the young researchers rose to speak in praise of Kritsman's approach to rural social studies and even went so far as to heckle Dubrovskii from their seats.[39] Moreover, Kritsman was supported by the statistician Nemchinov, who dubbed the head of the Agrarian Section "the leading worker in the field."[40] As a consequence, Dubrovskii's challenge was unsuccessful.

Having beaten back this first attack, the group in the Agrarian Section appeared safe.[41] But there were ominous signs. In his speech at the January meeting, Dubrovskii had called for the congruence of research findings and Party dicta. In defending Kritsman, the young researchers had paid no heed to that call. Their omission was understandable; in early 1928 the demand for such congruence appeared bizarre. Regrettably, before too long, it would become commonplace.

The Field of Rural Studies, Autumn 1928

Whatever its other results, the concession by the Organization-Production scholars did not weaken the position of agricultural economics in the field of rural social studies. For in ceding their point, the members of the Chaianov group never disclaimed the importance of the questions they were studying; they merely shifted the focus of their inquiry from the family farm to large-scale socialist units of cultivation. Consequently, agricultural economics continued to be the leading approach to the study of the countryside. Yet, over a decade after the Revolution, Marxist scholars had made little if any contribution to that specialty.

An intensive effort to rectify this situation by developing a uniquely Marxist agricultural economics began in late 1928.[42] On October 16, a conference was held in the Agrarian Institute of the Communist Academy to discuss the content and perimeters of such a specialty.[43] The proceedings of the conference and the discussion occasioned by them were given extensive coverage in the Institute's journal, *Na agrarnom fronte*.[44] For Marxist rural scholars, the topic of the October meeting was a new one. To be sure, these scholars (or at least the best-read among them) were conversant with the literature in agricultural economics,[45] but before late 1928 there had been no attempt to formulate a comprehensive science of agricultural economics that would be congruent with the tenets of Marxism.[46]

The task confronting the Marxist scholars was not susceptible to quick solutions. Consequently, it should come as no surprise to learn that the participants at the October conference devoted far more time to criticizing the established brand of agricultural economics than to charting new directions for the field. The criticisms were articulated in a variety of accents and terminologies, but beneath the rhetoric lay two common complaints. First, it was charged, the agricultural economics that held sway in Russia in the 1920s had been built on the analysis of the family farm studied in isolation from its environment. Speaker after speaker raised methodological objections to a science built on such foundations. The "bourgeois" analysis was termed "static" and was attacked because it bracketed out social reality.[47] A corollary objection, not stated but clearly implied, was that the family farm, whose features had served as the building blocks of the reigning science, was fact becoming an anachronistic economic unit. Second, it was objected, the established version of agricultural economics was too divorced from theory (read "Marxist theory"). No attempt was being made to find general economic laws that governed the operation of agriculture.[48] Instead the field was oriented to practice; and, as such, it was nothing more than a form of "agricultural technics" or "agronomy."[49]

The participants' quarrels with tradition were far more impressive than the panaceas they suggested. Indeed, in making recommendations for a Marxist science of agricultural economics, the speakers showed themselves to be at a very preliminary stage of conceptualization. For example, in contrast to the established science based on the analysis of the family farm, many speakers called for the grounding of agricultural economics on the study of capitalist agriculture. Although the originator of this suggestion touted his revision as a breakthrough in "historical" or "evolutionary" methodology,[50] he made no mention of the need to isolate the variables that defined the succession of systems of cultivation. To take another example: in the effort to minimize the practical orientation that colored established agricultural economics, most participants advocated a focus on theory. At this point, however, consensus ceased. Some speakers urged that agricultural economics be regarded as a separate discipline and that an effort be made to generate theory from its findings, while other speakers argued strenuously that agricultural economics be regarded as a branch of political economy.[51]

The 1928 conference was important not so much for its content—which was laced with hairsplitting distinctions and formulaic arguments—but rather for what it suggested about the state of Marxist scholarship on the countryside. To begin with, the stenographic report of the October meeting reveals the extent of the gap between the thinking of the leading Marxist scholars and the official designs for the countryside that were taking shape at the time. To a man, the Marxist social scientists who met in late 1928 agreed that the new science ought to be based on the study of capitalist agriculture, with only minor attention being devoted to the features of socialist cultivation. Ironically, these scholars were less in tune with the spirit of the age than their non-Marxist rivals, who earlier in the same year had taken steps to refocus their work around the study of large-scale socialist farming.

Second, the fact that Marxist rural scholars (even some associated with Kritsman) were now concentrating their energies on agricultural economics suggests that rural sociology, once recognized as the foremost Marxist approach to the study of the Soviet countryside, had passed its peak. The change of interest among Marxist scholars was most clearly reflected in the speech by one of the less-known participants at the conference, V. Ulasevich. Ulasevich took the term *agrarniki* ("agrarian experts"), which had come to serve as a shorthand symbol for rural sociologists, and redefined it to refer to "agricultural economists"![52] In no small measure, the move by Marxist scholars away from rural sociology was a function of the concerns of that specialty. With the regime placing ever greater emphasis on the construction of large-scale socialist farms, the study of the polarization of the peasantry into capitalist and proletarian cultivators (upon which the rural sociologists had concentrated since 1925) seemed marginal, if not outmoded. Moreover, with the Organization-Production scholars no longer a force in rural studies, the specialty of rural sociology lost its value as a weapon in the struggle for leadership in the field. In the course of the next two years, rural sociology would continue to decline in prestige in Marxist scholarly circles,[53] and efforts to forge a Marxist science of agricultural economics would intensify.[54]

Part 4
Aftermath and Conclusion

10. The Politicization of Rural Social Studies

As the controversy between the Organization-Production and Agrarian-Marxist groups drew to an end, there were changes in Party policy toward the countryside and toward social science. These changes were so fundamental as to constitute a new social context for rural inquiry.

Beginning in late 1928, concerted efforts were being made to draft the First Five-Year Plan.[1] Despite the fact that the country was in the throes of a severe grain crisis,[2] the Plan was drafted in a spirit of unbridled optimism. Indeed, each successive version of the plan projected a higher rate of growth. As planning agencies vied with one another to produce the most ambitious draft, there grew a determination to overcome the constraints in the rural sector, to bend reality to design. In that light, the "measures of extreme severity" that had been rationalized in early 1928 as a temporary expedient were not revoked, but were employed again the next year to collect the grain. Thus was laid the foundation for the eclipse of the New Economic Policy, an eclipse that would become complete in December 1929 with the announcement of the forced collectivization of agriculture.

The widening gap between existing conditions and projected goals did not go unnoticed. It gave rise to repeated questioning not only within the planning agencies[3] but also in scholarly circles. The questioning, however, did little to inhibit the formulation of unrealistic designs; rather, it served to generate within certain segments of the Party leadership an apprehension about, and consequently an intolerance of, opposition to the bold plans for the future. The fear of dissent was eventually reflected in Party policy toward social science. In May 1928, in the wake of the Shakhty trial, the Communist Academy was charged with the task of "securing the hegemony of Marxist-Leninist theory."[4] No mention was made of the need to preserve non-Marxist social inquiry. Thus the policy of complementarity that the Party had pursued since 1926 in its dealings with social science came to an end. Ironically, as we shall see, the attack on bourgeois social science triggered by the end of the policy of complementarity had very severe implications for Marxist social science.

This new social context became the background for the denouement to our story: the politicization of the field of rural inquiry. The politicization that began in late 1928 affected every aspect of the field—the structure and activities of its major institutions, the composition of its scholarly community, and the content of its theory and research. In this chapter we trace the process through which the field became politicized. We look not only at the stages of this process but at the interrelation between them.

Institutional Structure

The new emphasis on forging a Marxist science of society had a tangible effect on the institutional structure of the field of rural inquiry. In September 1928 the Agrarian Section was elevated to the status of an Institute of the Communist Academy.[5] Officially, the change was made in recognition of the achievements of the Section in studying rural social structure. Probably, however, the change was the result of the Party's understanding that the young researchers working in the Agrarian Section required additional stature if they were to challenge successfully the leadership of their former teachers.

At about the same time the Timiriazev Academy was reorganized. The first harbinger of the change was the appointment in June 1928 of M. E. Shefler as Director of the Academy.[6] Shefler, who had been a Party member since 1917, gave the signal for the reorganization just one month after his appointment. At the July meeting of the collegia of the Commissariat of Agriculture and the Commissariat of Enlightenment, he read a report that criticized the workings of the Academy.[7] This report culminated in the drafting of a five-year plan to revamp the Academy. The changes envisaged in the plan were many-faceted. New facilities were to be built, new facilities were to be added, new approaches to teaching were to be encouraged, and the increased involvement of students in practical work was to be encouraged. For our story, the most important aspect of the projected changes was the planned division of the economics faculty into a faculty of state farms and a faculty of collective farms. This division meant that there was no longer any faculty in which courses on presocialist agriculture could be taught. Thus the Organization-Production scholars, who had traditionally taught in the economics faculty, were to be deprived of their base. In the last three months of 1928, the reorganization of the Academy's faculty structure became a reality. It was followed closely by an attack on the research center dominated by the Organization-Production scholars, the Institute on Agriculture Economics. In February 1929 a proposal was made in the Presidium of RANION to integrate the Timiriazev Institute with the Institute of Land Consolidation and Migration.[8] Without doubt, the purpose behind the proposal was to ease out the members of the Organization-Production school without having to close down their institute.

The net effect of the organizational changes was to shift the balance between the two major institutions in the rural studies field. The Timiriazev Academy, which had been the most important research and teaching center, was diminished in stature; the Agrarian Section, which had been created but three years earlier, was aggrandized.

The Community of Scholars

The new policy toward the social sciences also affected the composition of the community of rural scholars. For the first time, in late 1928, Marxist credentials became a prerequisite for scholars who wished to study the Soviet countryside. Not surprisingly, the first victims of this new rule were the Timiriazev professors.

Organization-Production Scholars

When Chaianov set aside the traditional concerns of the Organization-Production school in March 1928 and undertook a study of socialist farming, he made no reference to the change in rural policy that had spurred his shift of focus. He simply styled himself a technical expert whose skills could be applied in a variety of socioeconomic settings.

Five months later, when Chelintsev prepared to follow Chaianov's lead, the position of the apolitical expert was no longer tenable. Consequently, Chelintsev prefaced his claim to expertise with a criticism of Organization-Production theory.[9] Reassessing the labor-consumption theory he had once espoused, he declared it "unnecessary and confusing" as well as "reactionary" in its implications.[10] In effect, Chelintsev's article was a confession of error. But it was a strangely impersonal confession, for it concentrated on the flaws in the theory and said nothing about his onetime adherence to the account he now denounced. Less than six months later, Chaianov was to issue a much more personal recantation. In an article published in a daily newspaper he presented what amounted to an intellectual autobiography.[11] Chaianov explained that he had championed the small-scale farm because he believed it more viable than either the capitalist or the socialist forms of agriculture. For the years 1912-1923, he insisted, his original stand had been correct. But he had prolonged his advocacy of family farming beyond the point of reason, he admitted. Chaianov concluded his article with a pledge to espouse the cause of large-scale socialist farms.[12]

With the benefit of hindsight, it is clear that these self-denunciations by the leaders of the Organization-Production group marked the true demise of the school. Yet at the time they were issued, the Timiriazev professors hoped to use the confessions to stave off total defeat. They knew that in the highly charged atmosphere of late 1928 and early 1929 they could not divorce expertise from politics; their only hope of preserving their position lay in "clarifying" their attitude toward their former work. Consequently they denounced their past in the hope of securing for themselves a measure of legitimacy for the future.

Initially, the "confessions" of both Chelintsev and Chaianov were accepted at face value. In a note following Chelintsev's "theoretical" article of August 1928, the editors of *Puti sel'skogo khoziaistva* expressed pleasure at the fact that Chelintsev had sided with the Marxists. They welcomed the convert, even though they noted that some of his ideas were still unorthodox.[13] Similarly, Chaianov's recantation was well received. In a brief paragraph that followed Chaianov's article of February 1929, the editors of *Sel'sko-khoziaistvennaia zhizn'* remarked that although Chaianov's account left certain questions "unanswered," he was clearly on the road to redemption.[14]

Ultimately, however, the genuineness of these confessions was challenged. The challenges stemmed from the fact that their earnest efforts notwithstanding, the Organization-Production scholars found it difficult to adjust their scholarship to official thinking about the rural sector. To take one example: while the kolkhozy were being commended by the Party on ideological grounds, Chelintsev persisted in treating these farms as units of cultivation whose performance ought to be measured by normal standards of efficiency.[15] Or, while the Party was stressing the pervasiveness of social antagonisms in the countryside, Chaianov was writing about the peasants moving peacefully and voluntarily into the collective farms ("self-collectivization").[16] In the course of 1929 tolerance of these views decreased sharply, and critics of the Timiriazev group began to insist that the original recantations by Chaianov and Chelintsev had been fraudulent, for the scholars had remained "un-Marxist."[17]

Retrained, monitored, denounced, the members of the Organization-Production school came to realize that despite their announced willingness to follow the line set by rural policy, they would not be permitted to continue their study of the countryside. In the field of rural inquiry, political allegiances were now determining the value of a scholar's contribution, and claims to truth were becoming group-based.[18] The relevant group, that of the Marxists, was simply closed to the Timiriazev professors. Consequently, during 1929 the Organization-Production scholars retreated one by one from the field they had once led.

Makarov went off to write propaganda articles that bore no relation to his former interests;[19] Chelintsev, though still at the Timiriazev Academy,[20] devoted himself to examining the technical aspects of farming, avoiding all mention of the socioeconomic forces in the rural sector;[21] and Chaianov published articles on the technology of the future.[22] By the end of 1929 the Timiriazev professors had virtually disappeared from the field of rural inquiry.[23] Not coincidentally, *Puti sel'skogo khoziaistva*, the journal to which the Chaianov group had submitted its most important articles, ceased publication at about the same time.[24] In its stead there appeared a new journal entitled *Sotsialisticheskaia rekonstruktsiia i sel'skoe khoziaistvo* [Socialist Reconstruction of Agriculture], which was the organ of four institutions: the Commissariat of Agriculture of the USSR, the Commissariat of Agriculture of the RSFSR, the Lenin Agricultural Academy, and the Timiriazev Agricultural Academy. The new journal devoted precious little space to agricultural policy and even less to the field of agricultural economics.

For some zealots, the elimination of the Organization-Production school as a force in rural studies was apparently insufficient. In 1930 Chaianov, Chelintsev, and Makarov were rounded up and arrested on the charge (never proven) that they had formed an opposition party, the Working Peasant Party.[25]

The exclusion of the Chaianov group from rural inquiry had far-reaching effects. It clearly impoverished the field of study, and, as we shall see, it profoundly altered the conditions of work for those scholars who remained.

The Agrarian-Marxists

As fate would have it, the Agrarian-Marxists had little time to enjoy their victory. Almost as soon as the Timiriazev professors began to retreat from the field, the Kritsman group found its own views under renewed attack.[26]

The attack was mounted in April 1929 at the Conference of Marxist-Leninist Scientific Research Institutes held in Moscow.[27] The conference opened with an address by Kritsman reviewing the accomplishments of Kubanin's study of the peasant household, which had been undertaken, it will be remembered, to show that there were no significant phenomena accounted for by the labor-consumption theory that could not be better explained using the Marxist approach. Kritsman gave Kubanin's work a firm endorsement. The analysis of the *dvor* from a Marxist perspective was a prerequisite to the effective refutation of the Organization-Production school, he claimed. "In neo-narodnik theory, the peasant *dvor* occupies a central position. To prove the untruth about this conception means to destroy the whole conception of the neo-narodnik school."[28] Moreover, he added, the study of the class structure of the *dvor* was indispensable to the formulation of sound policy on rural social change.[29]

Kritsman's presentation came in for a good deal of criticism.[30] Some members of his audience accused the speaker of taking an ahistoric approach that minimized the uniqueness of the Soviet period.[31] It was useful, they admitted, to oppose the Timiriazev professors' view that the family farm was a biological organism, but there was no reason to go to the opposite extreme and declare that the family farm was simply a microcosm of capitalist society.[32] That declaration had led Kritsman to overemphasize the amount of capitalism in the countryside and thus to blur the distinction between the capitalist and Soviet periods.[33] Other members of the audience focused their remarks on the implications of Kritsman's views for policy on the splintering of peasant households. They characterized the speaker as a "noninterventionist," who was content to allow the process of splintering to play itself out. In their view this process could be offset by the incorporation of family farms into socialist cooperatives.[34]

In the give-and-take that followed his address, Kritsman was staunchly defended by the younger members of his group. The Agrarian-Marxists insisted that the refutation of the Organization-Production school was a matter of priority, and they declared somewhat immodestly that the Agrarian Institute was doing the best job of refutation.[35] Moreover, they added, it was impermissible to require conceptual (as opposed to descriptive) studies to be revised every five years when the Soviet

Union embarked on a new phase of its development.[36] To this defense, Kritsman added only the observation that one could not tamper with history. While some of his critics had suggested that the family farm could be overcome by peaceful transition to socialism, he declared that the phase of capitalism with all its antagonisms could not be avoided.[37]

Although the April conference ended with resolutions commending the progress made by the researchers working in the Agrarian Institute,[38] the members of the Kritsman group had little cause to rejoice. Their opponents had leveled two very weighty charges against them. The first was that the Kritsman group had allowed the Timiriazev professors to define their Marxism for them. The irony of this charge was bitter indeed. For over half a decade the Agrarian-Marxists had steadfastly battled their teachers in the name of Marxism. Now that the Timiriazev professors no longer constituted a danger, that very service was being turned against Kritsman and his colleagues. Irony aside, there was more than a grain of truth to the accusation. As we saw above, the Agrarian-Marxists had shaped their research in part to refute the views of their teachers. Moreover, the Kritsman group could not easily set aside the work of its onetime mentors. As late as October 1929, well after the Organization-Production school had ceased to be a force in rural inquiry, a member of the Kritsman group drew up a proposal for a course of study in agricultural economics which included as suggested (rather than required) reading all the major writings of the Timiriazev professors.[39]

The second accusation against the researchers in the Agrarian Institute was that they held positions that conflicted with Party policy on the countryside. This charge was potentially much more serious than the first. Given the new enthusiasm for constructing large-scale socialist farms, it was likely to become increasingly difficult to insist that the Soviet rural sector had to pass through the stage of capitalism on its path to socialism.

However difficult the April conference was for the Kritsman group, it was not the worst attack they were to sustain. Before the year was out they were to be confronted by an assault far more grave in its implications than that they had just encountered.

In December 1929 the First All-Union Conference of Agrarian-Marxists convened in Moscow.[40] This conference, which was the analogue of a similar meeting among historians held the previous year,[41] brought together some three hundred delegates from all over the country.[42] Officially the conference was called to foster links between scholars working in the Agrarian Institute in Moscow and Marxist researchers working on the periphery.[43] However, the evidence suggests that the real purpose of the conference was to extend the hegemony of the Agrarian Institute (and thus of the Kritsman group, which dominated that Institute) over the field of rural studies. Thus, in preparation for the December meeting, scholars from the Institute were sent out to the provinces to "help" in the selection of delegates.[44] Moreover, the members of the Institute were designated in advance as the leaders of the new All-Union Society of Agrarian-Marxists, whose formation was announced at the December meeting.[45]

A more dramatic moment for a conference of rural scholars could not have been chosen. The meeting opened on December 20 against the background of an intensive campaign to make full-scale collectivization of agriculture into an immediate reality. The campaign had been set in motion by Stalin's article of November 7, "The Great Turn," which declared that the middle peasant had spontaneously turned toward collective farming.[46] In presenting goals as accomplished facts, Stalin forced the hand of his colleagues. From that point on, events moved with relentless speed. The Plenum of the Central Committee, which met from November 10-17, passed resolutions enjoining the hasty implementation of collectivization. To devise methods of implementing these resolutions, a Politburo commission under the new Minister of Agriculture, Iakovlev, was established on December 8. Just as the rural scholars were coming together in Moscow, that commission was preparing to submit its first proposals to the Politburo.[47]

In a curious way, the Moscow conference was remote from the political events swirling around it. Of course, collectivization was discussed, but it did not dominate the meeting— despite the fact that the delegates heard an address on rural policy by M. Kalinin, the president of the Central Executive

Committee.[48] The scholar-delegates were preoccupied by academic politics; they focused their attention on a question that concerned them directly—the question of who was a Marxist rural scholar.

The arguments over credentials at the December meeting were heated. Cross fire among Marxist researchers had clearly become common throughout the country, and the conference was witness to a series of regional disputes, which were aired in vivid detail.[49] It was, however, the confrontation within the Moscow contingent that occupied center stage. The main participants here were S. M. Dubrovskii, Deputy Director of the International Agrarian Institute,[50] and the followers of L. N. Kritsman, head of the Agrarian Institute that was hosting the conference. This was no parochial fight between feuding scholars. At stake was nothing less than the right to lead the community of Marxist rural scholars.

The confrontation between the Dubrovskii and Kritsman forces was not on the agenda. According to keynote speaker V. P. Miliutin, the December meeting had two tasks. First was the ideological task of refuting unacceptable or deviant views about Soviet rural policy. This was by no means simple, the vice-president of the Communist Academy told the delegates. Deviant views were rampant both within and without the Party; they had been expressed by the "bourgeois" school, the "neo-narodnik or petit bourgeois" school, and the Left and Right deviationists within the Party.[51] Second, there was the cognitive task of setting standards for future Marxist scholarship on the countryside.

Not long after Miliutin had completed his charge to the delegates, the clash between Dubrovskii and Kritsman came to the surface. In certain respects the December confrontation was a replay of old antagonisms. Dubrovskii, it will be remembered, had spearheaded an attack on Kritsman's work at the January 1928 meeting of the Communist Academy; moreover, he had figured prominently in the more recent criticism of Kritsman's work voiced at the April 1929 Conference of Marxist-Leninist Scientific Research Institutions. The December 1929 exchange between the two camps, however, had certain novel features. To begin with, institutional rivalries were superimposed upon intellectual disagreements. Dubrovskii, speaking on behalf of the International Agrarian Institute[52] took as his target not only Kritsman but the entire Kritsman group centered in the Agrarian Institute of the Communist Academy. Second, the tone of the interchanges between the two camps was more vituperative than before, a function of the stakes of the dispute. Finally, it was the Kritsman group that attacked Dubrovskii and not vice versa, as had been the case before.

Immediately after some bland remarks by Dubrovskii, Kubanin delivered a violent diatribe against him. The clear purpose of the attack was to challenge the authenticity of Dubrovskii's credentials as a Marxist. The evidence for this challenge that the members of the Kritsman group had culled was far from definitive. For example, Kubanin alleged that Dubrovskii was a covert member of the Right deviation; Sulkovskii pointed out that Dubrovskii held a position similar to that of Chaianov; and Kubanin added that in his early speeches Dubrovskii had paid insufficient attention to the goal of industrialization.[53] To add insult to injury, Vermenichev coined the term "Dubrovskiism," which he contrasted with Leninism.[54] The precise motive behind the attack on Dubrovskii remains unclear. It is possible that the Kritsman group, confident of its ability to control the conference, wanted to force Dubrovskii to air in public those criticisms he had been leveling in closed meetings in order that he be defeated before a prestigious assembly. It is also possible, however, that the Kritsman group, anticipating a new challenge by Dubrovskii, intended their attack as a preemptive strike.[55]

Whatever the reasoning of the Kritsman group, the bait they held out worked. Dubrovskii rose to answer the charges made against him and, in the process, lashed out against Kritsman and his school for deviations from orthodox Marxist analysis of the Soviet countryside. Most of Dubrovskii's attack centered on a single point: Kritsman's insensitivity to the heightening of class conflict in the period of transition to socialism.[56] This fundamental error, Dubrovskii alleged, affected Kritsman's work in several ways. First, it led him to develop a scheme of classification that underplayed the extent of social differentiation in the countryside.[57] Second, it led him to focus on the petit bourgeois peasant when Marxist scholars ought to be concentrating their attention on the kulak.[58] Third, it led him to historical distortions, the most important of which was the assessment of the *Kombedy* ("Committee of the Poor Peasants") movement as petit bourgeois rather than socialist in nature.[59] In addition to criticizing Kritsman's thought, Dubrovskii attacked the school that had gathered in the Agrarian Institute of the Communist Academy under Kritsman's leadership. He denounced these scholars for their effrontery in assuming that they were "the hub of the universe" (*pup zemli*) and intimated that there was something un-Marxist about this select group's having arrogated unto itself the title of "Agrarian-Marxist."[60]

Dubrovskii, a skillful polemicist under fire, had launched a forceful attack.[61] Although he had received little support from the delegates,[62] his attack could not remain unanswered. Kritsman was ill and unable to attend the conference,[63] and his younger colleagues had to take up the cudgels on his behalf. The young Agrarian-Marxists employed two tactics in making their case. First, they accused Dubrovskii of having misunderstood the thrust of Kritsman's work, of having failed to see that work in its proper perspective. For example, Kubanin claimed that to understand the true value of Kritsman's class analysis of the *dvor*, one had to see it as a refutation of the biological interpretation of the *dvor* advanced by the Organization-Production School.[64] Only because Dubrovskii had taken Kritsman's analysis of the *dvor* out of context, alleged Kubanin, had he failed to appreciate its essential value.[65] A second example was given by Gaister, who cited the interpretation of the agrarian revolution as petit bourgeois in character, an interpretation that he as well as Kritsman had espoused.[66] Gaister explained that in order to assess this interpretation properly, one had to understand, first, that it was not the *entire* October Revolution that was being thus evaluated and, second, that the designation of the agrarian revolution as "petit bourgeois" had been intended as a corrective to those who had overestimated the accomplishments of the *Kombedy* movement. Only because Dubrovskii had not understood the purpose or context of the interpretation of the agrarian revolution, urged Gaister, was he able to accuse Kritsman of being ahistorical.[67]

The second tactic employed by the young agrarianists to refute Dubrovskii was their denial that a Kritsman School of agrarian studies existed within the Agrarian Institute.[68] To a man, they attempted to prove that each of them approached the study of the countryside independently. Despite their efforts, however, the young researchers were not convincing; their impassioned defense of Kritsman gave the lie to their statement that there was no socially cohesive group working in the Agrarian Institute.

On 27 December, the last day of the conference, the participants heard a statement dictated by Kritsman from his hospital bed.[69] It is interesting to note that in his statement the ailing leader of the Agrarian-Marxists concentrated not on refuting Dubrovskii's specific charges but on demonstrating that, both as a researcher and as a theoretician, Dubrovskii was an opportunist.[70] Kritsman declared that Dubrovskii was forever climbing aboard the latest bandwagon, proclaiming dramatic shifts in policy instead of seeing continuities. In particular, Kritsman referred to Dubrovskii's "recent" espousal of two propositions: first, that the kulak was the greatest foe of the Soviet regime; and second, that capitalism was not a progressive force. Kritsman argued that these propositions had not been discovered by Dubrovskii; they had always been true. However, their utility depended upon the context in which they were asserted. To be sure, as compared to the petit bourgeois economic order, capitalism was progressive; but, as compared to the economic order that prevailed during the transition to socialism, capitalism was regressive. By taking statements out of context, alleged Kritsman, Dubrovskii was being intellectually "dishonest."[71] In fact, for intellectual honesty and restraint, by late 1929 there was little to choose between Kritsman and his supporters on the one hand and Dubrovskii on the other. Each side engaged freely in phrase-mongering and character assassination.

In the dispute over the leadership of the community of Marxist rural scholars, the Agrarian Institute group came out on top. The resolutions that brought the conference to an end "affirmed" a governing body for the All-Union Society of Agrarian-Marxists that included Kritsman, Gaister, Kubanin, Vermenichev, and Sulkovskii.[72] Moreover, in the resolutions of the conference the Institute and its journal *Na agrarnom fronte* were commended for having followed a politically correct line.[73] Dubrovskii was not thoroughly routed, however. A motion to censure him was not passed,[74] and Gaister's suggestion that the International Agrarian Institute be censured was similarly defeated.[75] The victory of the Kritsman group was thus a qualified one. In time it would be nullified.

Theory and Research in Rural Social Studies

Despite the fact that most of the discussion at the December meeting centered on the issue of credentials, its most important result was the establishment of nonscientific criteria for the assessment of rural research. During the first six days of the conference, there were occasional signs of a tendency to judge scholarship according to political criteria. For example, when Dubrovskii wished to cast scorn on Kritsman's scheme for classifying peasants, he did not trouble to assess its scientific merit; he simply pointed out that because it minimized the role of the kulak, upon whom the regime was focusing attention, it should therefore be declared "incorrect." Similarly, the Kritsman group accused Dubrovskii of having underplayed the importance of industrialization in a work written before the industrialization campaign had begun. Until the final day of the conference, such incidents were sporadic; however, on the seventh day, when Stalin appeared to address the delegates, official sanction was given to the use of political, rather than scientific, criteria for measuring the merit of scholarship.

Stalin's speech began rather innocuously.[76] He reminded his listeners of the importance of theory in the study of the countryside.[77] To this he added the not-surprising injunction that only Marxist theory be tolerated in Soviet work on the countryside. He then coupled this injunction with a stern denunciation of five "bourgeois" prejudices that he claimed were rampant in current rural inquiry.[78] Stalin's remarks on rural studies were but the prelude to the core of his address, the announcement that the kulaks were to be liquidated as a class.[79] Apparently Stalin's announcement was electrifying.[80] In a flash the assembled delegates understood that the debates they had been having for six days were irrelevant. The final arbiter of truth in all intellectual matters was not to be Marxist-Leninist theory, but rather the facts as created by the Communist Party through its rural policy. Henceforth, theory would merely celebrate those facts, and research would confirm the correctness of theory.

The enshrining of the new criteria of inquiry effectively destroyed rural studies as a field of social science in Russia. The record of that destruction emerges clearly from a comparison of the syllabus for a course in agricultural economics presented by Sulkovskii in October 1929[81] and the syllabus prescribed just one year later for all departments of agricultural economics.[82] Gone from the 1930 syllabus were references to Western writings in the field; gone were the suggested readings in Organization-Production research; gone indeed was all discussion of precapitalist agriculture. In their place appeared a list of books in which the writings of Marx and Lenin figured heavily. As Uzhanskii observed at the meeting of the heads of agricultural economics departments responsible for the 1930 syllabus, this was the time in which all agrarian experts had to be brought under the Party flag.[83]

The new standards for scholarly work unveiled at the December 1929 conference and enforced in the months that followed had their most profound impact upon the members of the Kritsman group. As we have indicated, these individuals did not anticipate the extent of the changes in official policy toward social science. In a sense, however, they were given a second chance, for at the conference of Agrarian-Marxists, the members of the Kritsman group were assigned the task of enforcing the new policy within rural studies. For this role of ideological watchdog, the group led by Kritsman proved itself unsuited. Consequently, like their teachers before them, most of the young researchers were forced to leave the field of rural inquiry. The saga of their departure is tinged with both irony and pathos. In September 1930 Kritsman lost his post as editor-in-chief of *Na agrarnom fronte*, although he remained a member of the editorial board. Toward the end of that year the attacks on Kritsman and his colleagues multiplied. At the end of 1930 there were recantations by Kritsman's co-workers,[84] and apparently a "scientific discussion" of Kritsman's work was planned for early 1931—although there is no evidence that such a discussion was ever held.[85] The final break occurred in early 1932, when the entire editorial board of *Na agrarnom fronte* was replaced, an action justified as necessary in the face of Kritsman's "anti-Leninism."[86] Thus disappeared the last vestige of the two groups of rural scholars responsible for the flowering of Soviet rural social studies in the NEP period.

In place of the two familiar groups of scholars, a new group of men came to prominence, men whose names were unknown in the field of rural social studies.[87] This group was heterogeneous in its composition. Some of its members were part of a new (third) generation on the rise—young undergraduates studying in the Timiriazev Academy.[88] Others hailed from newly created research and teaching institutions, which had played no role in the development of rural studies.[89] Still others were established researchers, who, seeing the opportunity, jumped aboard the bandwagon.[90] Despite differences in background and profile, these individuals shared a willingness to participate in or at least supervise the subordination of science to the dictates of the Party. The ascendancy of these Party minions was the final act in the destruction of rural social studies.

11. Reconsiderations

Having chronicled developments in the Soviet field of rural studies from 1923 through 1930, we now turn to consider certain important questions raised at the outset of this study. First, what were the effects of the dispute on the field of rural social studies? Specifically, how did the dispute affect the content of the field, the relations among its practitioners, and the structure of the profession? What facets of the dispute were most responsible for the effects observed? Second, what was the relationship between the period of controversy and the period of Cultural Revolution in the field of rural studies? In particular, what differences were there from the first to the second period in the impact of social factors on science and in the cohesion of the community of scholars? In discussing these questions, we will draw out the implications of our findings both for the study of scientific disputes and for an understanding of the viability of the NEP experiment in culture.

The Dispute and the Field of Rural Studies

In the development of rural social studies in Russia, the controversy between the Organization-Production and Agrarian-Marxist schools was no minor episode. The dispute left its mark on the intellectual content of the field, on relations among scholars engaged in studying the countryside, and on the structure of the profession.

One of the most important effects of the controversy was the substantial narrowing of the content of rural social studies. In its initial phase, it will be remembered, the dispute was the vehicle through which the boundaries of the field were extended beyond the traditional preoccupations with microeconomic issues to include sociological concerns. But in early 1927, when the controversy became a substantive disagreement over the nature of the family farm, that expansion ceased. All scholarly work not directly related to the disputed issues was set aside. To be sure, in the period 1927 to 1929 new studies were launched and new methods were essayed, but these were invariably linked to the question of the family farm. The willingness of the scholarly community to concentrate all its energies on this single issue was clearly a function of the centrality of that issue for official policy toward the countryside. But the fact that the boundaries of rural social studies were far from settled in this period probably facilitated the concentration of energy that led ultimately to the diminution of the scope of the field.

It is interesting to note that although the dispute ended by narrowing the content of rural social studies, the rank ordering of research perspectives in the field remained unchanged. Despite the concession by the scholars who had spoken on behalf of agricultural economics for over a decade, that specialty continued to be the dominant approach to the study of the countryside. Indeed, as the debate was coming to an end, we found the Agrarian-Marxists setting aside the rural sociology they had advocated so ardently and attempting to refine an agricultural economics that would be congruent with Marxism.

Further, the controversy strained relations, both intellectual and social, among rural scholars. The half decade during which the dispute was in progress was witness to a gradual polarization of scholars into two camps. The symptoms were several— a marked increase in intellectual posturing by scholars and a serious diminution in collaborative, or even cooperative, ventures. Some of these signs appeared as early as the differentiation debate of 1927, but it was only after that public meeting that divisions within the scholarly community became hard and fast. While the strains evident during the controversy pale by comparison with conditions in the post-1929 period, they were sufficiently profound as to make untenable the position of an unaffiliated scholar. On this point, the career of G. A. Studenskii was most illustrative. Studenskii, it will be remembered, began the decade as a member of the Chaianov group. His agreement with his colleagues was far from complete, and, at mid-decade, he made an effort to detach himself from the Organization-Production school in order to steer a middle course between it and the Agrarian-Marxist group. When his attempts to be nonpartisan were rebuffed by both schools, Studenskii decided to throw in his lot with the Kritsman group. Once again his overtures met with failure, for he was considered to have been tainted by his early association with the Timiriazev professors. Consequently, at the end of the decade, the hapless Studenskii had no intellectual home. The polarization of the community of scholars was clearly a by-product of the importance of the issue under dispute for official rural policy. But the process of polarization was greatly facilitated both by the lengthy duration of the dispute and by certain changes in the institutional structure of the rural studies field, notably the emergence of the Agrarian Section as an alternative to the Timiriazev Academy.

Finally, in the course of the dispute status and prestige were redistributed within the community of rural scholars. At the beginning the Organization-Production scholars were the undisputed leaders in the field; by mid-1928 the Agrarian-Marxists had taken their place. It is not clear that the dispute was the primary cause of the reallocation of status among rural scholars, since the Party had always had as its long-run goal the development of a group of scholars who would elaborate a Marxist science of society. What may be unequivocally asserted is that the rise of the Agrarian-Marxists to positions of prominence was *accelerated* by the existence of a controversy in their field. The fact that the Agrarian-Marxists were engaged in rivalry with their mentors compensated for their lack of experience and achievement and even lent them a certain amount of prestige. In any event, it should be noted that although the Agrarian-Marxists eventually became the leaders in the field of rural social studies, they never attained the *degree* of prestige their teachers had enjoyed. Indeed, just as the balance of status and power in the rural studies community was shifting in their direction, the Agrarian-Marxists found themselves facing a series of challenges from other Marxist scholars. In sum, the controversy in rural inquiry sapped the intellectual vitality of the field and strained the social fabric of the scholarly community. Devastating though these developments were, the field of rural inquiry might well have recovered from them; indeed, the history of science has recorded many instances in which a field of science is the more vibrant after the resolution of a dispute among its practitioners. In the case of Soviet rural studies, however, there was no opportunity for such recovery. The resolution of the scientific disagreement was followed almost immediately by the onset of the Cultural Revolution. In light of this sequence of events, we must ask to what extent the dispute in rural studies paved the way for the Revolution that followed. Or to put it another way, was the Cultural Revolution simply an intensification of trends that had existed earlier in the field, or was there a difference of kind between conditions in the field before and after mid-1928?

Mid-1928: Dividing Line or Bridge?

The assessment of the relation between the period of controversy and the period of Cultural Revolution in the field of rural social studies is not a simple matter. Certain dissimilarities in the conduct of rural inquiry from one period to another come immediately to mind, but the extent and implications of those dissimilarities remain to be discovered. To ascertain the degree to which the Cultural Revolution constituted a genuine departure from conditions that existed in the field while the dispute was in progress, we shall compare the periods before and after mid-1928 on two particular points: the impact of social factors on rural science, and the cohesion within the community of rural scholars.

Social Factors: Influence or Pressure on Rural Science?

Late in 1928, certain social factors began to act as a pressure on rural inquiry. Specifically, the Party adopted a social science policy according to which a researcher's status in the community of scholars was directly affected by his political beliefs and affiliations, and the results of research were required to be congruent with the Party's policy toward the countryside. With the introduction of this policy, the field of rural social studies became "politicized."

Did the impact of social factors on rural science in the period before mid-1928 differ substantially from what we have described above? With this question in mind, we shall examine in some detail the impact of social factors on the two major turning points in the dispute between the Chaianov and Kritsman schools: the change in the issues and conduct of the dispute in early 1927, and the resolution of the disagreement in mid-1928.

In early 1927, the controversy changed from a dispute over goals to a substantive disagreement. This change in issues received its major impetus from certain shifts of emphasis in the Party's policy toward the countryside. In particular, the Party's patent disenchantment with the individual farm sector and its concomitant emphasis on the creation of large-scale socialist units brought to the fore the two groups' differences of opinion over the nature of the family farm. That difference of opinion had always been latent, but now it loomed so large that it eclipsed all other disagreements between the two schools. The transition to a substantive dispute might have been inhibited by certain developments in the professional organization of rural studies, changes that occurred at mid-decade. The move by the Agrarian-Marxists from the Timiriazev to the Communist Academy divided the two schools physically from one another, giving each its own institutional base. This separation might well have made for the continuation of the dispute over goals or even for the resolution of the dispute by the departure of the specialty of rural sociology from the larger field of rural social studies. But the impact of the change in the professional organization of the field described here was far outweighed by the new emphasis in rural policy. Consequently, the separation of the contending groups into two institutions ended only by making the substantive dispute into a more equal, and therefore more heated, contest.

As the issues in the dispute shifted, there occurred important modifications in the behavior—both intellectual and social—of the disputants. On the intellectual level, each school replaced intermittent criticism with sustained and careful checking of its opponents' work. A variety of factors contributed to this. The Agrarian-Marxists were determined to launch a root-and-branch attack on their teachers' work, primarily because they realized that the emergence of a dispute over a single substantive issue rendered ineffective their old tactic of taking potshots at their rivals. Without doubt, the members of the Kritsman group were emboldened in their decision by certain changes that had occurred in the professional organization of their field—specifically, their recent move from the Timiriazev to the Communist Academy. Their new institutional base gave the Agrarian-Marxists the independence they needed to launch a full-scale critique of the writing of scholars commonly acknowledged as the leading figures in rural social studies. For their part, the Organization-Production scholars decided to devote more attention to the work of their former students, primarily because changes in official rural policy made clear the extent to which their work was out of tune with the new age. By pointing out the similarity between their research and that of their opponents, the members of the Chaianov group hoped to make a case for their own relevance. Their decision to adopt this new intellectual strategy was doubtless reinforced by certain alterations in the professional organization of rural inquiry. Earlier the Chaianov group had occupied the top posts in the community of scholars, but in 1925 they found their authority coming under increasing challenge from a new nucleus of scholars with its own institutional base.

The change in intellectual conduct was accompanied by a change in the social behavior of the disputants. By early 1927, members of the two groups no longer collaborated in research projects. The interchanges between the contending schools became increasingly heated in tone and polemical in accent, and even the payment of intellectual debts was used by each side as an occasion to score points for its position. The considerable shift in social relations was in the main the outgrowth of developments in the professional organization of rural studies. The move by the Agrarian-Marxists to the

Communist Academy brought to an end the teacher-student relations that had been responsible for the cordial tone of the pre-1927 period, and the collaborative research projects whose very existence had inhibited unrestrained criticism by either school against the other. But almost as important as the changes in the professional organization of the field were the shifts in rural policy which led to the emergence of the substantive dispute. The fact that the two schools were in direct conflict over a single point surely worked against the continuation of the spirit of toleration that had marked the first phase of the controversy.

In the spring of 1928, the substantive disagreement between the Chaianov and Kritsman schools was brought to an end by the concession of the Timiriazev professors. The main impetus to end the controversy seems to have come from certain changes in official rural policy. As the regime moved forward with the First Five-Year Plan, it became imperative to know which of the two schools was "correct" in its analysis of the countryside. In this new purposive mood, a resolution through stalemate would have been unthinkable; nor would the departure of either group from the field of rural social studies have settled the issue. Thus all signs pointed to a resolution by concession. That it was the Organization-Production scholars, and not their opponents, who made the concession should not be surprising, for since 1926 the work of the Timiriazev professors had been in conflict with the dominant emphasis in Party policy toward the countryside.

Our analysis of the important turning points in the rural studies controversy showed the dispute to have been strongly influenced by the social context of inquiry. In particular, changes of emphasis in official rural policy were found to have exerted considerable impact on the redefinition of the issues in the dispute, on the alteration of the conduct of the disputants, and on the resolution of the dispute. Although it was not the only factor at work here (both the professional organization of the field and the dynamics of the dispute itself were influential), official policy toward the countryside did play a major role in bringing about the developments cited.

Extensive and profound though it was, the influence of

official rural policy before mid-1928 cannot be considered to have constituted a pressure on science. The evidence suggests that while the controversy was in progress, rural scholars responded to changes in governmental rural policy because theirs was a field whose subject matter was of concern to practical policy and in which, therefore, a premium had been placed on knowledge that was "useful" in practice. In this period, "useful" research was defined as inquiry that bore on questions of importance to the regime. Agreement between research findings and Party policy was not a requirement; nor did the political affiliations of the investigator affect the reception accorded his work. In the aftermath of the Shakhty trial of May 1928, however, official policy toward social science changed. Now the findings of research on the country-side had to conform to the facts as created by the rural policy of the Communist Party. This shift in the Party's policy toward social science converted rural policy from an influence to a source of great pressure upon rural studies. That pressure was the more keenly felt because the new facts created by the Party's rural policy in late 1929 differed so strikingly from those that the rural scholars had come to take for granted during NEP.

Although the "politicization" of rural inquiry did not begin until late in 1928, the process had roots in developments that took place earlier in the same year—namely, the use of force ("measures of extreme severity") to collect grain from the peasantry and the Shakhty trial. Consequently, we must consider the possibility that in the early months of 1928 the Organization-Production scholars foresaw the impending politicization and, guided by their anticipation,[1] made their concession. It seems clear from the available evidence that the Chaianov group did foresee the increasing emphasis on large-scale socialist farming and altered the focus of its research accordingly, but its members did not foresee the change in official policy toward social science, in particular the rampant "credentialism" that would lead to their exclusion from the community of rural scholars. When the Organization-Pro-duction scholars first began to make their concession, it will be remembered, they attempted to style themselves as apolitical technical experts on farming. Only considerably later did they attempt to jump aboard the political bandwagon.

In failing to foresee the new policy toward social science introduced in late 1928, were the members of the Chaianov group oblivious to signs close to home? Specifically, were there elements within the community of scholars who were pushing for a policy along the new lines? To answer this question, we turn to examine the cohesion in the community of rural scholars before mid-1928.

Cohesion in the Community of Rural Scholars

The historical record shows clearly that shortly after the dispute in rural social studies came to an end, the community of rural scholars was rent asunder. Not only did members of opposing schools highlight their intellectual differences and cease social contact with one another, but even within schools all manner of intellectual and social ties were broken, as individual scholars attempted to secure their positions by disavowing their affiliations to the two great schools of inquiry.

How serious were the tensions among rural scholars prior to mid-1928? Was the infighting so bitter that the scholarly community was held together only by the action of an external force, or did the community cohere because of a certain degree of intellectual consensus and social solidarity among contending scholars? It may seem out of place to inquire about cohesion among scholars engaged in a dispute, but, as has been repeatedly pointed out, the true extent of the cohesiveness of a scientific community is revealed when its members are embroiled in dispute.

Our examination of the controversy in rural social studies showed profound intellectual disagreements between the Chaianov and Kritsman groups. They disagreed over theory, the best methods of research, and the rank ordering of questions in their field. Profound though these differences were, the Organization-Production and Agrarian-Marxists scholars did share a common framework of discourse, a framework defined by the premises underlying the New Economic Policy. The fact that the rival groups subscribed to the NEP premises allowed them to talk to, rather than past, each other. So successful was the dialogue between contending schools that at the end of the 1920s, the Agrarian-Marxists were accused of having allowed their opponents to define their Marxism for them. So completely did all the rural scholars share the NEP premises that both non-Marxists and Marxists alike were caught short by Stalin's announcement of forced collectivization in December 1929.

Not only was there intellectual consensus, but before late 1928 there was also considerable social solidarity among rural scholars belonging to opposing schools. To be sure, the members of each school were primarily loyal to their own subgroup, especially as the controversy began to gather force in the second stage; and from early 1927 there was a growing polarization of rural scholars into two camps. Nevertheless, until mid-1928 scholars of all stripes evidently had some feeling of identification with the field as a whole. Neither group sought to break away from rural social studies to create a new field in which its concerns would be dominant; nor did either group attempt to have the other excluded from the field of rural social studies. Rather, each seemed to accept the other as part of its profession.

The sources of this feeling of solidarity were several. To begin with, the fluid boundaries of rural social studies made it possible for two such diverse groups as the Chaianov and Kritsman schools to identify with a single field. The permissive effect of this definition was reinforced by the open-ended nature of rural policy itself in this period.[2] Furthermore, the organization of rural social studies in the first half of the 1920s encouraged both groups of scholars to share certain norms of scholarly work and professional conduct. Until 1926, it will be recalled, the Agrarian-Marxists studied with, and worked as research assistants to, the members of the Chaianov group. This early training and work experience socialized the young researchers quite profoundly. When the members of the Kritsman group sought to displace their rivals as leaders of the rural studies community, they did not suspend the rules of social science method or set aside their commitment to scholarship. Rather, they made every effort to best their former mentors by disproving the propositions of Organization-Production theory and by proposing alternative approaches to problems traditionally studied by the Timiriazev professors. Clearly, the young Marxists who conducted rural research in the years 1925-1929 did not have the uneasy relation to their profession described by Fitzpatrick as having been the case in the field of literature.[3] Far from being hostile to or even ambivalent about the canons of their profession, the Agrarian-Marxists showed themselves committed to retaining the established rules of scientific work.

The evidence of intellectual and social cohesion presented here has important implications for the historical questions to which this study is addressed. First, it bears directly on the interpretation of developments in rural social studies. We found no significant demand for "politicization" from rural scholars before 1929. Certainly, there were some scattered calls for more Marxist content in academic programs, but those calls were both few in number and ill-focused. We may therefore conclude that in this case the responsibility for the onset of the Cultural Revolution must be laid squarely at the door of the Communist Party and its minions—men with no scholarly credentials but with the requisite willingness (so welcome after 1929) to act as watchdogs over those who conducted inquiry. On this point our study supports the interpretation of the events of 1928 to 1931 advanced by such scholars as David Joravsky.[4]

The fact that our case supports the traditional view of the onset of the Cultural Revolution should not diminish the value of the new interpretation of that event. The transformation of Soviet culture at the end of the 1920s did not take place according to any single pattern. In some fields, like that described by Fitzpatrick, the young communist intellectuals chafed at the norms of their professions and at the first opportunity converted their disagreements with their non-Marxist (and sometimes Marxist) senior colleagues into all-out war. In other fields, such as the one we have examined, the infighting among intellectuals, however bitter, was contained by a certain intellectual and social cohesion within the profession; in these cases, the intervention of the Party and its deputies in scholarship set the Revolution in motion.

There were, in fact, variations in the development of the cultural professions under NEP, and students of the period must now begin the difficult task of identifying the factors that produced those variations. It is interesting in this regard to speculate on the differences between our case and that described by Fitzpatrick. Some of the divergence in the attitudes toward their profession held by writers and rural scholars may be attributed to variations in the socialization to which novices in the arts and social sciences were exposed. We may hypothesize that there was a greater premium placed on creativity and originality in the field of literature than in rural social studies. But in the case of rural studies, other factors played significant roles in fostering the allegiance of scholars to traditional norms. For example, the long history of the field affected the type of novice attracted to the study of the countryside; the fact that rural social studies had been conducted for nearly a decade in Russia discouraged those who sought a field with a small corpus of knowledge that could be quickly assimilated. Or, the government's acceptance of rural studies inhibited most potential rebels from jettisoning professional standards. Before 1929 government agencies regularly commissioned research from the leading rural scholars. Consequently, novices were educated in the belief that official recognition would be accorded those who extended, rather than destroyed, the corpus of research on the countryside. The salience of these specific factors in the case of rural social studies suggests that the division of fields into the categories of the arts, humanities, social sciences, and natural sciences would only be a first step toward explaining the variations in patterns of development.

Second, the cohesion evidenced among rural scholars during the controversy suggests that the NEP experiment in cultural pluralism was viable. To put it plainly, the facts of the rural studies case argue against the view that the coexistence of intellectual opposites under NEP was inherently unstable and that therefore some sort of revolution in culture was unavoidable. Our findings imply that although the rifts of 1923 to mid-1928 were serious, there was still an overriding commitment among rural scholars of all persuasions to the continuation of pluralism in the field. The Agrarian-Marxists, who might have been thought eager to oust their rivals from the discipline, proved disinclined to do so. Indeed, as late as October 1929, members of the Kritsman school were still acknowledging the value of their opponents' work. We may infer from this that the young Marxist students of the countryside were not seeking to eliminate social and intellectual diversity in scholarship; their main concern was to secure for Marxist theory (and for their group) the leading position in the field of rural studies.

A pluralism in which Marxism was the dominant, but not the only, approach to social inquiry would have met many needs. It would have satisfied the desire of the regime for research that was supportive and sound; it would also have fulfilled the desire of the Marxist scholars for hegemony in their respective fields. Despite its merits, this form of pluralism was never tried. In the realm of culture, then, as in other realms, the limits of the NEP experiment were not exploited.[5]

To Western scholars, the potential of NEP has been a question of great historical interest. For Soviet leaders, however, it is a question of political moment. As reformers within Soviet society are increasingly looking to the NEP period as a model,[6] the difference between heterodoxy and heresy becomes a live issue.

Appendixes

Organization-Production Scholars

A. V. Chaianov.[1] Born January 17, 1888; in 1913, was appointed to the faculty of the Petrovskii Agricultural Academy; between 1920 and 1922, headed the graduate seminar on agricultural economics of that Academy; between 1922 and 1930 served as Director of the Institute on Agricultural Economics of the Timiriazev Academy; in 1930, arrested together with other members of his group on the charge of having formed an opposition political party, the Working Peasants Party. The trial was scheduled for March 1931, and Chaianov was listed as one of the prominent defendants; however, there is no record of any trial having taken place. Chaianov did not appear after the Menshevik trial of 1931.

N. P. Makarov.[2] Born December 20, 1886; in 1912, joined the League for Agarian Reform; in the early 1920s visited Cornell University, where he was reportedly offered a post by Professor Warren; he declined the post and returned to Russia in 1923; in the academic year 1927-1928, headed the *kabinet* of Agricultural Economics, the section on livestock breeding, and the academic seminar on agricultural economics in the Institute of Agricultural Economics of the Timiriazev Academy; during the 1920s, worked in Gosplan; in 1930, arrested with Chaianov; after 1957, reappeared as the author of a book on the economy and organization of the Donbass region.

A. N. Chelintsev.[3] Born in 1874; well known as an economist before World War I; between 1914 and 1915, the head of the sector on farm organization of the Kharkov Society of Agriculture; during the 1920s, worked in Gosplan; in the year 1927-1928, head of the *kabinet* of local planning and head of the section on garden plots in the Institute of Agricultural Economics of the Timiriazev Academy.

G. A. Studenskii.[4] Born December 4, 1898; *Dotsent* in the Timiriazev Academy and Professor in the Samara Agricultural Institute; between 1928 and 1929, traveled to Germany to conduct research under the sponsorship of the International Agrarian Institute of the Peasant International; died in 1937.

A. A. Rybnikov.[5] Mentioned by Chaianov as one of the core members of the Organization-Production school; in the academic year 1927-1928, headed the *kabinet* on economic geography and location theory, the section on artisan industry, and the academic seminar on agricultural geography in the Institute on Agricultural Economics of the Timiriazev Academy.

A. N. Minin.[6] Mentioned by Chaianov as one of the core members of the Organization-Production school; for the year 1926-1927, listed as an out-of-town member (representing Voronezh) of the Institute on Agricultural Economics of the Timiriazev Academy.

Note to Appendixes A and B: It will be observed that some of the information in our biographies was obtained from a source listed as "interview with S. M. D. in Moscow, 1969." The respondant was Sergei Mitrofanovich Dubrovskii, a participant in the 1920s rural controversy. During 1969 the author was granted bi-weekly interviews with Dubrovskii.

Agrarian-Marxist (and Other Marxist) Scholars

Agrarian-Marxist Scholars

L. N. Kritsman.[1] Born June 3, 1890; in February 1921, attacked by Lenin for his advocacy of the "single economic plan"; from 1922 to 1937, a member of the Presidium of the Communist Academy; Director of the Agrarian Section and later of the Agrarian Institute of the Communist Academy; member of the Presidium of RANION; one of the founders of *Na agrarnom fronte*, the organ of the Agarian Section and between 1925 and 1930 served as its editor-in-chief; in 1930, traveled to America for the International Conference of Agricultural Economics; died in 1937 of kidney disease.

A. Gaister.[2] Born January 1899; between 1923 and 1927, studied in the historical section of the Institute of Red Professors under Pokrovskii; later moved to the Agrarian Section of the Communist Academy; in the academic year 1927-1928, head of the *kabinet* on agricultural relations in the Institute of Agricultural Economics of the Timiriazev Academy; in 1928, worked in Gosplan; in the same year, became Assistant Director of the Agrarian Institute of the Communist Academy; between 1928 and 1929, assistant to Popov in the Central Statistical Administration; in 1929, became a member of the Communist Academy; member of the editorial board of *Na agrarnom fronte* until 1931; died in 1937.

M. Kubanin.[3] Born June 1898; in the academic year 1926-1927, graduated from the historical section of the Institute of Red Professors; transferred to the Agrarian Institute of the

Communist Academy; in 1928, became a member of the Presidium of the Agrarian Institute; in 1935, appeared as an accuser against Voznesenskii, the head of Gosplan; died in 1937.

I. Vermenichev.[4] Graduated in economics from the Timiriazev Academy; in the academic year 1926-1927, listed as a graduate student in the Institute of Agricultural Economics of the Timiriazev Academy; transferred to the International Agrarian Institute under Dubrovskii and later moved to the Agrarian Institute of the Communist Academy; replaced Gaister in the Central Statistical Administration; died in 1937.

M. Sulkovskii.[5] Attended the Timiriazev Agricultural Academy; in the year 1928-1929, listed as a member of the Agrarian Institute of the Communist Academy; in 1928, became Secretary of that Institute; died in 1937.

Ia. A. Anisimov.[6] Born January 10, 1897; for the academic year 1926-1927, listed as a graduate student in the Institute on Agricultural Economics of the Timiriazev Academy; later a professor in that Academy.

K. Naumov.[7] Born March 5, 1897; for the year 1926-1927, listed as a graduate student in the Institute on Agricultural Economics of the Timiriazev Academy; later head of the section on collective farms in the Central Statistical Administration.

Other Marxist Scholars

A. Khriashcheva.[8] Born late 1890s; before 1917, head of the agrarian section of the statistical bureau in the *zemstvo* of Tula *guberniia*; married Popov, head of the Central Statistical Administration, where she later worked; died in early 1930s.

S. M. Dubrovskii.[9] Born March 15, 1900; in 1917, joined the Communist Party; in 1921, admitted to the Institute of Red Professors, where he worked under Pokrovskii; between 1924 and 1926, Dean of the Economics Faculty in the Timiriazev Academy; in 1925, became Assistant Director of the International Agrarian Institute, a post he retained until 1933; from 1934 to 1936, Dean of the History Faculty at Leningrad

University; from 1937 to 1954 he was in exile; rehabilitated in 1955 and later returned to the Institute of History of the Academy of Sciences in Moscow; died October 19, 1970.

V. S. Nemchinov.[10] Born in 1894; between 1928 and 1948, head of the *kafedra* of statistics in the Timiriazev Academy; in 1954 awarded the Stalin prize.

List of Research Reports

The following list of Research Reports of the Scientific Research Institute on Agricultural Economics of the Timiriazev Agricultural Academy was compiled from holdings in the Lenin Library in Moscow, the Fundamental Library of Social Sciences in Moscow, the Library of the Academy of Sciences in Leningrad, the Library of Congress in Washington, the Library of the Hoover Institution in Stanford, and the Widener Library of Harvard University. Although the list is not complete, it nevertheless represents the fullest enumeration found in any single place.

Between 1921 and 1930, fifty-four Research Reports were published. The first seven of these came out under the imprimatur *Vysshii seminar sel'sko-khoziaistvennoi ekonomii i politiki pri Petrovskoi Sel'sko-khoziaistvennoi Akademii;* from Report No. 8 on (i.e., after 1922), the works came out under the imprimatur *Nauchno-Issledovatel'skii Institut Sel'sko-Khoziaistvennoi Ekonomii.*

1. *Sbornik statei po voprosam sel'sko-khoziaistvennogo raionirovaniia i ekonomicheskoi geografii* (Moscow, 1921). A. V. Chaianov, "Opyty izucheniia izolirovannogo gosudarstva." N. Nikitin, "Khoziaistvennye raiony Evropeiskoi Rossii." A. V. Chaianov, "Nomograficheskie elementy ekonomicheskoi geografii."
2. *Metody bezdenezhnogo ucheta khoziaistvennykh pred-*

priiatii (Moscow, 1921). A. V. Chaianov, "Poniatii vygodnosti sotsialisticheskogo khoziaistva." A. L. Vainshtein, "Metodologiia khoziaistvennogo ucheta krupnykh predpriiatii."

3. S. Klepikov, *Pitanie russkogo krestianstva* (Moscow, 1921).

4. A. V. Chaianov, *Ekonomicheskie osnovy kul'tury kartoflia* (Moscow, 1921).

5. B. N. Knipovich, *K metodologii raionirovaniia* (Moscow, 1921).

6. N. Nikitin, *Sel'sko-khoziaistvennoe raionirovanie Moskovskoi gubernii* (Moscow, 1921).

7. A. V. Chaianov, A. Vainshtein, and I. Lopatin, *Optimal'nye razmery sel'sko-khoziaistvennykh predpriiatii* (Moscow, 1922).

8. G. A. Studenskii, *Ocherki po teorii krest'ianskogo khoziaistva* (Moscow, 1923).

9. I. Koniukov, *Evropeiskii sel'sko-khoziaistvennyi krizis 70-80-kh godov XIX veka* (Moscow, 1924).

10. A. V. Chaianov, *Organizatsiia krest'ianskogo khoziaistva* (Moscow, 1925).

11. A. V. Chaianov, *Sel'sko-khoziaistvennaia taksatsiia* (Moscow, 1925).

12. A. L. Vainshtein, *Issledovanie tesnoty vzaimnoi sviazi mezhdu tsenoi valovoi sboroi, urozhainostiiu i posevnoi ploshadi v S.A.S.Sh.* (Moscow, 1925).

13. A. Kotov, *Rynki i perspektivy kozhevennogo syr'ia v SSSR* (Moscow, 1925).

14. G. A. Studenskii, *Ocherki sel'sko-khoziaistvennoi ekonomii* (Moscow, 1925).

15. G. A. Studenskii, *Renta v krest'ianskom khoziaistve i printsipy ego oblozheniia* (Moscow, 1925).

16. Davidovich, Nekrasov, Obukhov, Rozov, Chaianov, and Chetverikov, *Problemy urozhaia* (Moscow, 1925).

17. B. Bruk, A. Vainshtein, S. Platovoi, K. Sazonov, and A. V. Chaianov, *Metody kolichestvennogo ucheta effekta zemleustroistva* (Moscow, 1925).

18. N. P. Makarov, *Organizatsiia sel'skogo khoziaistva* (Moscow, 1925).

19. I. I. Gontareva and V. I. Lebedeva, *Laboratornye zaniatiia*

po organizatsii i tsennostnym vychisleniiam v sel'skom khoziaistve (Moscow, 1925).

20. G. A. Studenskii, *Opyt issledovaniia krest'ianskogo khoziaistva tsentral'no-chernozemnoi oblasti* (Moscow, 1926).

21. A. V. Chaianov and S. Tumanovskii, *Ekonomicheskie osnovy polevoi kul'tury korneplodov i trav* (Moscow, 1926).

22. Ia. A. Anisimov, I. Vermenichev, and K. Naumov, *Proizvodstvennaia kharakteristika krest'ianskikh khoziaitsv razlichnykh sotsial'nykh grupp l'nianogo raiona* (Moscow, 1927).

23. A. V. Chaianov and V. Kratinov, *Metody taksatsionnykh issledovanii v sel'skom khoziaistve* (Moscow, 1927).

25. B. Grigoriev, *Predmetnyi ukazatel' materialov v zemskostatisticheskikh trudakh s 1860-kh po 1917 godakh* (Moscow, 1927).

26. G. A. Studenskii, *Problemy organizatsii krestianskogo sel'skogo khoziaistva* (Moscow, 1927).

27. L. I. Goretskii, S. M. Malyshev, A. A. Rybnikov, *Ekonomicheskoe vliianie Moskvy na organizatsii sel'skogo khoziaistva oblasti* (Moscow, 1927).

29. N. P. Makarov, ed., *Sebestoimost' produktov sel'skogo khoziaistva* (Moscow, 1929).

30. I. I. Gontareva, *Schetovodnyi analiz krest'ianskogo khoziaistva* (Moscow, 1928).

32. A. V. Chaianov, *K voprosu o sebestoimosti khlopka-syrtsa v khoziaistvakh srednei Azii* (Moscow, 1927).

34. A. Kotov, *Sushchnost' agrarnogo i sel'skokhoziaistvennogo krizisa* (Moscow, 1927).

36. V. E. Shprink, *Bibliograficheskii ukazatel' po voprosam khoziaistvennoi koniunktury* (Moscow, 1928).

40. K. V. Shuvaev, *Ot vymiraniia k vozrozhdeniiu* (Moscow, 1927).

43. A. V. Chaianov, *Sebestoimost' sakharnoi svekly* (Moscow, 1928).

47. A. V. Chaianov, *Biudzhetnye issledovaniia* (Moscow, 1929).

52. A. L. Vainshtein, *Problema ekonomicheskogo prognoza v eë statisticheskoi postanovke* (Moscow, 1930).

53. A. Kuplenskii, E. Rudakov, and M. Sulkovskii, *Klassovye gruppy krest'ianskikh khoziaistv i ikh proizvodstvennaia kharakteristika* (Moscow, 1930).

54. M. Sulkovskii, *Klassovye gruppy i proizvodstvennye tipy krest'ianskikh khoziaistv* (Moscow, 1930).

APPENDIX D
The "Minions"

O. M. Targulian.[1] Born September 1902; did his undergraduate and graduate work in the Timiriazev Academy; in 1925, while still a student, wrote a letter to the Academy journal, *Uspekhi agronomii*, protesting the absence of Marxist content in the curriculum; in the second half of the 1920s, was a member of the editorial board of *Puti sel'skogo khoziaista*; in late 1929 and 1930, attacked Chaianov and Chelintsev in print.

S. T. Uzhanskii.[2] Born May 1900; was *Dotsent* level II at Moscow State University; also affiliated with the Timiriazev Academy; in 1925 wrote to the journal *Uspekhi agronomii* protesting the absence of Marxist content in the curriculum of the Timiriazev Academy; in 1930, spoke out at the conference that condemned Kondratev and his associates.

I.D. Laptev.[3] Born August 1900; was a teacher in the Communist University of the Workers of the East.

D. P. Davydov.[4] Born September 1902; was a teacher and head of a *kafedra* at the Communist University of the Workers of China; in 1930, appeared as a speaker at the conference that denounced Kondratev and his associates; in early 1932, became a member of the editorial board of *Na agrarnom fronte*, replacing Kritsman and his group.

A. G. Silin.[5] Born August 1901; was an agricultural economist who did his graduate work in the Timiriazev Academy; later taught in the *kafedra* of the methodology of constructing long-range plans in the Timiriazev Academy.

A. S. Libkind.[6] Born June 1902; an agricultural economist by profession; was a senior research worker at the Agrarian Institute of the Communist Academy.

G. S. Gordeev.[7] Born September 1891; a professor in the Timiriazev Academy and head of the sector on Anglo-American countries in the International Agrarian Institute; in 1930, began to attack his former colleagues.

Note: This list is not comprehensive. Included here were those who were most vocal in the early period of the Cultural Revolution in rural studies (1930 and 1931) and whose careers appeared to be representative of the type of individual attracted to the role of watchdog in scholarship.

Notes

Notes

Chapter 1

1. Current Soviet writers on the Cultural Revolution are strangely silent about the events of 1928-1931. They portray the socialist Cultural Revolution as a gradual process that began in 1917. For a discussion of this issue, see Sheila Fitzpatrick, "Cultural Revolution in Russia 1928-1932," *Journal of Contemporary History* 9 (January 1974): 32-35.

2. Artists and intellectuals reacted in a variety of ways to the condemnation of inherited wisdom. Some sought out narrow, technical subjects whose pursuit would not bring them into contact (much less conflict) with the Party line in their fields. Others unveiled eccentric schemes in the hope that these would get a favorable reception in the new climate. For a discussion of the latter phenomenon, see Sheila Fitzpatrick, "Cultural Revolution as Class War," in *Cultural Revolution in Russia, 1928-1931*, ed. Sheila Fitzpatrick (Bloomington, Indiana, 1977).

3. For examples, see David Joravsky, *Soviet Marxism and Natural Science, 1917-1932* (New York, 1961); Edward Brown, *The Proletarian Episode in Russian Literature* (New York, 1953); Konstantin Shteppa, *Russian Historians and the Soviet State* (New Brunswick, N.J., 1962); and Raymond Bauer, *The New Man in Soviet Psychology* (Cambridge, Mass., 1952).

4. David Joravsky, "The Construction of the Stalinist Psyche," in Fitzpatrick, *Cultural Revolution in Russia*.

5. This hypothesis was first presented in Fitzpatrick, "Cultural Revolution in Russia," p. 35; and in Fitzpatrick, "Cultural Revolution as Class War."

6. Fitzpatrick, "Cultural Revolution as Class War." This contention had been made in the earlier article, Fitzpatrick, "Cultural Revolution in Russia," p. 35.

7. This provocative claim was made by Fitzpatrick in a paper delivered in August 1975 at a conference on Stalinism. See Sheila Fitzpatrick, "Stalinism and Culture" (Paper prepared for the Research Conference on Stalinism held in Bellagio, Italy, July 25-31, 1975), p. 5.

8. Soviet discussions of cultural life under NEP have generally been focused on the proletarianization of the intelligentsia (portrayed in statistical form). More recently, some work has been published on the institutionalization of science under NEP. See M. S. Bastrakova, *Stanovlenie Sovetskoi sistemy organizatsii nauki (1917-1922)* (Moscow, 1973); *Organizatsiia nauki v pervye gody Sovetskoi vlasti*, vol. 1 (Moscow, 1968); vol. 2 (Moscow, 1974).

9. For examples of the new focus of interest, see Fitzpatrick, *The Cultural Revolution in Russia.*

10. The traditional view of the Cultural Revolution as developed by its most eloquent exponent, David Joravsky, was based on a study of the natural sciences. The new view of the events of 1928-1931 presented by Sheila Fitzpatrick was developed on the basis of a study of literature and the arts under NEP.

11. The data were collected by those who worked for the statistical bureaus of the local governing councils (*zemstva*) in the countryside. For synopses of the information collected and methods used, see N. A. Svavitskii and Z. M. Svavitskii, *Zemskie podvornye perepisi, 1880-1913 gg.* (Moscow, 1926); N. A. Svavitskii, *Zemskie podvornye perepisi: obzor metodologii* (Moscow, 1961); E. Volkov, *Agrarno-ekonomicheskaia statistika Rossii* (Moscow, 1923).

12. For references to these works, see N. P. Makarov, *Krest'ianskoe khoziaistvo i ego evoliutsiia*, vol. 1 (Moscow, 1920), pp. 18-20, 52-53.

13. I. V. Iakushkin, ed., *Vysshaia Sel'skokhoziaistvennaia*

Shkola v SSSR (Moscow, 1948), pp. 10-40.

14. A brief assessment of the methodology in Soviet rural social studies will be offered in chapter 2. Detailed descriptions of the techniques used by researchers in the 1920s will be found in chapters 4 and 6.

15. The relationship between agricultural economics and rural sociology in America in the first two decades of the twentieth century is discussed in Henry C. and Anne Dewees Taylor, *The Story of Agricultural Economics in the United States, 1840-1932* (Ames, Iowa, 1952), pp. 80-101; Lowry Nelson, *Rural Sociology: Its Origins and Growth in the United States* (Minneapolis, Minnesota, 1969), pp. 30-32.

16. We owe to Florian Znaniecki the insight that intellectual disputes can often be struggles for prestige and position within the academic or scholarly community. See Florian Znaniecki, *The Social Role of the Man of Knowledge* (New York, 1946), p. 137.

17. As we shall see, the Cultural Revolution did not occasion any eccentric or utopian thinking in rural social studies. In the period 1928-1931, the subject matter of rural inquiry was treated in deadly earnest by all who dared to write or speak about it.

18. The first types of disputes to be examined systematically by sociologists of science were those that occurred among individuals, groups, or nations over the question of priority in scientific discovery. For the pioneering article in this genre, see Robert K. Merton, "Priorities in Scientific Discovery: A Chapter in the Sociology of Science," *American Sociological Review* 22 (1957): 635-659. The concern of sociologists of science with substantive disputes among scientists has been a more recent one. There were, of course, certain exceptions. As early as the 1960s, some sociologists were studying scientists' reactions to new substantive discoveries. Bernard Barber, "Resistance by Scientists to Scientific Discovery," *Science* 134 (1961): 596-602; Robert K. Merton, "Singletons and Multiples in Scientific Discovery: A Chapter in the Sociology of Science," *Proceedings of the American Philosophical Society* 105 (October 1961): 470-486.

19. Robert K. Merton, "Social Conflict over Styles of

Sociological Work," *Transactions of the Fourth World Congress of Sociology*, vol. 3 (Louvain, Belgium, 1961), pp. 21-36. On this point, historians of science have been more prolific. See, for example, Thomas Kuhn, *The Structure of Scientific Revolutions* (Chicago, 1962); Charles C. Gillespie, *The Edge of Objectivity: An Essay in the History of Scientific Ideas* (Princeton, New Jersey, 1969).

20. A thoughtful, if brief, discussion of the ways in which controversies gave rise to new specialties in science may be found in Warren O. Hagstrom, *The Scientific Community* (New York, 1965), pp. 187-194. Hagstrom suggests that specialties may emerge either as a result of the rebellion of a subgroup against the goals of its mother discipline or as a result of a subgroup's desire to reallocate prestige and redistribute resources within its discipline.

21. Robert K. Merton, "Insiders and Outsiders: A Chapter in the Sociology of Knowledge," *American Journal of Sociology* 78, no. 1 (July 1972): 9-48. According to Merton, the intellectual conduct of contending scientists may vary significantly. Scientists may check one another's work carefully and level reasoned criticisms, or they may simply scan the work, stereotype it, and launch polemical attacks.

22. The range of social conduct that disputants may adopt is considerable. They may communicate with one another with greater or less frequency; their contacts may be face-to-face or confined to exchanges in printed journals. On the basis of his research, Hagstrom hypothesized that there was a relation between the type of social contact scientists have and the control of the dispute. According to him, the more continuous the contact among disputants, the less likely the dispute is to get out of hand. Hagstrom, *The Scientific Community*, pp. 267-275.

23. Ibid.

24. Hagstrom suggests that a controversy will probably have more socially disruptive effects when the dispute has wide intellectual and programmatic scope, when decisions are made with difficulty, and when the dispute affects textbook education. Ibid., pp. 258-259.

25. An excellent review of this literature can be found in

Jonathan R. and Stephen Cole, *Social Stratification in Science* (Chicago, 1973), pp. 7-11. We have drawn considerably on that review in the discussion of the sociological literature that follows.

26. For a seminal study of this type, see Robert K. Merton, "Science, Technology and Society in Seventeenth Century England," *Osiris* 4, no. 2 (1938): 360-632; also A. Hunter Dupree, *Science in the Federal Government: A History of Policies and Activities to 1940* (New York, 1957); Simon Marcson, *The Scientist in Industry* (New York, 1960).

27. Sociologists of science have devoted most of their attention to this type of study. Some important examples of this literature are Robert K. Merton, "The Matthew Effect in Science," *Science* 159 (January 1968): 56-63; Cole and Cole, *Social Stratification*; Diana Crana, *Invisible Colleges* (Chicago, 1972); Joseph Ben David and Abraham Zloczower, "Universities and Academic Systems in Modern Society," *European Journal of Sociology* 3 (1962): 45-84; Norman W. Storer, Social System of Science (New York, 1966); Robert K. Merton, "Science and Technology in a Democratic Order," *Journal of Legal and Political Sociology* 1 (1942): 115-126; Nicholas C. Mullins, "The Development of a Scientific Specialty," *Minerva* 10 (January 1972): 51-82.

28. The effect on science of the demands made by the supporting agency has been discussed in Dupree, *Science in the Federal Government*, and Marcson, *The Scientist in Industry*.

29. In his study of science in seventeenth-century England, Merton considered the impact upon scientific interests of state policy in military and economic areas. Merton, "Science, Technology and Society."

30. For the range of questions that could be treated under this rubric, see Cole and Cole, *Social Stratification*, pp. 10-11.

31. This distinction is most clearly articulated in the writings of Robert Merton on science in Nazi Germany. See Robert K. Merton, "Science and the Social Order," *Philosophy of Science* 5 (1928): 321-337; Merton, "Science and Technology in a Democratic Order."

32. The two outstanding instances of such pressure in the contemporary period occurred in Nazi Germany and in Soviet

Russia between 1930 and 1953. There is evidence to suggest that in an earlier perod, the Catholic Church might have exerted a similar sort of pressure on science.

33. In the discussion of political pressures on science, we have followed Merton, "Science and the Social Order."

34. For an examination of the politicization of science, see Susan Gross Solomon, "Controversy in Social Science: Soviet Rural Studies in the 1920s," *Minerva* 13 (Winter 1975): 554-582.

Chapter 2

1. E. H. Carr and R. W. Davies, *Foundations of a Planned Economy*, vol. 1 in 2 pts., pt. 1 (London, 1973), p. 113. The *dvor* was a unit of land tenure and of cultivation.

2. The *obshchina* was an institution with deep roots in the pre-Revolutionary Russian countryside. The economic and social functions of this institution (termed the "land community" in the 1920s) are discussed in D. J. Male, "The Village Community in the USSR: 1925-1930," *Soviet Studies* 14, no. 3 (January 1963): 225-248.

3. Throughout the 1920s, the Soviet government attempted through legislation to halt this process, but its efforts met with little success. Carr and Davies, *Foundations*, vol. 1, pt. 1, pp. 113-120. Research on the causes of this process was conducted throughout the 1920s by Soviet scholars. One of the most controversial examples of this research will be described in chapter 8.

4. Moshe Lewin, *Russian Peasants and Soviet Power* (London, 1968), pp. 28-29. Apparently, after the Revolution, the production of agricultural implements and machines virtually ceased for a period of time. Carr and Davies, *Foundations*, vol. 1, pt. 1, p. 197.

5. The collective forms of agriculture did not prove themselves attractive to the peasantry. As late as 1927 these forms of farming accounted for but 2 percent of Russian agriculture. *Itogi desiatiletiia Sovetskoi vlasti v tsifrakh* (Moscow, 1927), pp. 120-121, as cited in Ihor Stebelsky, "Individualism and Collectivism in Soviet Agriculture Before Collectivization" (Paper presented to the Northeastern Slavic Conference of the

American Association for the Advancement of Slavic Studies in Montreal, May 6, 1971), p. 14.

6. The varieties of agricultural cooperation in which the Soviet peasants engaged are discussed in Carr and Davies, *Foundations*, vol. 1, pt. 1, pp. 144-157. The tradition of cooperation was a long-standing one; it dated back well before 1917. Geroid Tanquary Robinson, *Rural Russia Under the Old Regime* (New York, 1961), pp. 254-256.

7. Stebelsky, "Individualism and Collectivism," p. 4.

8. Among Russian Marxists writing in the twentieth century, the notion that agriculture was not subject to the same laws of scale as industry was never very popular.

9. These assumptions, never spelled out directly, were evident in the decrees passed during NEP. For the content of these decrees, see Lewin, *Russian Peasants*; Alec Nove, *An Economic History of the USSR* (London, 1969), pp. 83-160; and the appropriate sections of E. H. Carr, *A History of Soviet Russia*, 9 vols. (London, 1950-1973). The NEP assumptions were born of the lessons of War Communism.

10. The extent to which some of the difficulties experienced by the regime in dealing with the peasantry stemmed from its unrealistic assumptions about peasant psychology and behavior was the theme of a recent book by a Western historian. Teodor Shanin, *The Awkward Class: Political Sociology of Peasantry in a Developing Society: Russia 1910-1925* (Oxford, 1972).

11. The mix of ideological and pragmatic goals that underlay official support for the cooperatives during the 1920s was discussed in Robert F. Miller, "Soviet Agricultural Policy in the Twenties: The Failure of Cooperation," *Soviet Studies* 27, no. 2 (April 1975): 220-244.

12. The debates on the political level have been discussed at length in Stephen F. Cohen, *Bukharin and the Bolshevik Revolution* (New York, 1973); Lewin, *Russian Peasants*; Robert V. Daniels, *The Conscience of the Revolution* (Cambridge, Mass., 1960); and Richard B. Day, *Leon Trotsky and the Politics of Economic Isolation* (Cambridge, 1973). The debates on the bureaucratic level have been described in Carr and Davies, *Foundations*, vol. 1, pt. 2, pp. 787-898.

13. The governmental agencies with which the rural scholars were most frequently involved were the RSFSR Commissariat of Agriculture (*Narkomzem RSFSR*) and the State Planning Commission (*Gosplan*). But other agencies also sought the scholars' opinions and commissioned research work from them.

14. As we shall see, their status as experts became particularly important when the research activities of the scholars began to be suspect.

15. Shanin, *The Awkward Class*, p. 60.

16. E. H. Carr, *The Bolshevik Revolution*, vol. 2 (London, 1952), pp. 280-296; E. H. Carr, *Socialism in One Century*, vol. 1 (London, 1958), pp. 209-282.

17. The context in which Lenin made this argument will be described in chapter 5.

18. *Osnovy perspektivnogo plana razvitiia sel'skogo i lesnogo khoziaistva* (Moscow, 1924). This plan has not received much attention from Western historians of the Soviet Union. For a brief treatment, see Carr, *Socialism in One Country*, vol. 1, p. 522.

19. "Osnovy perspektivnogo plana razvitiia sel'skogo i lesnogo khoziaistva," *Puti sel'skogo khoziaistva* (hereafter cited as *PSKh*), 1925, no. 4, p. 186. The support for change came from L. N. Kritsman, the Marxist historian who would become the leader of the Agrarian-Marxist group.

20. Carr and Davies, *Foundations*, vol. 1, pt. 1, pp. 158-197. Throughout the first half of NEP, very little official interest was shown in collective forms of cultivation. In fact, there seems to have been some suspicion about state farms, despite the fact that these forms of cultivation were the most socialist in form.

21. Official policy toward social science in this period was paralleled by policy toward natural science. Loren Graham, *The Soviet Academy of Science and the Communist Party, 1927-1932* (Princeton, 1967); David Joravsky, *Soviet Marxism and Natural Science, 1917-1932* (New York, 1961); James Swanson, "The Bolshevization of Scientific Societies in the Soviet Union" (Ph.D. dissertation, Indiana University, 1968); M.S. Bastrakova, *Stanovlenie Sovetskoi sistemy organizatsii nauki (1917-1922)* (Moscow, 1973).

22. This is the view taken by a leading Western expert on the history of the Communist Party. Leonard Schapiro, *The Communist Party of the Soviet Union* (London, 1964), pp. 341-342.

23. A. Udal'tsov, "Ocherk istorii Sotsialisticheskoi Akademii," *Vestnik Sotsialisticheskoi Akademii*, no. 1 (1922), pp. 13-39. For a detailed treatment of the Academy in its first decade, see *Deiatel'nost' Kommunisticheskoi Akademii* (Moscow, 1928).

24. Some of the centers joined the federation RANION (Russian Association of Scientific Research Institutes for the Social Sciences), which was created in 1923. At its height, RANION had fifteen such institutes under its jurisdiction. In many of these, noncommunists and communists worked side by side. Joravsky, *Soviet Marxism and Natural Science*, pp. 68, 69, 331.

25. This point is made in Sheila Fitzpatrick, "The 'Soft' Line on Culture and Its Enemies: Soviet Cultural Policy, 1922-1927," *Slavic Review* 23, no. 2 (June 1974): 267-288.

26. Joravsky, *Soviet Marxism and the Natural Sciences*, pp. 66-67; Schapiro, *The Communist Party*, p. 343.

27. The ranking of the Party's concerns is evident from the fact that in the pre-1926 period most of the confrontations between the Party and the actors and institutions it labeled "deviant" occurred in the economic and political spheres.

28. The "hands-off" attitude that characterized Party policy toward the social sciences in this period was mirrored in the Party's treatment of the arts. Sheila Fitzpatrick, *The Commissariat of Enlightenment* (Cambridge, England, 1970).

29. The year 1925 was one of great growth for the Communist Academy. In January of that year there were four research sections under the Academy: State and Law, Soviet Construction, Literature and Art, and Scientific Method. One year later, the number of sections had increased to seven: State and Law, Literature and Art, Scientific Method, Natural and Precise Sciences, Economics, Agrarian Studies, and an office on the history of agrarian movements, which had the status of a section. "Kratkii otchet o deiatel'nosti Kommunisticheskoi Akademii," *Vestnik Kommunisticheskoi Akademii*, no. 15 (1926), p. 305.

30. In the summer of 1927, the Party Central Committee conducted a formal review of the work of the Communist Academy. Joravsky, *Soviet Marxism and the Natural Sciences*, p. 88.

31. Carr and Davies, *Foundations*, vol. 1, pt. 1, p. 53.

32. For an analysis of the background to and setting of the Shakhty trial, see Kendall Bailes, "Stalin and the Revolution from Above: The Formation of the Technical Intelligentsia, 1928-1934" (Ph.D. dissertation, Columbia University, 1971); Jeremy Azrael, *Managerial Power and Soviet Politics* (Cambridge, Mass., 1966).

33. The Bolsheviks, plagued by a shortage of dedicated communists who possessed the technical and administrative skills necessary to run an industrializing country, had expended a great deal of effort to convince these specialists to offer their services to the new regime. For details, see S. A. Fediukin, *Velikii Oktiabr' i intelligenstiia. Iz istorii vovleche-niia staroi intelligentsii v stroitel'stvo sotsializma* (Moscow, 1972).

34. Cohen, *Bukharin*, pp. 278-279.

35. Ibid., pp. 281-283.

36. The Academy was named after the Petrovsko-Razumovskoe estate upon which it was situated. The estate, 714 *desiatins* (approximately 1,928 acres), was purchased for 250,000 rubles. *Moskovskaia Sel'skokhoziaistvennaia Akademiia imeni Timiriazeva 1865-1965* (Moscow, 1969), pp. 15-17.

37. From 1865 to 1891 the institution was known as the Petrovskii Agricultural Academy. Between 1894 and the spring of 1917 it was called the Moscow Agricultural Institute, and from 1917 to 1923 it was again known as the Petrovskii Agricultural Academy. The changes of names were often accompanied by structural revisions.

38. The Petrovskii Academy was closed by the Tsarist government between 1891 and 1894 in retaliation for political dissidence among students. *Moskovskaia Sel'skokhoziaistvennaia Akademiia*, pp. 63-64. Student radicalism flared up again in 1905, but no official action was taken against the institution as a whole.

39. The Revolution did not bring immediate peace to the Academy. For the first few years after 1917 there were notable

administrative reorganizations and staff changes. For a somewhat glossed over, but still revealing, account of the developments of this period, see ibid., pp. 109-116.

40. The academy was renamed in honor of K. A. Timiriazev, who had taught in the department of botany and physiology. Timiriazev had earned the gratitude of the Bolshevik leaders by announcing his support for the new regime at an early date. Ibid., 116.

41. The Academy was under the joint jurisdiction of the RSFSR Commissariat of Agriculture and the Main Committee of Professional Technical Education of the RSFSR Commissariat of Enlightenment (*Glavprofobr Narkomprosa RSFSR*). The Commissariat of Agriculture used the research facilities of the Academy and called many of the Academy's staff for consultations on prospective policy measures.

42. This journal began publication in 1925 and ceased at the end of 1929. It superseded two previously existing journals: *Sel'skoe i lesnoe khoziaistvo*, the organ of the Commissariat of Agriculture, and *Uspekhi agronomii*, the journal of the Timiriazev Academy. In 1929 *Puti sel'skogo khoziaistva* was itself replaced by *Sotsialisticheskaia rekonstruktsiia i sel'skoe khoziaistvo*, which continued publication until 1935.

43. In recruiting students, Academy representatives made a conscious effort to draw in those with worker and peasant backgrounds. Consequently, the proportion of such students in the Academy jumped from 39.6 percent in 1917-1918 to 79.5 percent in 1927. O. M. Targulian, "Akademiia za desiat' let," *PSKh*, 1927, no. 10, p. 52.

44. A. V. Chaianov, *Petrovsko-Razumovskoe v ego proshlom i nastioashchem: putevoditel' po Timiriazevskoi Sel'skokhoziaistvennoi Akademii* (Moscow, 1925), p. 47.

45. Apparently the plan to introduce the faculty structure in the Academy occasioned intense debate. The plan's opponents argued that the fragmentation of instruction into faculties would mitigate against the "universalist" education that was the aim of the Academy. The plan's proponents submitted that the faculty structure would actually increase the opportunity for cross-disciplinary education. *Moskovskaia Sel'skokhoziaistvennaia Akademiia*, pp. 126-127.

46. The faculty of agricultural economics and policy replaced the old economics section of the Petrovskii Academy. The creation of the new faculty was rationalized as a device to end the divorce of the study of the economics of agriculture (which had traditionally been taught in universities) from the study of farming. P. A. Mesiatsev, ed., *Programmy i uchebnyi plan fakul'teta sel'skokhoziaistvennoi ekonomii i politiki Petrovskoi Sel'sko-Khoziaistvennoi Akademii* (Moscow, 1923), p. 3.

47. The forestry faculty was incorporated into the Moscow Institute of Forestry Technology in the summer of 1923. At about the same time the fisheries faculty became a section of the agronomy faculty of the Timiriazev Academy. *Moskovskaia Sel'skokhoziaistvennaia Akademiia*, 127.

48. The changes in faculty structure introduced in late 1928 will be discussed in chapter 10.

49. The faculty structure of the Timiriazev Academy became a model for similar institutions. In 1923 the Leningrad Agricultural Institute, founded one year earlier, adopted the three-faculty organization. *Zapiski Leningradskogo Sel'sko-Khoziaistvennogo Instituta* 1 (1924): 261.

50. For the history of the Petrovskii seminar and the story of its conversion into an institute, see Mesiatsev, *Programmy i uchebnyi plan*, pp. 135-143.

51. The Institute on Agricultural Economics, hereafter known as the Timiriazev Institute, was not the only research center separate from but attached to the Timiriazev Academy. The Scientific Research Institute on Soil Science enjoyed similar status. Targulian, "Akademiia za desiat' let," p. 58.

52. The preoccupation with the research and activities of centers outside Russia was characteristic of the members of the Timiriazev Institute (and of the Petrovskii seminar that preceded it). This explains the extensive reviews of the work of such foreign centers found in the bulletin of the Timiriazev Institute. For one example, see "Kratkii obzor tsentrov ekonomicheskoi mysli v oblasti sel'skogo khoziaistva v Evrope i drugikh stranakh," *Biulleten' Gosudarstvennogo Nauchno-Issledovatel'skogo Instituta Sel'sko-Khoziaistvennoi Ekonomii*, 1927, nos. 1-2, pp. 53-61. Reflecting its concern with

international scholarship in agricultural economics, the Timiriazev Institute included among its members several leading American and German scholars. The role of these men appears to have been mainly ceremonial. For a list of the non-Soviet members of the Institute, see ibid., p. 54.

53. Publication of the Institute *trudy* began in 1921 and ceased in 1930. In the space of those nine years, fifty-four studies were published. A list of most of the studies in this series is provided in appendix C. Institute research was carried out in departments, each staffed by a few professors and some technical personnel. The projects that emanated from these departments were both collective and individual.

54. Graduate student instruction was carried out through a series of compulsory and optional seminars. Students were expected to learn both English and German, to conduct a research project, and to write a Master's essay.

55. The consulting work was done in sections that combined scientific researchers from the Institute and staff from the government agencies. Sometimes these sections were linked to the Institute's research departments; sometimes they were directly attached to the Collegium of the Institute. "Materialy po nauchnoi rabote Instituta Sel'sko-Khoziaistvennoi Ekonomii," *Biulleten' Gosudarstvennogo Nauchno-Issledovatel'skogo Instituta Sel'sko-Khoziaistvennoi Ekonomii*, 1928, nos. 1-4, p. 133. For an indication of the range of institutions that commissioned studies, see the chart that describes the work of the Institute's sections in the year 1928. "Tablitsa B, Sektsii Nauchno-issledovatel'skogo Instituta Sel'sko-Khoziaistvennoi Ekonomii," ibid., p. 136.

56. This structure was replicated in each of the union republics. Graham, *The Soviet Academy of Sciences*, p. 69.

57. This group of scholars is described by Jasny in his book on the leading Soviet economists of the 1920s. Naum Jasny, *Soviet Economists of the Twenties: Names to be Remembered* (Cambridge, 1972), pp. 196-204.

58. For a discussion of the attributes of "cosmopolitanism" in scholarship, see Alvin Gouldner, "Cosmopolitans and Locals: Towards an Analysis of Latent Social Roles," *Administrative Science Quarterly* 2 (December 1957): 281-306; and

(March, 1958): 444-480.

59. The political orientation of this group of scholars is far from clear. Some Western historians have suggested that during the period of the Provisional Government, the Organization-Production scholars were in some way linked to the Socialist Revolutionary (SR) Party. Carr and Davies, *Foundations*, vol. 1, pt. 1, p. 20; Basile Kerblay, "A. V. Chayanov: Life, Career, Works," in *A. V. Chayanov on the Theory of Peasant Economy*, ed. Daniel Thorner, Basile Kerblay, and R. E. F. Smith (Homewood, Illinois, 1966), pp. xxxvi-xxxvii; Herbert J. Ellison, "The Socialist Revolutionaries," *Problems of Communism* 16 (June 1967): 7. But the Soviet sources we consulted did not support the identification of the Chaianov group with the SR Party. For example, at a conference called in 1930 to denounce deviance among academics, the Organization-Production scholars were not referred to as "former SRs," even though there was a good deal of name-calling at the meeting. *Kondrat'evshchina* (Moscow, 1930). Further, a recent Soviet article analyzing the agrarian policy of the Provisional Government lists these scholars simply as members of the Organization-Production school, while other individuals active at the same time were listed as SRs. N. K. Figurovskaia, "Bankrotstvo 'agrarnoi reformy' burzhuaznogo vremenogo pravitel'stva," *Istoricheskie zapiski* 81 (1968): 30-31.

60. The nature and the extent of the leadership of A. V. Chaianov, who was in fact the youngest member of the group, will be assessed in chapter 3. For Chaianov's biography and those of the other members of his group, see appendix A.

61. For examples of the discontent, see *Uspekhi agronomii*, 1925, no. 1, pp. 228-230, 234-235.

62. In 1925, the Agrarian Marxists averaged twenty-four years of age, and the Organization-Production scholars thirty-nine.

63. Some of the Agrarian-Marxists were doing graduate work in the Timiriazev Academy as late as the academic year 1926-1927. *Biulleten' Gosudarstvennogo Nauchno-Issledovatel'skogo Instituta Sel'sko-Koziaistvennoi Ekonomii*, 1927, nos. 1-2, p. 62.

64. To some degree at least, Miliutin's success was a function of the fact that in 1925 there was a general expansion of the research units in the Academy.

65. "Protokol obshchego sobraniia chlenov Kommunisticheskoi Akademii, 2-ogo iiuniia 1925 goda," *Vestnik Kommunisticheskoi Akademii*, no. 12 (1925), p. 369.

66. *Deiatel'nost' Kommunisticheskoi Akademii*, p. 15.

67. The Agrarian Section tried very hard to attract these students. For example, in 1926 a special seminar on rural social structure was organized, and invitations were issued to some of the Timiriazev students. "Deiatel'nost' Kommunisticheskoi Akademii za ianvar'-iiun' 1926," *Vestnik Kommunisticheskoi Akademii*, no. 17 (1926), p. 305.

68. Kritsman had been active in both political and scholarly life since the immediate post-Revolutionary days. For his biography, as well as those of the other members of his group, see appendix B.

69. For the attributes of "localism" in scholarship, see Gouldner, "Cosmopolitans and Locals."

70. On one such trip, two of the younger members of the group, M. Kubanin and A. Gaister, went to Frankfurt to visit the *Institute für Sozialforschung*. *Deiatel'nost' Kommunisticheskoi Akademii*, p. 17.

71. When the research unit was originally founded, there were two large collective projects on its agenda: the history of the agrarian revolution in Russia and the social stratification of the peasantry. In 1925 clear priority was given to the first project; within two years the second project, with which the Agrarian-Marxists were identified, had usurped that position of primacy. "Deiatel'nost' Kommunisticheskoi Akademii za ianvar'-iiun' 1926," p. 301.

72. This journal, founded in 1925, continued to appear for a decade. From 1925 to 1930 its editor-in-chief was L. N. Kritsman.

73. For example, in the second half of 1926 the Council of the National Economy of the USSR (*Sovnarkom SSSR*) charged the Agrarian Section with the task of producing a draft for legislation on land use and consolidation. M. Pokrovskii, "O deiatel'nosti Kommunisticheskoi Akademii," *Vest-*

nik Kommunisticheskoi Akademii, no. 22 (1927), p. 13. For the text of the charge, see "Vypiska iz protokola No. 168 zasedaniia Soveta Narodnykh Komissarov SSSR ot 29 iiuniia 1926 goda," *Na Agrarnom Fronte* (hereafter NAF), 1926, nos. 5-6, p. 93. As we shall see in chapter 6, the researchers in the Agrarian Section placed more stress on their scholarly work than on their roles as consultants.

74. For the story of the change and some speculation as to the reasons behind it, see chapter 10.

75. Among those who sent greetings when the Institute was officially opened were Professor A. V. Chaianov of the Timiriazev Institute on Agricultural Economics and Professor Geroid Tanquary Robinson of Columbia University in New York. "Mezhdunarodnyi agrarnyi institut i ego rabota za iztekshii god," *Agrarnye problemy* no. 2 (November 1927), p. 178.

76. "Otkrytie mezhdunarodnogo agrarnogo instituta," ibid., no. 1 (July 1927), p. 174. The Rome Institute had been functioning since 1906. For the fullest description of that institute, see Asher Hobson, *The International Institute of Agriculture: An Historical and Critical Analysis of Its Organization, Activities, and Policies of Administration* (Berkeley, 1931).

77. "Otkrytie mezhdunarodnogo agrarnogo instituta," p. 176.

78. At its opening the Institute boasted 112 workers; that number included both trained specialists and volunteers. "Mezhdunarodnyi agrarnyi institut," p. 185.

79. When it was founded only one of the Institute's four departments (that devoted to "the study of the experience of the Russian Revolution and economic construction in the USSR") was specifically focused on Russia. The other three departments ("the economy," "the international peasant movement," and "land law and policy") were charged with the task of culling data on agriculture throughout the world.

80. For the biography of Dubrovskii, see appendix B.

81. In America the concern with research methods in rural social studies began in the mid-1920s. In 1925 the Social Science Research Council set up an Advisory Committee on

Economic and Social Research in Agriculture. That committee, which included the leading figures in both agricultural economics and rural sociology, was responsible for the publication of some twenty volumes on research in different subareas of the field. For the introductory volumes of this extensive research report, see *Research Method and Procedures in Agricultural Economics*, 2 vols. (n.p., 1928).

82. In the United States research in farm management preceded research in any other area of agricultural economics. John Black, ed., *Research in Farm Management: Scope and Method*, Publications of the Advisory Committee on Social and Economic Research in Agriculture of the Social Science Research Council, no. 13 (New York, 1932), p. 3. For a discussion of the complex relation of farm management studies to research in agricultural economics in the period 1910-1920, see Henry C. and Anne Dewees Taylor, *The Story of Agricultural Economics in the United States, 1840-1932* (Ames, Iowa, 1952), pp. 80-101. The early studies in farm management were practical in their orientation, probably because the leaders in the field had been trained as natural scientists or agronomists rather than as economists. H. C. M. Case and D. B. Williams, *Fifty Years of Farm Management*; (Urbana, Illinois, 1957), p. 14. Descriptions of the research conducted in the United States in the first two decades of the twentieth century may be found in Case and Williams, *Fifty Years*; in Black, ed., *Research in Farm Management* and in Merrill K. Bennet, *Farm Cost Studies in the United States* (Stanford, 1928).

83. For some brief overviews of the development of agricultural economics in Germany, see Immanuel Fauser, "German Approach to Farm Economic Investigations," *Journal of Farm Economics* 8, no. 3 (July 1926): 289-297; Asher Hobson, "Agricultural Economics in Europe," *Journal of Farm Economics* 9, no. 4 (October 1927): 423-424; Walter Roth, "Farm Budgeting in Germany," *Journal of Farm Economics* 11, no. 4 (October 1929): 623-632.

84. The contrast between the American and German approaches to the study of agricultural economics was brought out most strikingly in Sigmund von Frauendorfer, "Development, Methods, and Results of Agricultural Economic Re-

search in the United States," *Journal of Farm Economics* 10, no. 3 (July 1928): 286-311. Von Frauendorfer was a German scholar affiliated with the International Institute of Agriculture in Rome.

85. The term "family farm" has been used in economic literature to describe enterprises quite different from the Russian economic unit. For a discussion of this point, see Daniel Thorner, "Chayanov's Concept of Peasant Economy," in Thorner, Kerblay and Smith, *A. V. Chayanov on the Theory of Peasant Economy*, pp. xi-xxiii.

86. The great landholdings of the nobility had begun to disappear well before 1917. Many of the nobles had rented their lands to peasants, and others sold their holdings outright. According to one Western scholar, between 1877 and 1915 the nobles lost three-sevenths of the lands they had held in 1877. Robinson, *Rural Russia*, p. 261. After the Revolution, the remaining landowners' estates were distributed, with 86 percent of this land going to the peasants. E. H. Carr, *The Bolshevik Revolution*, vol. 2 (London, 1966), p. 53.

87. For an account of the work experiences of these scholars, see Basile Kerblay, "A. V. Chayanov: Life, Career, Works," in Thorner, Kerblay, and Smith, *A. V. Chayanov on the Theory of Peasant Economy*, p. xxviii; George L. Yaney, "Agricultural Administration in Russia from the Stolypin Reform to Forced Collectivization: An Interpretive Study," in *The Soviet Rural Community*, ed. James Millar (Urbana, Illinois, 1971), pp. 3-35.

88. A detailed study of these reforms can be found in George L. Yaney, "The Imperial Russian Government and the Stolypin Land Reforms" (Ph.D. dissertation, Princeton University, 1961).

89. A. V. Chaianov, *Osnovnye idei i metody raboty obshchestvennoi agronomii* (Moscow, 1922), p. 12.

90. In the period 1908 to 1915 there was a good deal of communication among agricultural officials. The Congress of Agronomists of the winter of 1911, the regular meetings of the Circle of Agronomy in the period 1908-1912, and the pages of the *Agronomicheskii zhurnal* (edited between 1913 and 1917 in Kharkov) provided numerous opportunities for the exchange

of information and views. The intellectual climate of these years is described in Chaianov, *Osnovnye idei i metody raboty*, pp. 3-4.

91. The substance and implications of the new theory for the study of economics will be discussed in full in chapter 3. The research conducted by the Chaianov group will be described in chapter 4.

92. To be sure, the microeconomic studies done by this group had implications for the analysis of the national economy; however, only under the duress of a challenge did the Organization-Production scholars bring out those implications.

93. For a discussion of this earlier tradition in the field, see Makarov, *Krest'ianskoe khoziaistvo i ego evoliutsiia* (Moscow, 1920), pp. 1-36.

94. Ibid., pp. 37-56.

95. The relationship between the practical orientation of the established agricultural economics in the 1920s and its institutional setting was discussed at the end of the decade by scholars arguing for a new approach to the field.

96. For summaries of these studies, commissioned in 1924 and 1925, see chapter 6.

97. In their attitude toward the new work, the Russian agricultural economists differed strikingly from their American counterparts, who had faced a similar situation in the period 1910-1920. In the United States agricultural economics often acted as an "elder brother" to rural sociology, guiding it through its period of gestation. Lowry Nelson, *Rural Sociology: Its Origin and Growth in the United States* (Minneapolis, 1969), pp. 30-32.

98. These studies had been commissioned by Zemplan, the division of the RSFSR Commissariat of Agriculture charged with planning.

99. By the time the Agrarian-Marxists were doing their graduate work, sociology had ceased to be taught in Soviet Russia. For a brief period after the Revolution it had flowered there. In Leningrad there was a Sociological Society and courses were offered at the university in a number of facets of the discipline. But by mid-1923 this activity had come to an end. In Moscow there was a chair of sociology in the Depart-

ment of Social Sciences at Moscow State University, but in 1924 that department was closed. Elizabeth Ann Weinberg, *The Development of Sociology in the Soviet Union* (London, 1974), pp. 3-4.

100. The leader of the group, L. N. Kritsman, has been cited in a recent book as one of the three leading empirical sociologists of the 1920s. B. A. Chagin, *Ocherk istorii sotsiologicheskoi mysli v SSSR (1917-1969)* (Leningrad, 1971), p. 104.

101. The form of stratification defined by the Agrarian-Marxists as "social" was termed "occupational" by one of the pioneers of rural sociology in the United States, Pitirim Sorokin. According to Sorokin, the agricultural population is stratified occupationally "from the standpoint of domination and control on the one hand and subjection and execution on the other," Pitirim Sorokin, Carle Zimmerman, and Charles Galpin, eds., *A Systematic Sourcebook in Rural Sociology* (Minneapolis, 1930), p. 362.

102. Sorokin's contribution to American rural sociology cannot be overestimated. For a highly laudatory review by one of the field's most creative scholars, see T. Lynn Smith, "Sorokin's Rural-Urban Principles," *Pitirim A. Sorokin in Review*, ed. Philip J. Allen (Durham, North Carolina, 1963), pp. 188-206.

103. Perhaps understandably, in his section on rural stratification Sorokin made no mention of Agrarian-Marxists scholarship. He did cite Russian sources but referred to works written either by prerevolutionary Russian Marxists or by members of the Organization-Production school. Ibid., p, 365.

104. For an examination of American rural sociology in this period, see Nelson, *Rural Sociology*; Edmund deS. Bruner, *The Growth of a Science: A Half-Century of Rural Sociological Research in the United States* (New York, 1957).

105. Some idea of the content of Soviet ethnography in the 1920s may be obtained from Stephen P. and Ethel Dunn, *The Peasants of Central Russia* (New York, 1967), pp. 13-31. Ethnography had a long tradition in Russia. As early as 1864 there was a Society of Admirers of Natural Science, Anthropology, and Ethnography at Moscow University. In 1867 it organized an ethnographic exhibit. Alexander Vucinich,

Science in Russian Culture, 1861-1917 (Stanford, 1970), p. 81.
106. The development of Agrarian-Marxist theory will be discussed in detail in chapter 5. The content and methodology of the research done by the Kritsman group will be the topic of chapter 6.

Chapter 3

1. The Organization-Production scholars never explored the possibility that the behavior they had noted stemmed from motives different from those they had identified. This earned the group much criticism.

2. A. V. Chaianov, *Lën i drugie kul'tury v organizatsionnom plane krest'ianskogo khoziaistva nechernozemnoi Rossii*, vol. 1 (Moscow, 1912), p. xiv. This study grew out of a conference held in January 1911 under the joint sponsorship of the All-Russian Society of Flax Producers and the Moscow Society of Agriculture. Chaianov worked on the original study and then reworked the data for his book.

3. Chaianov, like his colleagues in the school, assumed that the peasant regarded all work as a sacrifice of leisure and, in deciding to work at all, was consciously trading leisure for other values. Commenting on this assumption, a Western economist has noted that below a certain level of income, leisure is not a meaningful concept. James Millar, "A Reformulation of A. V. Chayanov's Theory of the Peasant Economy," *Economic Development and Cultural Change* 18 (January 1970): 225.

4. The theory of the Organization-Production scholars contained an early version of the notion of the backward-sloping supply curve of labor, which was to play so important a role in the work of certain economic anthropologists writing in the 1940s. For an acknowledgment of the contribution of Chaianov to the development of this idea, see J. H. Boeke, *The Structure of the Netherlands Indian Economy* (New York, 1942), p. 18.

5. A. V. Chaianov, *Ocherki po teorii trudovogo khoziaistva* (Moscow, 1912-1913), pp. 31-32.

6. Ibid., p. 23.

7. Ibid., p. 48.

8. The *uezd* was a subdivision of the *guberniia*.
9. The *guberniia* was an administrative unit in Russia.
10. A. V. Chaianov, *Biudzhety krest'ian Starobel'skago uezda* (Moscow, 1915). This study will hereafter be known as *Starobel'sk*. A companion piece devoted to methodology appeared at the same time. See A. V. Chaianov, *Opyt razrabotki biudzhetnykh dannykh po sto odnomu khoziaistvu Starobel'skogo uezda Khar'kovskoi gubernii* (Moscow, 1915).
11. On the basis of research, the Organization-Production scholars would later reject the notion of a standard consumption budget. Their critics, however, never took note of this rejection and continued to accuse these scholars of espousing the original hypothesis.
12. Implicit in Chaianov's interpretation was the assumption that, if necessary, production could always be expanded by the farmer's intensifying his labor, engaging in crafts, or, as was done in Starobel'sk, renting land. No mention was made of the possibility of a scarcity of land or employment in crafts or of the existence of laws prohibiting the rental of land. Chaianov was not unaware of the extent to which his analysis depended on his assumptions. A. V. Chayanov, "Peasant Farm Organization," in *A. V. Chayanov on the Theory of Peasant Economy*, ed. Daniel Thorner, Basile Kerblay, and R. E. F. Smith (Homewood, Ill., 1966), p. 68.
13. The "biological analogy" inherent in Chaianov's treatment would come under attack in the second stage of the controversy.
14. Chaianov, *Starobel'sk*, p. 92.
15. Chaianov acknowledged that this calculation was rooted in the assumption that the family paid its members the market wage for labor. Ibid., p. 118.
16. In his "Peasant Farm Organization," published in 1925, Chaianov suggested that the rejection of classical economics was implicit in his school's work from the very beginning. The evidence from *Starobel'sk* hardly supports this contention.
17. A. V. Chaianov, *Lën i drugie kul'tury*, p. vii.
18. N. P. Makarov, *Krest'ianskoe khoziaistvo i ego evoliutsiia* (Moscow, 1920).
19. Under this rubric, Makarov subsumed both the Marx-

ists and the populists of the 1890s. In so doing, he muted important differences between the two groups, which will be described in chapter 5.

20. Ibid., pp. 17-36.

21. Ibid., pp. 48-52.

22. At this point Makarov was referring to the pre-Revolutionary Marxist scholars.

23. Makarov, *Krestianskoe khoziaistvo*, 54. Makarov even went so far as to propose a synthesis between the two approaches, making very clear, however, that in such a synthesis the Organization-Production approach would be the dominant element.

24. In the first part of the decade, the Agrarian-Marxists criticized the omissions in the Organization-Production approach. Only beginning in 1927 did they address themselves to the validity of the Timiriazev professors' theory.

25. That these differences of opinion played a role in postponing the codification of theory seems likely, given the fact that despite the turbulent events of the period, the Timiriazev scholars managed to carry out a startling array of research projects between 1915 and 1924.

26. A. N. Chelintsev, *Opyt izucheniia organizatsii krest'-ianskogo sel'skogo khoziaistva na primere Tambovskoi gubernii* (Kharkov, 1919), p. 243.

27. G. A. Studenskii, *Ocherki po teorii krest'ianskogo khoziaistva* (Moscow, 1923), pp. 13-17.

28. In fact, Studenskii tried to detach the group's theory from its dependence upon the labor-consumption balance. Ibid., p. 13. In 1923, Studenskii was the group maverick; later he was to move beyond the Organization-Production school altogether.

29. This publication later appeared as the first five chapters of A. V. Chaianov, *Organizatsiia krest'ianskogo khoziaistva* (Moscow, 1925), a work we have cited in its English version as Chaianov, "Peasant Farm Organization."

30. Chaianov, "Peasant Farm Organization," p. 48.

31. Ibid.

32. Ibid., p. 119.

33. In 1920 Makarov had taken a similar stand. He had

claimed that were it not for the limited resources available to the family farm, this economic unit could become oriented toward acquisition. Makarov, *Krest'ianskoe khoziaistvo*, pp. 43-44.

34. In 1921 Chaianov added socialist agriculture to the forms of farming for which no objective calculation of labor could be made. See A. V. Chaianov, "Metody bezdenezhnogo ucheta khoziaistvennykh predpriiatii," *Trudy vysshego seminariia sel'sko-khoziaistvennoi ekonomii i politiki pri Petrovskoi Sel'sko-khoziaistvennoi Akademii*, vol. 2 (Moscow, 1921). Underlying this position was Chaianov's view that the socialist economy, in its ideal form, was but a variant of the family farm. It was, he claimed, a single, natural, consuming work farm. Ibid., p. 13. This definition of the socialist farm was anathema to the Marxists, who stressed the superiority of the socialist over the natural economy and who emphasized production rather than consumption.

35. Makarov, citing with approval Chaianov's analysis, attributed the inability to value family farm labor objectively to the nonacquisitive psychology of the peasant. Makarov, *Krest'ianskoe khoziaistvo*, pp. 83, 86. Studenskii traced the same inability to a different cause, namely, the organizational integrity of the family farm structure. Studenskii, *Ocherki po teorii krest'ianskogo khoziaistva*, p. 38.

36. Makarov, *Krest'ianskoe khoziaistvo*, pp. 83-84. Makarov admitted that the situation was very different when the family farm used capital from outside sources.

37. Chaianov, "Metody bezdenezhnogo ucheta," p. 19.

38. Although he did not mention Chaianov by name, it is clear that Studenskii was here taking issue with the Director of the Timiriazev Institute, who had submitted that the family farm aimed at obtaining the greatest gross return.

39. Studenskii, *Ocherki po teorii krest'ianskogo khoziaistva*, pp. 42-43.

40. It is significant that these scholars never considered the possibility that a scarcity rent existed for the family farm. This may be explained by the fact that the group's model of the family farm was based on the assumption of an absence of scarcity in land.

41. A. N. Chelintsev, *Est'-li zemel'naia renta v krest'ianskom khoziaistve?* (Kharkov, 1918), pp. 9-11.

42. Ibid., pp. 12, 14.

43. Ibid., p. 90.

44. Makarov, *Krest'ianskoe khoziaistvo*, p. 84.

45. Studenskii, *Ocherki po teorii krest'ianskogo khoziaistva*, p. 40. Somewhat later Studenskii would attempt to work out a way to calculate rent in a peasant economy. G. A. Studenskii, *Renta v krest'ianskom khoziaistve i printsipy eë oblozheniia* (Moscow, 1925).

46. The reasons why Chaianov chose to publish this seminal work in German remain obscure. Since most of his colleagues and critics read German, the article was nevertheless widely read.

47. This article, which never appeared in Russian, was translated into English as A. V. Chayanov, "On the Theory of Non-Capitalist Economic Systems," in Thorner, Kerblay, and Smith, *A. V. Chayanov on the Theory of Peasant Economy*, pp. 1-29.

48. Chaianov, "On the Theory of Non-Capitalist Economic Systems," p. 1.

49. Ibid., p. 4.

50. Ibid., p. 7.

51. Ibid., p. 8. Chaianov's 1924 position on differential rent resembled closely that espoused by Makarov and Chelintsev; however, the reasons Chaianov offered in support of that position were more consonant with the theory he was proposing.

52. Chaianov did allow that certain concepts of traditional economics were applicable to the family farm, namely, land prices, commodity prices, prices for circulating capital, and capital formation. Ibid., p. 11.

53. Ibid., p. 5.

54. Ibid.

55. Ibid., p. 7

56. Ibid.

57. Elsewhere, Chaianov described the growth of the school's determination to formulate a new theory as follows: "At first special explanations and interpretations were given

separately in each specific instance. But this introduced into the theory of private economic undertakings such a number of complications that, finally, it seemed more convenient to generalize them and to construct a separate theory of the family undertaking working for itself." Chaianov, "Peasant Farm Organization," p. 38.

58. Chaianov, "On the Theory of Non-Capitalist Economic Systems," p. 28.

59. The economists whose works they knew best were Ernst Laur, F. Aeroboe, who was actually a corresponding member of the Timiriazev Institute, and F. Waterstradt.

60. The Organization-Production scholars had closest contact with Henry C. Taylor, who was the first Chief of the Bureau of Agricultural Economics in the United States, and with George F. Warren of Cornell University.

61. Both *Sel'skoe i lesnoe khoziaistvo* and its successor *Puti sel'skogo khoziaistva* (*PSKh*) had regular sections devoted to reviewing foreign studies of farming.

62. Individual scholars often forwarded autographed copies of their research to foreign libraries. Chaianov, in his capacity as Director of the Timiriazev Institute, made a regular practice of sending his colleagues' works abroad.

63. Most often, members of this group (notably Chaianov, Makarov, and Studenskii) published their works in German. Occasionally, an article by one of these scholars would appear in English or French.

64. The distribution of status and authority within the Soviet community of rural scholars was described in chapter 2.

65. For an appreciation of Chaianov's sensitivity to these foreign critics, see Kerblay, "A. V. Chayanov: Life, Career, Works," p. liii.

66. Other Agrarian-Marxists later lent their support to this criticism.

67. This work has been cited here as Chaianov, "Peasant Farm Organization."

68. Although the new work was the most finished version of the Organization-Production theory, it was rarely referred to by the group's critics, who preferred to level their attacks at earlier formulations.

69. Apparently A. Weber had made this charge in a conversation with Chaianov. Chaianov, "Peasant Farm Organization," p. 41.

70. This argument was offered by A. Skalweit in a review of Chaianov's *Die Lehre* (1923). The review was published in a journal in April 1924. Chaianov, "Peasant Farm Organization," p. 68.

71. Chaianov did acknowledge that where nonpartible inheritance was the rule, the demographic factor would be less important than in Russia. Ibid.

72. Ibid., p. 117. Emphasis in original. Chaianov's description of the arguments offered by Kurt Ritter.

73. Ibid.

74. Ibid., p. 42.

75. Ibid., p. 117.

76. Ibid., p. 37.

77. G. Meerson, "Semeino-trudovaia teoriia i differentsiatsiia krest'ianstva na zare tovarnogo khoziaistva," pt. 1, *NAF*, 1925, no. 3, p. 49. For a consideration of the relationship between the group's use of the biological analogy and its position on rural differentiation, see Teodor Shanin, *The Awkward Class: Political Sociology of Peasantry in a Developing Society: Russia, 1910-1925* (Oxford, 1972), pp. 101-106.

78. L. N. Kritsman, "Sovremennaia melkoburzhuaznaia politicheskaia ekonomiia," in *Proletarskaia revoliutsiia i derevnia*, ed. L. N. Kritsman (Moscow, 1929), pp. 548-567. This article was originally written as the preface to a collection of articles by Chaianov entitled *Ocherki po teorii trudovogo sel'skogo khoziaistva*, which appeared in 1924.

79. In the 1924 article, Chaianov had accorded some role in the determination of farm activity to market forces. Chaianov, "On the Theory of Non-Capitalist Economic Systems," p. 6.

80. Chaianov, "Peasant Farm Organization," p. 249. Chaianov intimated that the focus on socioeconomic differentiation was a thing of the past and the emphasis on demographic differentiation the wave of the future. Ibid., p. 245.

81. Ibid., p. 225.

82. Ibid., p. 237.

83. Ibid.

84. Ibid., p. 240.

85. Not all Agrarian-Marxist challenges were answered by the Chaianov group. Between 1925 and early 1928, the Agrarian-Marxist G. Raevich wrote a series of articles that criticized both the notion that the family farmer was a nonacquisitive economic actor and the contention that the family farm received no surplus income. See G. Raevich, "Teoriia krest'ianskogo khoziaistva i poniatiia 'rabotnik'," *NAF*, 1925, nos. 11-12, pp. 23-34; G. Raevich,"K issledovaniiu krest'ianskogo dokhoda," pt. 1, *NAF*, 1926, no. 3, pp. 3-17; pt. 2, *NAF*, 1926, no. 5-6, pp. 5-15; pt. 3, *NAF*, 1928, no. 1, pp. 40-49. Raevich's challenges were never answered, probably because by the time they were issued the attention of the Chaianov group had turned to other matters.

Chapter 4

1. It is difficult to determine with precision the way in which the Chaianov group ranked its research work, for that ranking varied considerably with the audience to which it was addressed. For example, compare A. V. Tchayanov, "Agricultural Economics in Russia," *Journal of Farm Economics* 10 (October 1928): 543-549, an article aimed at publicizing in America the work of the Timiriazev professors; and A. V. Tchayanoff, "L'Etat Actuel de L'Economie et de la Statistique Agricole en Russie," *Revue D'Economie Politique*, no. 42 (January-February 1928), pp. 82-96, a piece designed to acquaint French readers with the group's endeavors.

2. In detailing that lineage, the Timiriazev professors stressed both the elements of continuity and novelty in their use of budget data. The first history of the budget method written by a member of this group came out in 1915. A. V. Chaianov, *Opyt razrabotki biudzhetnykh dannykh po sto odnomu khoziaistvu Starobel'skago uezda Khar'kovskoi gubernii* (Moscow, 1915). Seven years later that history was republished with the addition of several new chapters written by Studenskii; it appeared as A. V. Chaianov and G. A. Studenskii, *Istoriia biudzhetnykh issledovanii*, Second and Enlarged Edition (Moscow, 1922). Seven years after that, the third history appeared. Actually completed in 1927, this version was a

reprint of the entire 1922 text, with the addition of a large section on the methodology of budget research. A. V. Chaianov, *Biudzhetnye issledovaniia: istoriia i metody* (Moscow, 1929). In the same year, there appeared in print another history of the budget method written by a supporter-turned-critic of the Chaianov group. See G. A. Studenskii, *Osnovnye voprosy metodiki biudzhetnykh i schetovodnykh issledovanii* (Samara, 1929).

3. Chaianov, *Biudzhetnye issledovanii*, p. 50. This account appeared in both the 1915 and 1922 versions of the history. Matseevich was to become the editor of *Agronomicheskii zhurnal*, the organ around which the nucleus of the Chaianov group was clustered between 1913 and 1917.

4. Ibid., pp. 50-51. Chaianov strengthened his appeal by giving a recitation of the frustrations encountered by the agronomist charged with the task of restructuring the family farm without any hard data on its organization.

5. Chaianov admitted his doubts in 1912 after conducting his first experiment with budget research. A. V. Chaianov, *Lën i drugie kul'tury v organizatsionnom plane krest'ianskogo khoziaistva nechernozemnoi Rossi*, 2 vols. (Moscow, 1912-1913) 1: viii. This experiment was only a partial one, for information on the natural (i.e., nonmonetary) budget of the farm was not culled.

6. The form designed by the Moscow economists bore strong resemblances to the bookkeeping method pioneered by E. Laur in Switzerland. Chaianov, *Biudzhetnye issledovaniia*, p. 55. For the details of this form, see ibid., pp. 65-66.

7. This form was endorsed by all the Organization-Production scholars. In 1913, Chelintsev urged agronomists to adopt it in their work. A. N. Chelintsev, *Uchastkovaia agronomiia i schetovodnyi analiz krest'ianskogo sel'skogo khoziaistva* (Samara, 1914). Teams of agronomists did in fact test the form in studies of farm organization in the Moscow, Chernigov, and Poltava *gubernii*. Chaianov, *Biudzhetnye issledovanii*, p. 66.

8. Chaianov admitted that there were two other possible responses by the farmer to an increase in consumption pressure: he could intensify production, or he could supplement his income from farming with revenue from crafts. In the Starobel'sk region, however, neither of these options proved viable.

9. For a summary of the findings on labor organization, see A. V. Chaianov, *Biudzhety krest'ian Starobel'skago uezda* (Moscow, 1915), pp. 88-89; for a capsule version of the findings on the use of inventory, see ibid., p. 69.

10. Ibid., pp. 55-56.

11. The origin and development of this proposition were described in chapter 3.

12. So confident was Chaianov of the success of his 1915 study that he sat down to write the first history of the budget method. Chaianov, *Opyt razrabotki*. His pride in the Starobel'sk study was reflected in the history he wrote in 1922, but it did not reappear in the 1929 version—for reasons that will be detailed in chapter 8.

13. For the fullest version of this criticism, see S. N. Prokopovich, *Krest'ianskoe khoziaistvo* (Berlin, 1923). Prokopovich was a non-Party Marxist who subjected Chaianov's work to detailed scrutiny.

14. For the distinction between confirming and testing a hypothesis, see Karl Popper, *Conjectures and Refutations* (New York, 1965), p. 36. Popper contends that confirmation of a proposition is no guarantee of its scientific status; only the unsuccessful attempt to falsify a hypothesis can count as a test of its validity.

15. In late 1927 Chaianov wrote of his Starobel'sk study, "The whole analysis was guided by the desire to test the effect of the size and composition of the family on its economic activity." Chaianov, *Biudzhetnye issledovaniia*, p. 282.

16. The years 1915-1919 saw a proliferation of budget studies, but these were mostly replications of Chaianov's work. For a list of such studies, see ibid., pp. 80-81.

17. A. N. Chelintsev, *Opyt izucheniia organizatsii krest'ianskogo sel'skogo khoziaistva na primere Tambovskoi gubernii* (Kharkov, 1919).

18. A. N. Chelintsev, *Teoreticheskie obosnovaniia organizatsii krest'ianskogo khoziaistva* (Kharkov, 1919).

19. The role of the market is discussed in both of Chelintsev's 1919 works. The more detailed discussion is in *Teoreticheskie*.

20. As early as 1910 Chelintsev had asserted that a farm

would respond to the demands of the market only with the type of product it was capable of furnishing. See A. N. Chelintsev, "Ocherki po sel'sko-khoziaistvennoi ekonomi," *Sel'skoe khoziastvo i lesovodstvo*, no. 134 (October 1910): pp. 700, 733-734.

21. This contention called into question the widely held belief that the quantity of peasant grain deliveries could be affected by market incentives.

22. This conclusion appears in both of Chelintsev's 1919 works; the more suggestive treatment was that advanced in *Opyt izucheniia*, pp. 158-159. In asserting that crafts was the occupation of the badly off farmer, Chelintsev was clearly influenced by his adherence to the Organization-Production tenet that the family farmer was a nonacquisitive being. For, in itself, the fact that peasants were farmers first and craftsmen second says nothing definitive about the reasons why peasants engage in craftwork. They may be forced to do so by economic need, or they may desire to do so because of an urge for gain.

23. Ibid., pp. 270-276.

24. Chelintsev's use of budget research was too blatant even for his colleagues. Assessing the 1919 works, Chaianov remarked that they provided new information only to agronomists. Chaianov, *Biudzhetnye issledovaniia*, p. 299.

25. Those critics had deplored what they regarded as the Timiriazev professors' penchant for considering the family farm in isolation from its environment.

26. Chaianov, "Peasant Farm Organization," p. 69.

27. Ibid., p. 126. Here Chaianov was refuting one of Chelintsev's core assertions—an assertion that he himself had made earlier—namely, that a farm would offer for sale only those products that natural conditions permitted.

28. According to Chaianov, the peasant would compare the wages he would receive in farming against those he could receive from craftwork and then make his decision. Ibid., p. 108. In saying this, Chaianov was explicitly rejecting Chelintsev's contention that craftwork was a residual occupation.

29. Ibid. Here Chaianov was casting doubt on the belief held by some Organization-Production scholars that the family farmer was immune to the lure of gain.

30. Chaianov put it this way: "Thanks to its contact with the

market, the farm is able to throw out of its organizational plan all production sectors that give little income and in which the product is obtained on the farm with greater effort than that required to obtain its market equivalent by other forms of economic activity which give greater income." Ibid.

31. Chaianov's 1925 contention that the family farm could survive in competition with capitalist agriculture was the more devastating, because he made it *after* he had explored the impact of the market upon precapitalist agriculture.

32. Similarly, Chaianov's 1925 attempt to modify the theory of the family farm failed to appease his detractors.

33. For their part, the members of the Organization-Production school had always insisted that the budget method was neutral and not linked to, though helpful for, the articulation of their theory.

34. In a report read to the Graduate Seminar of the Petrovskii Agricultural Academy on October 17, 1919, regionalization studies were traced to the work of K. I. Arsen'ev in 1818. N. P. Nikitin, *Khoziaistvennye raiony evropeiskoi Rossii* (Moscow, 1919), p. 37.

35. Chelintsev, "Ocherki po sel'sko-khoziaistvennoi ekonomii," 263.

36. Ibid.

37. Ibid., 251-286.

38. A. N. Chelintsev, *Sel'sko-khoziaistvennye raiony evropeiskoi Rossii kak stadii sel'sko-khoziaistvennoi evoliutsii i kulturnyi uroven' sel'skogo khoziaistva v nikh* (Moscow, 1911).

39. In 1916 Chelintsev presented a set of thirteen indicators to a conference of statisticians interested in farm typologies. B. N. Knipovich, *K metodologii raionirovaniia* (Moscow, 1921). In 1918 he published a large regionalization study, in which only six indicators were used. The results were reported in A. N. Chelintsev, *Sostoianie i razvitie russkogo sel'skogo khoziaistva po dannym sel'sko-khoziaistvennoi perepisi 1916 goda i zhelezno-dorozhnykh perevozok* (Moscow, 1918).

40. This modication allowed him to go beyond the description of a given region as "an average pig-raising area with an above-average ratio of tubrous plants to sown land." Moreov-

er, he was now able to compare one region to another.
41. That resistance derived mostly from the fact that to make his case, Chelintsev had adopted an extreme position, leaving his critics with the impression that he wanted to omit natural indicators altogether. Chelintsev corrected this impression in an address he delivered to the Imperial Free Economic Society. For a report of his remarks by the staunchest of his critics, see B. N. Knipovich, "Sel'sko-khoziaistvennoe raionirovanie," *Trudy Zemplana*, vol. 3, pt. 1 (1925), p. 44.

42. See, for example, Chaianov's preface to N. Nikitin, "Sel'sko-khoziaistvennoe raionirovanie Moskovskoi gubernii," *Trudy vysshego seminariia sel'sko-khoziaistvennoi ekonomii i politiki pri Petrovskoi Sel'sko-khoziaistvennoi Akademii*, vol. 6 (Moscow, 1921). Makarov claimed that the regionalization studies were even more important than the budget research conducted by the members of the Organization-Production school. N. P. Makarov, *Krest'ianskoe khoziaistvo i ego evolutsiia* (Moscow, 1920), p. 48.

43. Not all of the Timiriazev professors were convinced that the study of intrafarm dynamics was sufficient unto itself. Makarov suggested that it might be advantageous to combine the typology based on economic indicators favored by the Organization-Production scholars with the social (interfarm) indicators used by the Marxists. This combination, he argued, would produce a more complete farm typology. Makarov, *Krest'ianskoe khoziaistvo*, pp. 159-160.

44. This form of historical study was not done by American researchers engaged in regional analysis. At most, they offered an historical overview of the region they were studying. Henry C. and Anne Dewees Taylor, *The Story of Agricultural Economics in the United States 1840-1932* (Ames, Iowa, 1952) pp. 281-282.

45. Contrary to the accusations made by their opponents, the members of the Organization-Production school were not oblivious to the virtues of complex farm machinery. They did not believe, however, that such machinery could be applied under all circumstances. See, for example, N. P. Makarov, *Usloviia i predely primeneniia traktorov v sel'skom khoziaistve* (Moscow, 1922); N. P. Makarov, *Kak Amerikanskie*

fermery organizuiut svoe khoziaistvo (Moscow, 1921). Toward the end of the decade they were to set aside their cautious
attitude for reasons that were not strictly scientific.
    46. To the members of the Chaianov group, the voluntary
nature of the rural cooperatives was very important. They
would continue to insist upon this criterion even when such
insistence became dangerous.
    47. A. V. Chaianov, *Osnovnye idei i formy organizatsii
krest'ianskoi kooperatsii* (Moscow, 1919). A second edition of
this work appeared in 1927.
    48. Chaianov's experience in organizing the cooperatives
was discussed in Basile Kerblay, "A. V. Chayanov: Life, Career,
Works," in *A. V. Chayanov on the Theory of Peasant Economy*, ed. Daniel Thorner, Basile Kerblay, and R. E. F. Smith
(Homewood, Ill., 1966), pp. xxxiv-xxxv. Even before the
war, Chaianov had been interested in the problem of cooperation. In 1913 he had organized a seminar on cooperation in the
Petrovskii Academy. Two years later he published his notes for
this seminar. See A. V. Chaianov, *Kratkii kurs kooperatsii*
(Moscow, 1915). These notes were revised and republished in
1919.
    49. A. V. Chaianov, *Kratkii kurs kooperatsii*, 3d. rev. ed.
(Moscow, 1925); A. V. Chaianov, "Sel'skokhoziaistvennaia
kooperatsiia, kak forma sel'skokhoziaistvennogo proizvod-
stva SSSR," *Ekonomicheskoe obozrenie*, 1925, no. 5, pp. 58-
67; Chaianov, "Peasant Farm Organization," pp. 263-269. Of
these three treatments of the subject, the last constituted the
most fundamental departure from Chaianov's 1919 stand.
    50. Chaianov did not ignore the new horizontally organized
farms that had been created under the Soviet regime. While not
denying that they could be useful, he said, "This process is
taking place on a considerable scale, but it is not, and cannot
be, of such a massive size that we could be able to construct on
it our whole policy of agricultural concentration." Chaianov,
"Peasant Farm Organization," p. 267. In support of his
preference for vertical concentration, Chaianov cited the
opinion of "all agricultural organizers." Ibid., pp. 265-266.
    51. Ibid., p. 265.
    52. Ibid., pp. 268-269.

53. Chaianov, "On the Theory of Non-Capitalist Economic Systems," p. 24. In particular, Chaianov was dubious about the ability of socialist agriculture to motivate the peasant to work.
54. Chaianov, "Peasant Farm Organization," p. 269.
55. Ibid. Neither the definition nor the prediction of the transition to socialism from the vertical cooperatives occurred in Chaianov's 1925 article or monograph. This suggests that the final few pages of "Peasant Farm Organization" may have been added at the last moment.
56. Chaianov's linking of socialism to the cooperatives owed something to Lenin's 1923 writings. A full discussion of these writings and their impact will appear in chapter 5.
57. A review of Chaianov's *Kratkii kurs kooperatsii* was published in 1925. The reviewer took Chaianov to task for what he claimed was an unorthodox view of socialism. See *NAF*, 1925, no. 4, pp. 181-182. The reviewer, identified by his initials, may well have been the young Agrarian-Marxist S. Uzhanskii.
58. For some general reference works on location theory, see W. Isard, *Location and Space Economy* (Cambridge, Mass., 1962); C. Ponsard, *Histoire des Theories Economiques Spatiales* (Paris, 1958).
59. This pioneering work can be consulted in English. See Peter Hall, ed., *Von Thunen's Isolated State* (Oxford, 1966).
60. The Organization-Production stand on intensity had a long history. As early as 1912, in a report delivered to the Imperial Free Economic Society, Chelintsev inveighed against the "undue" emphasis on the market as the determinant of intensity, and he urged recognition of demographic forces as independent on-farm factors to which both prices and market demand adjusted themselves. Chelintsev's remarks were cited in Prokopovich, *Krest'ianskoe khoziaistvo*, p. 218.
61. The Timiriazev professors were not alone in their esteem for von Thunen. The German economist's work provoked research among Russian economists of different stripes. Some devoted their attention to clarifying the concept of agricultural intensity; other concentrated upon developing intricate measures of intensity; and still others focused on the problem of price formation.

62. A. V. Chaianov, "Opyty izucheniia izolirovannogo gosudarstva," *Trudy vysshego seminariia selsko-khoziaistvennoi ekonomii i politiki*, vol. 1 (Moscow, 1921).

63. The author's aspirations for the model were clearly detailed in the preface. The virtual replication by Chaianov of von Thunen's title leaves little doubt that the author intended his work to be seen as the companion piece to von Thunen's study.

64. Chaianov regarded the family farm as not being privately owned in the sense that it was nearly always part of the repartitional commune.

65. Chaianov, "Opyty izucheniia izolirovannogo gosudarstva," chapter 1.

66. Ibid., pp. 25, 30.

67. The perennial discussions had become more frequent since 1917. They dominated the agenda of the Land Reform Commission of the Main Land Committee (*Glavnyi Zemel'nyi Komitet*) in 1917; they had been part of the deliberations of the League for Agrarian Reform in the same year; and they had recurred at the All-Russian Congress of Land Redistributors in 1920-1921. See A. V. Chaianov, "Optimal'nye razmery zemledel'cheskikh khoziaistv," *Problemy zemleustroistva, optimal'nye razmery zemledel'cheskogo khoziaistva, kolichestvennyi uchet effekta zemleustroistva* (Moscow, 1922), p. 3.

68. The relevant works of these economists were K. Werner, *Über zeitgemassen Landwirtschaftsbetriebe* (1904); V. Stebel, "Einfluss der Grundstücksentfernung auf Wirtschaftsaufwand," *Fühlings Landwirtschaft*, 1909, nos. 1-2.

69. Here Chaianov was referring specifically to the debate among Russian economists after the turn of the twentieth century.

70. Chaianov, "Optimal'nye razmery," p. 6.

71. The method involved a division of farm costs into those that increased with the addition of new land, those that decreased with the addition of new land, and those that were not affected by the addition of new land. For a detailed exposition of the method, see Chaianov, "Optimal'nye razmery," pp. 14, 15.

72. For the long-fallow system, 1,800 to 2,000 *desiatins* was

found to be optimal; for the grain fallow without dung fertilizer, 800 to 900 was declared ideal; for the grain fallow with dung fertilizer, 500 to 600 was found to be optimal; and for the most intensive type of farming, crop rotation, the optimum was declared to be no higher than 200 to 250.

73. See L. N. Kritsman, review of Chiainov, *Optimal'nye razmery*, in *Vestnik Sotsialisticheskoi Akademii*, no. 3 (1923), pp. 401-407. This review was reprinted as "Krupnoe i melkoe khoziaistvo v zemledelii," in Kritsman, *Proletarskaia revolutsiia*, pp. 533-539.

74. Chaianov, "Optimal'nye razmery," p. 6.

75. Ibid.

76. Ibid., p. 4.

Chapter 5

1. Likewise, in refining their research methodology, the Agrarian-Marxists were much influenced by what they identified as the novel conditions of the NEP period.

2. The principal Marxist writers in this dispute were P. Struve, V. I. Lenin, S. Bulgakov, and M. Tugan-Baranovsky. The principal populist writers were N. Danielson, V. Vorontsov, and S. Iuzhakov. For detailed analysis of this fascinating debate, see Arthur P. Mendel, *Dilemmas of Progress in Tsarist Russia: Legal Marxism and Legal Populism* (Cambridge, Mass., 1961); Richard Kindersley, *The First Russian Revisionists* (Oxford, 1962); Richard Pipes, *Struve: Liberal on the Left* (Cambridge, Mass., 1970); Theodore von Laue, "The Fate of Capitalism in Russia: The *Narodnik* Version," *American Slavic and East European Review* 13 (1954): 11-29; Solomon Schwarz, "Populism and Early Marxism on Ways of Economic Development of Russia (the 1880's and 1890's)" in *Continuity and Change in Russian and Soviet Thought*, ed. E. J. Simmons (Cambridge, Mass., 1955), pp. 40-63.

3. Of all the commentators on this debate, only Richard Kindersley contends that the populists and Marxists diverged in their analysis of the extent to which capitalism had penetrated the Russian economy. No evidence supporting Kindersley's view has been found.

4. Schwarz has termed the populists' view "economic romanticism," thus underscoring the nostalgia for the past that ran through populist thought. Schwarz, "Populism and Early Marxism," p. 43.

5. This contention of the populists was based on the assumption that over time the peasant's income would gradually decrease. Because his products would compare unfavorably with sophisticated factory manufactures, he would soon be deprived of revenue from crafts. And Russia's inability to compete on the world grain market would lead to falling prices for grain. The reduction in income from crafts and grain would make industrial goods more costly for the peasant, who, under such circumstances, could hardly be expected to generate a substantial demand for these goods. Mendel, *Dilemmas*, pp. 47-48.

6. Several decades earlier, when Marxism first spread to Russia, Russian socialists sought guidance from Marx on the role of the *artel'* and the commune in the transition to socialism. In his early contact with the Russian socialists (among them Danielson), Marx had entertained with favor the idea that Russia might skip the capitalist stage of development and, on the basis of the communal spirit manifested in the rural institutions, might effect the transition to socialism directly. Later, Marx added the stipulation that a world revolution must succeed developments in Russia. For the details of the correspondence between Marx (and later Engels) and the Russian socialists, see Schwarz, "Populism and Early Marxism," pp. 47-54.

7. Among the populists, there were differences as to what form the socialist economy was to take. Some (whom Mendel has termed "minimalists") advocated the intensification of efforts to improve agriculture, the preservation of the traditional rural institutions, and the dependence of industrial development upon the purchasing power of the peasantry. Others (whom Mendel has termed "maximalists") advocated the immediate introduction of modern technology and urged the creation of large-scale units of production organized on socialist lines. Mendel, *Dilemmas*, p. 228. In their polemic with the populists, the Marxists ignored the "maximalist" position

and focused on the "minimalist" stand.

8. In particular, the Marxists charged that the rural commune, upon which the populists had pinned their hopes for socialism, was an institution that served only to tie to the land peasants who were not self-sufficient and who should have been part of the industrial labor force. Further, the Marxists rejected the populist dream of a fusion between agricultural and industrial work on the grounds that such a fusion would inhibit the growth of large-scale industry.

9. Among the Marxists, the strongest proponents of industrial socialism were Struve and Lenin, for whom progress was synonymous with industrial development.

10. See V. I. Lenin, "The Development of Capitalism in Russia," *Collected Works,* vol. 3 (Moscow, 1960-1970). Lenin's work was written in the heat of the 1890s controversy, yet in approach it belonged to the literature of the next century. For Lenin did not address himself to the question, so prominent in the 1890s, of whether capitalism ought to be allowed or encouraged to spread. Instead, he focused his work on the empirical question of the effects of capitalism upon the social structure of the countryside.

11. This point was made by both Struve and Lenin, who contended that crafts, which the populists had always identified as part of popular production, were in fact an embryonic form of capitalist industry.

12. See V. I. Lenin, "The Economic Content of Narodism and the Criticism of it in Mr. Struve's Book," *Collected Works*, vol. 1, p. 379.

13. Unlike the populists, the Marxists believed that capitalism would flourish of its own accord so long as the government did not impede its spread. They maintained that there would be no problem of markets for industrial goods because the very existence of industry would stimulate a demand for producer's goods. Moreover, they argued, if the rural sector were to become capitalist, it would bring into the industrial labor force those peasants whom the populists predicted would remain on the land and thus aggravate the problem of rural overpopulation.

14. It should be noted that there was a substantial difference

between Lenin and Struve on the question of the ills accompanying capitalism. Lenin was inclined to stress the negative by-products of capitalism, while Struve was inclined to underscore its positive aspects. Pipes explains this difference as a function of the variations in exposure to Western capitalism of Lenin and Struve. Struve had traveled widely in the West, whereas Lenin's contacts outside Russia were more limited. See Pipes, *Struve*, pp. 125-128.

15. The success of the Russian Marxists has been explained by Mendel as a result of the fact that these thinkers endorsed the path that Russia was already traveling. To the intelligentsia, weary after years of struggling against the tide, the optimism preached by the Russian Marxists was attractive indeed.

16. The populist strand of thought did not die out completely in Russia. At the beginning of the twentieth century, it found a new base in the Socialist Revolutionary (SR) Party. For a detailed study of the ideology of this party, see Oliver Radkey, *The Agrarian Foes of Bolshevism* (New York, 1958).

17. In outlining the widely held scenario of rural capitalization, we have drawn upon the work of a Western historian of Soviet Russia. See Teodor Shanin, *The Awkward Class: Political Sociology of Peasantry in a Developing Society: Russia 1910-1925* (Oxford, 1972), p. 1.

18. This proposal was submitted to the Tenth Party Congress on March 15, 1921. V. I. Lenin, "Report on the Substitution of a Tax in Kind for the Surplus Grain Appropriation System," *Collected Works*, vol. 32, pp. 214-238.

19. Ibid., p. 218.

20. Ibid., pp. 215-217, 224, 234.

21. V. I. Lenin, "The Tax in Kind," *Collected Works*, vol. 32, p. 334. Lenin's conviction that socialism could not be built without these preconditions owed much to the failure of the policy of War Communism.

22. Lenin, "Report on the Substitution of a Tax in Kind," pp. 214-215.

23. The label "retreat" was most likely to be applied by those who had regarded War Communism as a socialist offensive. Lenin himself vacillated in his attitude toward the policy of June 1918 to March 1921. When he introduced NEP, Lenin

termed War Communism a "makeshift," "peculiar" policy. Seven months later, when he was rethinking NEP, Lenin acknowledged that his new policy was a "retreat." Compare Lenin, "The Tax in Kind," and V. I. Lenin, "The New Economic Policy and the Tasks of the Political Education Departments," *Collected Works*, vol. 23, p. 63.

24. As a Western historian of the period has pointed out, one of the most striking differences between the two policies was that in 1918 Lenin had not thought in terms of free trade or market relations. Stephen F. Cohen, *Bukharin and the Bolshevik Revolution* (New York, 1973), p. 135.

25. Lenin, "Report on the Substitution of a Tax in Kind," p. 219.

26. Lenin, "The Tax in Kind," p. 345.

27. Ibid., p. 346.

28. Ibid., p. 349. At the time he proposed it, Lenin did not see anything problematic about the "reversion" of concession industries to the Soviet state. Events would prove him to have been very naïve on this point.

29. Ibid., p. 348.

30. Ibid.

31. Ibid.

32. Ibid., p. 349. Lenin emphasized that however long the period required to effect the transition, no force should be used to bring the small commodity producer to socialism.

33. "At present petty-bourgeois capitalism prevails in Russia and it is *one and the same road* which leads from it to both large-scale capitalism and to socialism, through *one and the same* intermediary station called 'national accounting and control of production and distribution.'" Lenin, "The Tax in Kind," p. 335.

34. Ibid., p. 333, 350.

35. In Lenin's view the petit bourgeoisie opposed socialism because it was wedded to small-scale production and because it resented any interference in production or distribution. Ibid., p. 331.

36. Lenin, "Report on the Substitution of a Tax in Kind," p. 215.

37. Lenin's ambivalence was pointed out by Lewin in his

lucid and interesting discussion of NEP. Moshe Lewin, *Lenin's Last Struggle* (New York, 1968), pp. 24-28. The interpretation of NEP presented here owes much to Lewin's treatment.

38. V. I. Lenin, "Political Report to the Central Committee of the R.C.P. (B.) March 27," *Collected Works*, vol. 33, pp. 280-285. Lenin had actually mentioned stopping the retreat a few weeks earlier in a speech delivered to the Communist group of the All-Russian Congress of Metal Workers. V. I. Lenin, "The International and Domestic Situation of the Soviet Republic," *Collected Works*, vol. 33, pp. 219-221.

39. According to Lenin, not one single profitable agreement had been concluded. V. I. Lenin, "To the Fourth Congress of the Communist International," *Collected Works*, vol. 33, p. 425.

40. V. I. Lenin, "Letter to the Fifth All-Russian Congress of Trade Unions," *Collected Works*, vol. 33, p. 370. This letter was written on September 22, 1922.

41. V. I. Lenin, "On Cooperation," *Collected Works*, vol. 33, pt. 1, pp. 467-471; pt. 2, pp. 472-475.

42. Ibid., pt. 1, p. 470; ibid., pt. 2, p. 474.

43. Ibid., pt. 2, p. 474.

44. This shift in attitude toward the cooperatives Lewin has termed a "doctrinal *volte face*." Lewin, *Lenin's Last Struggle*, p. 114.

45. Lenin, "On Cooperation," pt. 2, 473.

46. Ibid., pt. 1, 471.

47. For a discussion of this debate, see E. H. Carr and R. W. Davies, *Foundations of a Planned Economy*, 3 vols. (London, 1969), vol. 1, pt. 2, pp. 921-924.

48. It is difficult to say whether Kritsman's colleagues shied away from theory because they had formed an image of themselves as researchers or because they were aware of the problems inherent in constructing the new theory.

49. Kritsman, review of Chaianov, *Optimal'nye razmery*. See also Kritsman, "Sovremennaia melkoburzhuaznaia politicheskaia ekonomiia."

50. Kritsman would resume the attack in 1927. The hiatus of approximately two years allowed him the time to refine the Agrarian-Marxist approach to rural studies.

51. L. N. Kritsman, "Lenin i put' k sotsializmu," in Krits-man, *Proletarskaia revoliutsiia*, pp. 13-19.

52. L. N. Kritsman, "Soiuz proletariata i bol'shinstva krest'-ianstva v SSSR posle pobedy revoliutsiia," ibid., pp. 26-46. The original place of publication of this article is not known.

53. Kritsman, "Lenin i put' k sotsializmu," p. 17.

54. It should be noted that Lenin derived these "insights" by assertion, not induction.

55. In Kritsman's opinion, the idea of installing large-scale socialist agriculture in the form of state farms was impractical, given the level of development of the Soviet economy in 1925. Kritsman, "Soiuz proletariata," p. 34.

56. To Kritsman, the problem of the disparity between the two sectors of the economy was the most important obstacle confronting the Soviet regime in its attempt to transform the socioeconomic structure of Russia. Kritsman, "Lenin i put' k sotsializmu," p. 17.

57. Kritsman suggested that the cooperative route might be appropriate to other nations in which the majority of the population was engaged in small commodity production. Ibid., pp. 16-17.

58. Ibid., p. 17.

59. Kritsman expressed this conviction indirectly. He suggested that, if unreformed, peasant attitudes would support the continuance of the capitalist route. Kritsman, "Soiuz proletariata," p. 35.

60. Ibid., p. 45.

61. Kritsman's notion of the source of cultural change among the peasantry differed somewhat from that of Lenin. In his 1923 articles Lenin spoke of the cultural revolution growing out of the peasant's positive exposure to the cooperatives; Kritsman envisaged the peasant coming to the cooperatives as a result of his bitter experience with individual farming.

62. Kritsman noted the persistence of traditional attitudes as early as 1925. He recounted that under the influence of the promise of a small piece of land, "the vast majority of agricultural laborers . . . went over not to the cooperatives but to individual farming." Kritsman, "Soiuz proletariata," p. 41.

63. A large study Kritsman had been conducting revealed

that the cooperatives designed for marketing and retailing were
being used almost exclusively by the rich peasants, whereas the
other strata in the countryside were ignoring these institutions.
L. N. Kritsman, ed., *Sel'skoe khoziaistvo na putiakh vostano-
vleniia* (Moscow, 1925), p. 717, as cited in E. H. Carr, *Socialism in One Country*, 2 vols. (London, 1958) 1: 299.

    64. The first of these projects Kritsman undertook on his
own. See. L. N. Kritsman, *Klassovoe rassloenie v sovetskoi
derevni (po dannym volostnykh obsledovanii)* (Moscow,
1926). This work was reprinted in its entirety in Kritsman,
Proletarskaia revoliutsiia, pp. 117-268. This project served as
the point of departure for several others that Kritsman directed. These will be discussed in detail in the following chapter.

    65. The methodology refined by the Agrarian-Marxists was
an important part of their work. Its development will be
discussed in chapter 6.

    66. The Agrarian-Marxists did not coin the epithet. It was
first used by the "bourgeois" economist, L. N. Litoshenko, in
his work *Evoliutsiia i progress krest'ianskogo khoziaistva*
(Moscow, 1923). In applying this epithet Litoshenko was
inveighing against the predilection of the Chaianov group for
small-scale agriculture, a predilection that reminded him of the
preference of the narodniks of the 1880s and 1890s. The
members of the Chaianov group objected strenuously to this
appellation, claiming that they had little in common with the
populists of the late nineteenth century. G. A. Studenskii, a
sometime member of the school, claimed that a "total lack of
taste" prompted Litoshenko to coin the term. See G. A.
Studenskii, *Ocherki po teorii krest'ianskogo khoziaistva*
(Moscow, 1923), p. 17. For a discussion of the link between the
Chaianov group and the "bourgeois economists" who were
committed to one or another variety of capitalist future for
Russia, see N. K. Figurovskaia, "Razgrom burzhuaznykh i
melkoburzhuaznykh agrarnykh teorii, 1917-1930" (Candidate's thesis, Moscow State University, 1961).

Chapter 6

    1. This criticism cannot be completely taken at face value.
In part, at least, it was an early sign of the struggle for power

within the community of Marxist rural scholars, a struggle that would take shape in the second half of the decade.

2. "Diskussiia o klassovykh gruppirovkakh krest'ianskikh khoziaistv v Komakedemii," pt. 1 *NAF,* 1928, no. 5, p. 135.

3. A. I. Khriashcheva, *Gruppy i klassy v krest'ianstve* (Moscow, 1924), p. 15. Khriashcheva repeated this point in the revised edition of this work, which appeared under the same title in 1926.

4. L. N. Kritsman, "K voprosu o klassovom rassloenii sovremennoi derevni," pt. 1, *NAF,* 1925, no. 2, p. 49. This was first of three articles later reprinted as L. N. Kritsman, *Klassovoe rassloenie v sovetskoi derevni (po dannym volostnykh obsledovanii)* (Moscow, 1926).

5. In his discussion of the effect of the land redistribution of 1918-1921 upon the examination of rural social structure, Kritsman drew liberally on a study of War Communism in which he was engaged. This study appeared in monograph form as L. N. Kritsman, *Geroicheskii period velikoi russkoi revoliutsii* (Moscow, 1925).

6. Ibid., p. 49. In making this judgment, Kritsman was taking a position on the nature of War Communism, arguing that it was not socialist in character, but part of the transition to socialism. Kritsman's assessment of War Communism drew upon an early article by Lenin, in which the future leader explained that the division of land for private use among peasant proprietors was not socialism but the result of "unfavorable conditions" in the agrarian revolution. V. I. Lenin, "The Agrarian Programme of Social Democracy in the First Russian Revolution, 1905-1907," *Collected Works* (Moscow, 1960-1970), vol. 13, pp. 258-259.

7. After the Revolution poor peasants had been able to use the inventory of the better-off farmers, but this policy had ended in 1919, leaving the poor peasants in essentially the same condition vis-à-vis the means of cultivation as they had been prior to 1917.

8. On the basis of a study he had done using secondary material, Kritsman asserted that there was a glaring disparity between the formal equality of the peasantry (measured by the distribution of arable land) and the actual class structure of the

rural sector (measured by the distribution of herds and inventory). Kritsman, "K voprosu o klassovom rassloenii," pt. 1, p. 49.

9. Kritsman explained that he had made the independent peasant the center of his analytic framework for reasons of simplicity and elegance. Ibid., p. 52.

10. These ruses were occasioned by the fact that, save under exceptional circumstances, the hire and lease of land and labor were illegal until 1925. Therefore most peasants were forced to dissemble in order to obtain the resources necessary to farm their plots.

11. Kritsman, "K voprosu o klassovom rassloenii sovremennoi derevni," pt. 2, *NAF*, 1925, nos. 7-8, p. 7.

12. Apparently, members of the Organization-Production school looking at this situation had analyzed it as an instance of the division of labor. See Vermenichev's contribution to the 1928 debate over methodology. "Diskussiia o klassovykh gruppirovkakh krest'ianskikh khoziaistv," *NAF*, 1928, no. 5, p. 144.

13. Kritsman, "K voprosu o klassovom rassloenii," pt. 2, p. 7.

14. Ibid., p. 8.

15. These three farms did not bother to mask their social relations. Kritsman believed that as time went on, such farms would become increasingly rare. Ibid., p. 18.

16. For a biography of Nemchinov, see appendix B.

17. In the 1920s there was a good deal of interaction between social researchers working in the Agrarian Section of the Communist Academy and statisticians conducting studies in the Central Statistical Administration (TsSU). The effect of this interaction on Soviet rural sociology is an intriguing question, which remains to be explored. There have been studies of the links between social researchers and statisticians in other national settings. For example, see Suzanne P. Schad, *Empirical Social Research in Weimar Germany* (The Hague, 1972); David Elesh, "The Manchester Statistical Society: A Case of Discontinuity

in the History of Empirical Social Research," in *The Establishment of Empirical Sociology*, ed. Anthony Obershcall (New York, 1972); Stephen Cole, "Continuity and Institutionalization in a Science: A Case Study of Failure," ibid., pp. 73-129.

18. V. S. Nemchinov, "O statisticheskom izuchenii klassovogo rassloeniia derevni," *Biulleten' ural'skogo oblastnogo statisticheskogo upravleniia*, 1926, no. 1, pp. 25, 26.

19. The valuation of the means of production was actually not a simple matter; it involved several points of discretion. For example, land in excess of the "consumption norm" was to be valued at the level of local land rent; both basic capital and circulating capital had to be valued to include amortization; and labor had to be valued to include different types of work, agricultural and crafts (*promysly*). Ibid., p. 30.

20. Ibid., p. 36.

21. Nemchinov compared the results he obtained using his method to classify 835 farms in the Troitskii district with the results obtained by using the two traditional indexes and the well-worn method of calculation. He concluded that his method was superior. Ibid., pp. 33-34.

22. Ibid., p. 36. Such modesty was typical of Nemchinov. It was also a clever strategy for an innovator not to try to preempt the entire field but to claim superiority on the basis of expertise in a more limited area.

23. Kritsman was implicitly criticizing the *zemstvo* statisticians, who tended to see the farm in isolation. For his criticism in detail, see L. N. Kritsman, "Ob analize klassovoi struktury krest'ianstva," in Kritsman, *Proletarskaia revoliutsiia*, pp. 301-310. This article appeared originally as the preface to a research project conducted by Gaister.

24. L. N. Kritsman, "O statisticheskom izuchenii klassovoi struktury sovetskoi derevni," pt. 1, *NAF*, 1926, no. 2, pp. 3-10. This was the first of four articles published under the same title in the same journal. The second was in *NAF*, 1927, no. 7, pp. 3-22; the third in *NAF*, 1927, nos. 8-9, pp. 3-17; and the final article in *NAF*, 1927, no. 10, pp. 3-17. The entire set of articles

was reprinted in Kritsman, *Proletarskaia revoliutsiia*, pp. 433-504.

25. Kritsman, "O statisticheskom," pt. 1, p. 10.

26. For case 1, Nemchinov had estimated that the entrepreneurship indicators totaled 37.2 percent. Kritsman calculated as follows:

Own labor on own farm   x   *Own means of production*
(in rubles)   *on own farm* (in rubles)

Total labor on own farm   Total of own means of
(in rubles)   production (in rubles)

$$\frac{365.00}{365.00 + 351.00} \quad x \quad \frac{104.58 + 499.66}{104.58 + 499.66 + 11.0}$$

$$51\% \times 97.9\% = 49.9\%$$

Thus the entrepreneurship percentage was 50.1. For case 2, Nemchinov had estimated that the dependence indicators totaled 123.3 percent. Kristman calculated as follows:

Own labor on own farm   x   *Own means of production*
(in rubles)   *on own farm* (in rubles)

Total own labor   Total means of production
(in rubles)   on own farm (in rubles)

$$\frac{213.33}{213.33 + 266.67} \quad x \quad \frac{10.67}{10.67 + 29.23}$$

$$45.5\% \times 26.8\% = 11.97\%$$

Thus the dependence percentage was approximately 88. Ibid., pp. 9-10.

27. One of Kritsman's colleagues, Raevich, had doubts about the claims made on behalf of this methodology. He maintained that the substance of social relations was human interaction, not the correspondence between labor and the means of production. See G. Raevich, "K voprosu o priemakh izucheniia sotsial'no-ekonomicheskikh tipov sovremennoi derevni," *Vestnik statistiki,* 1927, no. 1, pp. 104-113. Kritsman devoted an entire article to a response. See Kritsman, "O statisticheskom," pt. 2, pp. 3-14.

28. Ia. Anisimov, I. Vermenichev, and K. Naumov, *Proizvodstvennaia kharakteristika krest'ianskikh khoziaistv razlichnykh sotsial'nykh grupp* (Moscow, 1927).

29. Ibid., p. 13.

30. Ibid., p. 17.

31. This was the very region that Chaianov had studied in 1911.

32. Although it was the companion piece of the Volokolamsk project, the Penza study was never regarded by the Agrarian-Marxists as part of their corpus of work. In all probability this was due to the fact that Studenskii took a leading role in the Penza research.

33. In the preface Chaianov admitted that both Chelintsev and Studenskii faced substantial difficulties because their own concerns focused on the internal structure of the farm. Anisimov, *Proizvodstvennaia*, p. 10.

34. In thanking Chaianov, who wrote the foreword to the book, the authors indicated their ambivalence: "Despite theoretical differences of view on the peasantry and different ways of studying it . . . the competent help of A. V. Chaianov . . . never put the authors in a difficult position." Ibid., p. 31.

35. Apparently the authors expected to publish the results of the statistical surveys as well as the budget data. Ibid., pp. 29-31. However, no such publication ever appeared.

36. Fifty-two of these they analyzed on their own; the data on eight others they took from Chaianov's 1911 study of the region.

37. Such purification was deemed necessary because of the

previous condemnation by the Agrarian-Marxists of the budget work done by their mentors.

38. Anisimov, Vermenichev, and Naumov, *Proizvodstvennaia kharakteristika*, p. 39.

39. Ibid., p. 33.

40. Ibid., p. 49.

41. The authors explained that the statistical survey turned up more peasants in the middle groups because in a survey it was harder to discern the way in which inventory was leased. Ibid., p. 47.

42. I. Vermenichev, A. Gaister, and G. Raevich, *710 khoziaistv Samarskoi derevni* (Moscow, 1927). The inside flyleaf dated the book in 1927; moreover, the final chapter was dated September 1927. However, the outside cover dated the book in 1928. We had decided to accept the earlier date since all published references to the book date it in 1927.

43. Ibid., p. v. Similar expeditions were sent to the *gubernii* of Voronezh and Moscow. In addition to sponsoring inquiry the Central Statistical Administration conducted its own research on the countryside. For most of the 1920s, one of the key figures conducting this research was A. I. Khriashcheva.

44. Ibid., pp. 38, 39.

45. Ibid., p. 43.

46. The authors did not establish a parallelism between the hire and sale of labor on the assumption that a working day to a capitalist farm was hardly the equivalent of a working day to a proletarian farm. Kritsman approved this assumption. Ibid., p. xi.

47. The same composite score could be achieved by a number of routes. For example, Kritsman derived the score of −5 in eighty-five different ways. Ibid., pp. ix-x.

48. Compiled from ibid., pp. 42, 44.

49. Ibid., pp. 44-45.

50. Ibid., p. xi.

51. Ibid., pp. xi, xii.

52. In 1927, before the book appeared, three articles published the findings of the Samara study. These articles, written by the authors of the Samara project, were printed in issue no. 8-9 of *Na agrarnom fronte*. The substance of these articles was

then included, without any change, in the book itself. The advance publication of the Samara results might have been due either to the researchers' desire to sent up a trial balloon to test the opinion of the scholarly community before the full-scale study was published or to the impatience of young scholars to publish their findings.

53. The results showed that 54.5 percent of the farms were involved in the hire and sale of labor. Vermenichev, Gaister, and Raevich, *710 khoziaistv*, p. 50. Further, 80.4 percent of the farms rented cattle and inventory, and 47.3 percent leased these means of production. Ibid., p. 62. Finally, 23.3 percent rented land, while 21.6 percent were involved in its leasing. Ibid., p. 81.

54. This finding emerges from Kritsman's preface of the Samara study. Ibid., pp. xi-xiv.

55. A. I. Gaister, *Rassloenie Sovetskoi derevni* (Moscow, 1928).

56. Ibid., pp. iii-xxxi. In addition to commenting on the findings of Gaister's study, Kritsman used the foreword to review the history of agricultural statistics in Russia, setting his group's work in perspective and linking it to Lenin's classic study of 1899.

57. The members of this project were Vermenichev, Gaister, Kritsman (who headed it), Raevich, and (as of 1927) Nemchinov. Ibid., p. xxxii. In the period under study, this Commissariat sponsored a wide range of research on the countryside, most of which appears to have been conducted by researchers working for the local organs of the Commissariat itself. S. N. Ikonnikov, *Sozdanie i deiatel'nost' ob"edinennykh organov TsKK-RKI v 1923-1934 gg.* (Moscow, 1971), pp. 424-441.

58. Gaister, *Rassloenie*, p. x.

59. Kritsman termed Gaister's work "a step forward" and predicted that it would facilitate further work on rural stratification. Ibid., p. xxxi.

60. Ibid., p. 102. Here Gaister had to tread carefully, for in 1899 Lenin had clearly used statistics (collected by the *zemstva*) based on natural indexes. Gaister obviated the problem by pointing out that although Lenin had used such statistics, he had bemoaned their inadequacy. Ibid., pp. 102-105.

61. Ibid., p. 25.
62. Ibid., pp. 105-106.
63. The attack appeared in Vol'f's foreword to M. Gurevich, *Voprosy sovremennogo krest'ianskogo khoziaistva Ukrainy* (Kharkov, 1927). Cited in Gaister, *Rassloenie*, pp. 105-109. For information about Vol'f, see Moshe Lewin, *Russian Peasants and Soviet Power* (London, 1968), p. 352.
64. Gaister, *Rassloenie*, chapter 8.
65. Ibid., p. xxxi.

Chapter 7

1. The exact date of the meeting is not known; however, an article published in 1929 by one of the participants referred to the session has having occurred in the spring of 1927. M. Sulkovskii, "Evoliutsiia i raspad neonarodnichestva," *NAF*, 1929, no. 11-12, p. 84. Since the first installment of the verbatim transcript of the meeting was published in the April issue of the Timiriazev Academy's journal, we assume that the session took place within the first three months of 1927. For the full stenographic report of the meeting, see N. P. Makarov, "Differentsiatsiia krest'ianskogo khoziaistva," *PSKh*, 1927, no. 4, pp. 103-113; A. N. Chelintsev, "K voprosu o differentsiatsii krest'ianskogo khoziaistva," ibid., pp. 113-132; A. V. Chaianov, "O differentsiatsii krest'ianskogo khoziaistva," *PSKh*, 1927, no. 5, pp. 109-122; N. D. Kondrat'ev, "K voprosu o differentsiatsii derevni," ibid., pp. 123-140; Ia. A. Anisimov, "Differentsiatsiia krest'ianskogo khoziaistva," *PSKh*, 1927, no. 6, pp. 126-128; S. T. Uzhanskii, "Differentsiatsiia krest'ianstva," ibid., pp. 129-136; N. N. Sukhanov, "O differentsiatsii krest'ianskogo khoziaistva," ibid., pp. 137-147; "Preniia po dokladu o differentsiatsii krest'ianskogo khoziaistva," *PSKh*, 1927, no. 8, pp. 103-127; "Preniia po dokladu o differentsiatsii derevni," *PSKh*, 1927, no. 9, pp. 118-133; I. Vermenichev, "O differentsiatsii krest'ianstva," *PSKh*, 1928, no. 1, pp. 105-113. The discussion at this session has not been extensively described in the Western literature on the Soviet Union. For some brief treatments, see Teodor Shanin, *The Awkward Class; Political Sociology of Peasantry in a Developing Society: Russia 1910-1925* (Oxford, 1972), p. 60; E. H. Carr and

R. W. Davies, *Foundations of a Planned Economy*, 3 vols. (London, 1969), vol. 1, pt. 1, pp. 20-21.

2. The debate over policy was closely linked to a struggle for power in the Party. For details, see Moshe Lewin, *Russian Peasants and Soviet Power* (London, 1968), pp. 41-80.

3. These debates were canvassed in ibid., pp. 41-43; E. H. Carr, *Socialism in One Country*, 2 vols. (London, 1958) 1: 224-226, 236-240.

4. The keynote speakers were N. P. Makarov, A. N. Chelintsev, A. V. Chaianov, and N. D. Kondrat'ev. All but the latter were members of the Organization-Production school. Toward the end of the decade, critics would link Kondrat'ev's name to the Chaianov group, but the evidence shows that he was never part of this group.

5. The respondents in order of appearance were Ia. Anisimov, S. Uzhanskii, N. Sukhanov, G. Raevich, G. S. Gordeev, I. Nazimov, A. Sivogrivov, M. Sulkovskii, A. Gaister, and I. Vermenichev. Of these ten, at least seven were known to be affiliated with the Kritsman group.

6. The affinities between the Organization-Production analysis and an equilibrium model of development are discussed in Shanin, *The Awkward Class*, p. 108.

7. Chelintsev had been the director of the Volokolamsk study, a major project on rural stratification, but his directorship had been more nominal than real.

8. According to Shanin, most statisticians working in the 1920s were sympathetic to this desire.

9. Among others, Makarov mentioned Kritsman's work by name. Makarov, "Differentsiatsiia krest'ianskogo khoziaistva," p. 108.

10. Ibid., p. 107.

11. Chelintsev, "K voprosu o differentsiatsii," p. 116.

12. Ibid., p. 127.

13. Chaianov, "O differentsiatsii," p. 114.

14. Chaianov professed to be disinterested in demographic differentiation for its own sake; he claimed to prefer the demographic explanation on purely heuristic grounds. This profession strikes the reader as somewhat disingenuous.

15. To ensure that Chaianov's views received adequate

review, after printing the text of his speech the editors of the Timiriazev Academy's journal added their own critique. See "Ot redaktsii," *PSKh*, 1927, no. 5, pp. 121-122.

16. Lenin's ambivalence toward capitalism was discussed in chapter 5.

17. This argument was most clearly spelled out by Chaianov. Chaianov, "O differentsiatsii," pp. 120-121.

18. Makarov, "Differentsiatsii krest'ianskogo khoziaistva," pp. 103-105. Chelintsev, "K voprosu o differentsiatsii," p. 122. In making this argument, both keynote speakers stressed the fact that they were adopting a macroeconomic perspective, thus twitting their Marxist critics.

19. Makarov, "Differentsiatsiia krest'ianskogo khoziaistva," pp. 103-105; Chelintsev, "K voprosu o differentsiatsii," p. 122.

20. Makarov, "Differentsiatsiia krest'ianskogo khoziaistva," p. 104.

21. The argument was much weaker when applied to areas of extensive cultivation, a fact recognized by the keynote speakers themselves. Chelintsev, for example, admitted that if all land were used to grow grain, the family farm would have little chance of survival. Chelintsev, "K voprosu o differentsiatsii," p. 122.

22. Of the ten respondents, seven criticized Chaianov's speech, and four of these drew particular attention to this point.

23. Anisimov, "Differentsiatsiia krest'ianskogo khoziaistva," p. 126. Anisimov stated his claim cleverly. He said that if Chaianov were consistent, he would have to deny the existence of socioeconomic differences.

24. In viewing these two accounts of differentiation as monocausal, we are following the lead of Shanin. Shanin, *The Awkward Class*, p. 116.

25. This belief had been expressed in 1910 by Sukhanov. See N. N. Sukhanov, *K voprosu ob evoliutsii sel'skogo khoziaistva* (Moscow, 1909). The same assertion was repeated fourteen years later in N. N. Sukhanov, *Ocherki po ekonomike sel'skogo khoziaistva* (Petrograd, 1923). As one of the respondents at

the 1927 conference, Sukhanov was not at all anxious to be identified with the keynote speakers. Some of the others commentators did, however, make reference to Sukhanov's earlier work.

26. See the remarks of A. Sivogrivov in "Preniia po dokladu o differentsiatsii krest'ianskogo khoziaistva," p. 125. Sivogrivov argued that there had never been a case in history where industrial capital had hindered the development of capitalism in agriculture.

27. Ibid.

28. This argument was made by Gordeev. See ibid., p. 110.

29. For a discussion of the intellectual as "fighter for truth," see Florian Znaniecki, *The Social Role of the Man of Knowledge* (New York, 1940), pp. 137-148.

30. The reasons for Kritsman's absence were never given.

31. Lewin has demonstrated convincingly that although there was considerable support for the collectivization of farming at this Congress, no clear line emerged from the meeting. For a discussion of the "ambiguous" nature of this Congress, see Lewin, *Russian Peasants*, pp. 198-213.

Chapter 8

1. Later in the decade, the right of this group to speak on behalf of Marxism would be challenged.

2. Their humiliation at the 1927 meeting left a lasting impression upon the Agrarian-Marxists. Well after the debate had ended, they continued to replay the arguments, attempting to furnish new evidence for their original position. For example, see I. Vermenichev, "Klassovoe rassloenie i klassovye pozitsii burzhuaznyikh i melkoburzhuaznykh teoretikov," pt. 1, *NAF*, 1927, no. 4, pp. 78-88; pt. 2, *NAF*, 1927, no. 7, pp. 37-53; M. Sulkovskii, "Evoliutsiia i raspad neonarodnichestva," *NAF*, 1929, nos. 11-12, pp. 76-97.

3. The Kritsman group did not cease its work on rural differentiation. It continued to work on the studies already in progress, and in early 1928 the group met to consider the progress that had been made. It should be noted, however, that in this period none of the core members of the group undertook

new research on peasant stratification.

4. M. Kubanin, "Sotsial'no-ekonomicheskaia sushchnost' problemy drobimosti," *NAF*, 1928, no. 1, pp. 10-32; M. Kubanin, "Sotsial'no-ekonomicheskaia sushchnost' problemy drobleniia krest'ianskikh khoziaistv," pt. 1, *NAF*, 1928, no. 8, pp. 11-36, and pt. 2, *NAF*, 1928, no. 11, pp. 7-27. These articles were followed by the publication of a book on the same subject. See M. Kubanin, *Klassovaia sushchnost' protsessa drobleniia krest'ianskikh khoziaistv* (Moscow, 1929).

5. The question of the splintering of peasant households was discussed by rural scholars of all stripes during NEP. To a man they deplored the results of such splintering; they differed, however, on the causes of and remedies for it.

6. Kubanin reworked the results of a study of forty-five farms conducted by the State and Law Sector of the Communist Academy in 1926. Kubanin, "Klassovaia sushchnost'," p. 52. His willingness to use secondary analysis may have stemmed from a desire to get quick results that could be used against the Timiriazev professors.

7. Kubanin described the head of the farm as holding "terrifying power" over his kin. Ibid., p. 61. This image differed sharply from that of the benevolent administrator put forward by the Timiriazev professors.

8. Apparently Khriashcheva had earlier analyzed the grievances of the family members and had concluded that each member simply wanted a larger amount of the income. Kubanin rejected this finding, claiming that the issue for the family members was not simply distributive, but redistributive. Ibid.

9. As the source for this rendition of history, Kubanin cited the results of a questionnaire that had been part of the 1926 study. Respondents were asked whether they believed there was any correlation between the way a farm was governed and its economic level. Most agreed that the poorer farms were more "democratic," while the better-off farms were more likely to be run in an authoritarian fashion. Ibid., p. 65.

10. Ibid., p. 70.

11. Ibid.

12. Kritsman had noted the tenacity of the peasant as early as 1925. Kritsman, "Soiuz proletariata."

13. A Western historian writing on the 1920s recently drew attention to this. See Teodor Shanin, *The Awkward Class: Political Sociology of Peasantry in a Developing Society: Russia 1920-1925* (Oxford, 1972), p.45.

14. Khriashcheva made this point in an article written in response to Kubanin's 1928 articles. See A. I. Khriashcheva, "Usloviia drobimosti krest'ianskikh khoziaistv," *Ekonomicheskoe obozrenie*, 1928, no. 9, p. 107. Kubanin retaliated by calling Khriashcheva a "narodnik under the guise of a Marxist." Kubanin, *Klassovaia sushchnost'*, pp. 62-63.

15. Khriashcheva, "Usloviia drobimosti," p. 107.

16. Kritsman's approval was registered in the foreword to Kubanin's book and in an address given to the Conference of Marxist-Leninist Scientific Research Institutes in April 1929, described above, pp. 160-162.

17. Kubanin's awareness of his role as innovator was evident. Kubanin, *Klassovaia sushchnost'*, p. 33.

18. V. Lubiako and K. Naumov, "K voprosu o postroenie organizatsionnykh planov sovkhozov," *PSKh*, 1927, no. 12, pp. 3-8.

19. Ia. A. Anisimov, "Postanovka nekotorykh voprosov ob organizatsii sel'skogo khoziaistva v proshlom," *PSKh*, 1928, no. 1, pp. 3-17.

20. Ia. A. Anisimov, "Osnovnye polozheniia organizatsionno-proizvodstvennoi shkoly v uchenie ob organizatsii krest'-ianskogo khoziaistva," *PSKh*, 1928, no. 2, pp. 3-15. Anisimov directed his attack at the work of Chelintsev and Makarov, even though Prokopovich, upon whose critique Anisimov relied, had devoted his book to a refutation of Chaianov's writings.

21. Ia. A. Anisimov, "K postanvoke nekotorykh voprosov ob organizatsii sel'skogo khoziaistva primenitel'no k usloviiam SSSR," *PSKh*, 1928, no. 4-5, pp. 16-26. Anisimov referred in particular to Chelintsev's Tambov study of 1919 and to Makarov's 1925 study, which appeared as N. P. Makarov, *Organizatsiia sel'skogo khoziaistva* (Moscow, 1925).

22. Within planning agencies the emphasis on teleological designs for the future was apparent as early as 1927. See the speech by the Gosplan economist Strumilin at the Second

Gosplan Conference of March 1927. *Perspektivy razvërtyvaniia narodngo khoziaistva SSSR na 1926/1927-1930/1931* (Moscow, 1927), p. 1. According to Strumilin, planning should be treated as an art not a science.

23. For a striking contrast to Anisimov's articles, see the work of Sivogrivov on the science of farm organization. A. Sivogrivov, "Predmet, metod, i zadachi organizatsii sel'skogo khoziaistva," *PSKh*, 1928, no. 3, pp. 3-21. Sivogrivov, one of the most relentless critics of the Timiriazev professors at the differentiation debate, was apparently also in the process of writing a work on farm organization. The article he published in early 1928 was polemical in tone, lacking in analytic nuance, and devoid of any concrete suggestions for reshaping the field.

24. The Agrarian-Marxists faced the same problem when they attempted to refine a uniquely Marxist science of agricultural economics. For the details of that attempt, see chapter 9.

25. For some reasons, this work was especially slow in being published. It did not appear until mid-1929.

26. A. V. Chaianov, *Biudzhetnye issledovaniia: istoriia i metody* (Moscow, 1929), p. 6.

27. Ibid., p. 299. The results of Studenskii's research were published in two volumes. See G. A. Studenskii, *Opyt issledovaniia organizatsii krest'ianskogo khoziaistva tsentral'no-chernozemnoi oblasti* (Moscow, 1926); G. A. Studenskii, *Problemy organizatsii krest'ianskogo sel'skogo khoziaistva* (Samara, 1927). Studenskii's work, which purported to be both a study of differentiation and a budget inquiry, satisfied neither the Timiriazev professors nor the members of the Kritsman group.

28. Chaianov, *Biudzhetnye issledovaniia*, p. 295. Chaianov's assessment would be repeated in the history of the budget method published in 1929 by Studenskii. See G. A. Studenskii, *Osnovnye voprosy metodiki biudzhetnykh i schetovodnykh issledovanii* (Samara, 1929). In Studenskii's hands, the main innovators in the field were the Agrarian-Marxists, while the Organization-Production scholars received only passing mention.

29. Chaianov, *Biudzhetnye issledovaniia*, p. 282.

30. A. V. Chaianov, *Krest'ianskoe svekloseianie tsentral'-*

no-chernozemnoi oblasti (Moscow, 1929).
31. Ibid., p. viii.
32. Ibid., p. ix.
33. The particular target of Chelintsev's attack was the *Narkomzem* long-range plan of 1925.
34. In general Chelintsev was in favor of small units for planning. He regarded the *uezd*, which had been the basis of the 1925 Narkomzem targets, as too large; he much preferred the small *volost'*. See A. N. Chelintsev, "K metodologii sel'sko-khoziaistvennogo raionirovaniia," *PSKh*, 1928, nos. 4-5, p. 26.
35. A. N. Chelintsev, "Sel'sko-khoziaistvennye raiony, poraionnye perspektivy sel'skogo khoziaistva i napravlenie meropri'atii sel'sko-khoziaistvennoi politiki," pt. 1, *PSKh*, 1927, no. 9, pp. 35-57; pt. 2, *PSKh*, 1927, no. 11, pp. 42-68.
36. Chelintsev, "Sel'sko-khoziaistvennye raiony," pt. 1, pp. 35-36.
37. Ibid., p. 41.
38. A. V. Chaianov, *Optimal'nye razmery sel'sko-khoziaistvennykh predpriiatii,* 3d ed. rev. (Moscow, 1928. See p. 236, n. 67.
39. When a German edition of this work came out in 1930, it had a hastily prepared preface, in which the optima listed were much greater than those that had appeared in 1928. These changes were clearly made at the last minute, for they were not reflected in the text of the work.

Chapter 9

1. M. Sulkovskii, "A. V. Chaianov, *Optimal'nye razmery sel'sko-khoziaistvennykh predpriiatii,*" *NAF*, 1928, no. 4, pp. 145-149.
2. Ibid., p. 148.
3. Ibid., p. 147.
4. Ibid., p. 149.
5. L. N. Kritsman, "Optimal'nye razmery sel'sko-khoziaistvennykh predpriiatii," *Vestnik Sotsialisticheskoi Akademii*, no. 3 (1923), pp. 401-406.
6. Ibid., p. 406.
7. That commitment was given official sanction in a resolution enjoining the "gradual transformation of individual hold-

ings into large-scale farming enterprises (that is, communal cultivation of the land based on intensified agriculture and increased mechanization)," as cited in Moshe Lewin, *Russian Peasants and Soviet Power* (London, 1968), p. 206. Clearly, much of the impetus for this resolution came from the grain shortages of the winter 1927-1928, which pointed up the shortcomings of the family farm sector. E. H. Carr and R. W. Davies, *Foundations of a Planned Economy*, 3 vols. (London, 1969), vol. 1, pt. 1, p. 187.

8. In April 1928 the Politburo appointed a commission headed by Kalinin, whose task it was to consider the formation of sovkhozy. Apparently that commission called a series of experts, among whom were Chaianov and Makarov. Carr and Davies, *Foundations*, vol. 1, pt. 1, p. 187.

9. A. V. Chaianov, "Metody sostavleniia organizatsionnykh planov sel'sko-khoziaistvennykh predpriiatii v usloviiakh sovetskoi ekonomii," *Biulleten' Gosudarstvennogo Nauchno-Issledovatel'skogo Instituta Sel'sko-Khoziaistvennoi Ekonomii*, 1928, nos. 1-4, pp. 5-15.

10. The author recommended that sovkhoz plans be designed in relation both to regional targets set by planning authorities and to the criteria of profitability. One member of the audience, K. I. Naumov, criticized Chaianov for including criteria of profitability, which, he alleged, smacked of capitalist approaches to planning. Ibid., p. 14.

11. He had articulated that skepticism as late as 1925. For specific references, see chapter 4, note 50.

12. A. V. Chaianov, "Segodniashnii i zavtrashnii den' krupnogo zemledeliia," *Ekonomicheskoe obozrenie* (1929, no. 9), pp. 39-51.

13. Basile Kerblay, "A. V. Chayanov: Life, Career, Works," in *A. V. Chayanov on the Theory of Peasant Economy*, ed. Daniel Thorner, Basile Kerblay, and R. E. F. Smith (Homewood, Illinois, 1966), p. lxii.

14. For the relevant works by Makarov, see chapter 4, note 45.

15. A. V. Chaianov, "Vozmozhnoe budushchee sel'skogo khoziaistva," in *Zhizn' i tekhnika budushchego*, ed. A. Kolman (Moscow, 1928), pp. 260-285.

16. Ibid., p. 285. No note to this effect appeared after any of the other essays in the collection.

17. A. V. Chaianov [Ivan Kremnev], *Puteshestvie moego brata Alekseia v stranu krest'ianskoi utopii* (Moscow, 1920), pp. 27-37. The utopia, which was written by Chaianov under a pseudonym, depicted Russia in 1984 as a country in which proletarian power and urban culture had been destroyed by an irate peasantry. By the end of the 1920s, the book had become a rarity in Russia. This work has now been translated. See Ivan Kremnev [A. V. Chaianov], "The Journey of My Brother Alexei to the Land of Peasant Utopia," *Journal of Peasant Studies* 4, no. 1 (October 1976): 63-117.

18. A. N. Chelintsev, "K voprosu o predmete, zadachakh, i metodakh organizatsii sel'skogo khoziaistva," *PSKh*, 1928, no. 9, pp. 12-21, A. N. Chelintsev, "O printsipakh stroitel'stva i proizvodstvennykh tipov kolkhozov," *PSKh*, 1928, no. 11, pp. 22-38.

19. Chelintsev, "O printsipakh."

20. A. N. Chelintsev, "K teorii organizatsii sel'skogo khoziaistva massy krest'ianskikh khoziaistv," *PSKh*, 1928, no. 8, pp. 23-32.

21. For the precise content of Chelintsev's criticisms of the theory he had once espoused, see chapter 10.

22. Chelintsev, "K teorii," p. 27.

23. M. Sulkovskii, "Evoliutsiia i raspad neonarodnichestva," *NAF*, 1929, nos. 11-13, pp. 76-97. Sulkovskii's interpretation was repeated by Kerblay. See Kerblay, "A. V. Chayanov: Life, Career, Works," p. lxix.

24. Present and participating were L. N. Kritsman, I. Vermenichev, K. Naumov, A. Gaister, Ia. Anisimov, and G. Raevich. The guests included N. N. Sukhanov, the non-Party Marxist; V. S. Nemchinov, the Marxist statistician; S. M. Dubrovskii, the Deputy Director of the International Agrarian Institute; and Vinogradov, about whom little is known.

25. L. N. Kritsman, "Klassovye gruppirovki krest'ianskikh khoziaistv," *NAF*, 1928, no. 4, pp. 114-135. This speech was followed by discussion. See "Diskussiia o klassovykh gruppirovkakh krest'ianskikh khoziaistv v Komakademii," pt. 1, *NAF*, 1928, no. 5, pp. 124-146; pt. 2, *NAF*, 1928, nos. 6-7, pp.

178-201; pt. 3, *NAF*, 1928, no. 8, pp. 102-110.

26. Kritsman, "Klassovye gruppirovki," p. 114.

27. Kritsman claimed that the grouping according to the amount of arable land gave a deceptive picture of peasant social structure; it tended to show a swollen central group and shrunken polar groups. As evidence, Kritsman referred to a study of pre-Revolutionary Russian peasantry, which appeared as *Materialy po istorii agrarnoi revoliutsii v Rossii* (Moscow, 1928). The study showed that even for the period 1911-1917 (before the land redistribution), the arable land index gave evidence of a more leveled countryside than did the combined index of inventory and herds applied to the same sample of farms for the same period. Kristman, "Klassovye gruppirovki," pp. 121-125. Kritsman's relation to this study was not tangential; he was the editor of *Materialy* and an original member of the Commission that had undertaken the research. An interview in Moscow in 1969 with another member of that Commission yielded the information that this Commission was always referred to as "Kritsman's Commission." Interview with S. M. Dubrovskii, February 17, 1969.

28. Kritsman contended that the indicator of herds, while more reliable than that of arable land, did not show the true extent of proletarianization, for it did not account for many of the inverted social relations among the peasantry. Kritsman, "Klassovye gruppirovki," p. 132.

29. In Kritsman's view, of all the classifications by natural indicators, the one based on the value of the means of production (employed by Gaister in 1928) was the most reliable. Kritsman's judgment was grounded on the fact that the latter classification gave results that were closest to those obtained by using the socioeconomic typology.

30. Of the three studies, Kritsman preferred the Volokolamsk project and was most critical of Gaister's study. Kritsman, "Klassovye gruppirovki," pp. 134-135.

31. Dubrovskii was no stranger to the Agrarian-Marxists, having been Dean of the Economics Faculty at the Timiriazev Academy in 1924-1926, when many of them were doing their graduate work there. For Dubrovskii's biography, see appendix B.

32. These labels were used ambiguously throughout the 1920s. See Lewin, *Russian Peasants*, pp. 41-80.

33. "Diskussiia," pt. 1, pp. 125, 128-129.

34. Dubrovskii asked rhetorically whether every time *Narkomzem* gave complex machinery to a *seredniak*, it risked converting him into a kulak. Ibid., p. 129.

35. Ibid., p. 131. Kritsman's position would come under fire several times in the next two years.

36. To further legitimate this study, the Agrarian-Marxists reminded their audience that in 1899 Lenin himself had examined the extent to which peasants farmed their land with rented inventory and hired labor. "Diskussiia," pt. 2, p. 198.

37. Ibid., pp. 198, 186.

38. "Diskussiia," pt. 1, pp. 144, 146.

39. The support from the young researchers was emotional as well as intellectual. As Gaister put it, "It is good to err in good company." "Diskussiia," pt. 2, p. 200.

40. "Diskussiia," pt. 3, p. 109.

41. In the wake of the January attack, the Kritsman group continued its work as before. Throughout 1928 reports of that work appeared in the journals. For example, see K. Naumov and D. Shadrin, "Opyt postroeniia klassovoi gruppirovki krest'ianskikh khoziaistv," *NAF*, 1928, no. 4, pp. 10-33; M. Sulkovskii, "Opyt sotsial'no-klassovoi gruppirovki krest'ianskikh biudzhetov podsolnechnogo raiona," *NAF*, 1928, no. 5, pp. 52-63.

42. The first effort in this direction by a Marxist scholar occurred earlier in the same year. P. Liashchenko, "Predmet i metod sel'sko-khoziaistvennoi ekonomii," *NAF*, 1928, no. 2, pp. 11-27. This article was referred to repeatedly at the October conference.

43. The two keynote speakers at the conference, M. Sulkovskii and S. Uzhanskii, were members of the Kritsman group. The remaining participants were Marxists scholars with different institutional affiliations.

44. The keynote addresses were reported as M. Sulvoskii, "Predmet i metod sel'sko-khoziaistvennoi ekonomii," *NAF*, 1928, no. 12, pp. 36-48; S. Uzhanskii, "Sel'sko-khoziaistvennaia ekonomika kak akademicheskaia distsiplina," ibid., pp.

49-59. The two keynote speakers had worked on their presentations together but differed on important points, and thus each presented his views separately. The keynote speeches occasioned much comment, both at the October meeting and afterward. See G. Raevich, "K popytkam obosnovaniia teoreticheskoi sistemy sel'sko-khoziaistvennoi ekonomii," *NAF*, 1929, no. 1, pp. 14-20; Ia. Miroshkhin, "O predmete i metode sel'skokhoziaistvennoi ekonomii," *NAF*, 1929, no. 2, pp. 20-33; V. Ulasevich, "Predmet i metod sel'sko-khoziaistvennoi ekonomii," *NAF*, 1929, no. 4, pp. 64-81; E. Rudakova, "O predmete sel'skokhoziaistvennoi ekonomii," *NAF*, 1930, no. 10, pp. 70-91.

45. In the period 1925-1929, *Na agrarnom fronte* carried reviews of Russian and Western books on agricultural economics and occasional articles refuting non-Marxist treatments of such core concepts as rent, profit, and intensity.

46. In a preface to Laishchenko's article of February 1928, the editors of *Na agrarnom fronte* acknowledged the inexperience of Marxist scholars in this area. "Ot redaktsii," *NAF*, 1928, no. 2, p. 11.

47. The most coherent expression of this objection came from Sulkovskii. Sulkovskii, "Predmet i metod," p. 43. In its substance, this criticism was not new; much earlier in the decade it had been leveled by Kritsman against the Organization-Production scholars.

48. Ibid.

49. In his early article on agricultural economics, Liashchenko had attributed the practical orientation of that specialty to the fact that it was taught in specialized academies rather than in a university setting. Liashchenko, "Predmet," p. 12. It should be noted that not all the speakers at the October meeting shared the distaste for the practical orientation of agricultural economics. One participant warned lest the specialty become too far removed from agronomy. Miroshkhin, "O predmete," p. 31.

50. Sulkovskii, "Predmet i metod," p. 43.

51. The dissensus on this point is discussed in Ulasevich, "Predmet i metod," pp. 64-74.

52. Ibid., p. 64.

53. The decline of rural sociology is best documented in the work plans of the Agrarian Institute of the Communist Academy, once the bastion of the new specialty. In a report on the work of the Institute in the year 1928-1929, the activities of the Section on social stratification were featured. *Kratkii otchët o rabote Kommunisticheskoi Akademii za 1928-1929 gg.* (Moscow, 1929), p. 10. Just a year later, the work plan of the same Agrarian Institute listed the activities of the Section on social stratification in fourth place and indicated that the Institute's first task was the study of socialist cultivation. *Plan rabot Kommunisticheskoi Akademii na 1929/1930 god* (Moscow, 1930), pp. 19, 20.

54. The most notable achievement in this direction was the publication of the first Marxist textbook on agricultural economics in 1929. G. S. Gordeev, *Osnovnye problemy sel'sko-khoziaistvennoi ekonomii* (Moscow, 1929). A year later, that textbook was denounced as reflecting "Right-opportunistic" views.

Chapter 10

1. For the development of the Plan, see E. H. Carr and R. W. Davies, *Foundations of a Planned Economy*, 3 vols. (London, 1969), vol. 1, pt. 2, pp. 787-898.

2. The extent of the crisis is described in Moshe Lewin, *Russian Peasants and Soviet Power* (London, 1968), pp. 344-353. One Western scholar suspected that Stalin reported the figures in such a way that the crisis appeared worse than it was. Jerzy Karcz, "Second Thoughts on the Grain Crisis," *Soviet Studies* 23 (April 1967): 399-434.

3. As a consequence of the questioning, the non-Party experts were ejected from Gosplan.

4. This mandate is described in Sheila Fitzpatrick, "Cultural Revolution in Russia, 1928-1932," *Journal of Contemporary History* 9, no. 1 (1974): 47.

5. "Deiatel'nost' Kommunisticheskoi Akademii," *Vestnik Kommunisticheskoi Akademii*, no. 30 (1929), p. 252.

6. See the biography of Shefler, *PSKh*, 1928, no. 6, p. 113.

7. *Moskovskaia Sel'skokhoziaistvennaia Akademiia imieni Timiriazeva 1865-1965* (Moscow, 1969), p. 138.

8. "Vypiska iz protokola zasedaniia prezidiuma RANION o sliianii institutov sel'skokhoziaistvennoi ekonomii i zemleustroistva i pereseleniia," dated February 1, 1929, *Organizatsiia Sovetskoi nauki v 1926-1932 gg. Sbornik dokumentov* (Leningrad, 1974), p. 315.

9. A. N. Chelintsev, "K teorii organizatsii sel'skogo khoziaistva massy krest'ianskikh khoziaistv," p. 27.

10. Ibid., p. 26.

11. A. V. Chaianov, "Ot klassovoi krest'ianskoi kooperatsii k sotsialisticheskoi rekonstruktsii sel'skogo khoziaistva," *Sel'sko-khoziaistvennaia zhizn'*, February 15, 1929, pp. 2-3.

12. Ibid., p. 2. Later in the same year Chaianov tried to convince his readers that he had championed the cause of socialist agriculture as early as 1920.

13. "Ot redaktsii," *PSKh*, 1928, no. 8, p. 31.

14. "Ot redaktsii," *Sel'sko-khoziastvennaia zhizn'*, February 15, 1929, p. 30.

15. A. N. Chelintsev, "O printsipakh stroitel'stva i proizvodstvennykh tipov kolkhozov," *PSKh*, 1928, no. 11, pp. 22-38.

16. Chaianov, "Segodniashnii i zavtrashnii den' krupnogo zemledeliia," *Ekonomicheskoe obozrenie*, 1929, no. 9, p. 42. Only through self-collectivization, he insisted, could technological revolution be accomplished without a social catastrophe.

17. For an example of such criticism, see O. M. Targulian, "Kolkhoznoe stroitel'stvo po Chelintsevu i samo-kollektivizatsii po Chaianovu," *PSKh*, 1930, no. 9, pp. 8-25. For the biography of Targulian, see appendix D.

18. For a discussion of the effects on the conduct of science of claims to group-based truth, see Robert K. Merton, "Insiders and Outsiders: A Chapter in the Sociology of Knowledge," *American Journal of Sociology* 78, no. 1 (July, 1972).

19. N. P. Makarov, "Problema kul'turnoi revoliutsii v derevne i shkola krest'ianskoi molodezhi," *PSKh*, 1929, no. 5, pp. 103-111.

20. Chelintsev was the only leader of the Organization-Production School to have been renamed as a professor in the economics faculty of the Timiriazev Academy for the year

1929, "Khronika," *PSKh*, 1929, no. 4, p. 143. Calls for his dismissal from this post were heard in late 1929. For example, see the speech by Gordeev in *Trudy pervoi vsesoiuznoi konferentsii agrarnikov-Marksistov* (Moscow, 1930), pp. 99-100.
21. A. N. Chelintsev, "Zhivotnovodstva i kormovoi vopros," pt. 1, *PSKh*, 1929, no. 2, pp. 34-56; pt. 2, *PSKh*, 1929, no. 3, pp. 20-43; pt. 3, *PSKh*, 1929, no. 4, pp. 21-37.
22. Chaianov, "Segodniashnii i zavtrashnii"; A. V. Chaianov, "Tekhnicheskaia organizatsiia zernovykh fabrik," *Ekonomicheskoe obozrenie*, 1929, no. 12, pp. 95-101.
23. The exception to this rule was Chelintsev, who wrote an article that appeared as late as February of 1930. See A. N. Chelintsev, "Spetsializatsii sel'skogo khoziaistva po raionam SSSR," *Sotsialisticheskaia rekonstruktsiia i sel'skoe khoziaistvo*, 1930, no. 3, pp. 54-80.
24. The demise of this journal came rather suddenly. In the final issue in 1929, plans were announced for the first issue of 1930. That issue never appeared.
25. See *Kondrat'evshchina* (Moscow, 1930), the record of a conference called in October 1930 to discuss the Kondrat'ev group, whose membership was alleged to include leaders of the Organization-Production School; *Wreckers on Trial* (London, 1930), which is the record of the trial of the Industrial Party in November-December 1930; Naum Jasny, *Names to be Remembered* (Cambridge, 1972), p. 200. A recent book by a Soviet author provides more detailed information on the charges against the group. Apparently, this party was alleged to have nine underground groups in Moscow, centered primarily in the Commissariats of Agriculture and Finance, in the newspaper *Bednota*, in the Timiriazev Academy, and in research institutes on agricultural economics. Further networks were "uncovered" in the provinces, with Social Revolutionaries and kulaks being among the members. Total enrollment in the party was estimated at 100,000 to 200,000. See Roy A. Medvedev, *Let History Judge* (New York, 1971), pp. 113-114.
26. This was not the first time the Kritsman approach had been criticized. For the critique leveled fifteen months earlier, see chapter 9.
27. The conference was reported in some detail in the

journal of the Agrarian Institute of the Communist Academy. See "Analiz krest'ianskogo dvora," pt. 1, *NAF*, 1929, no. 7, pp. 96-106; pt. 2, *NAF*, 1929, no. 8, pp. 83-106.

28. "Analiz krest'ianskogo dvora," pt. 1, p. 97.

29. Ibid., pp. 100-101.

30. Kritsman's speech was based on Kubanin's study, yet the critics concentrated their attack on the speaker, not on the author. To be sure, this was in part due to the fact that Kubanin's study had not yet appeared in print when the conference met, although articles from the work had been published.

31. Objections against Kritsman's view of history were to intensify. In 1930 he was accused of having underrated the socialist aspects of the agrarian revolution and the *Kombedy* (Committee of Poor Peasants) movement. See Z. Liviant, "V osnovnom voprose revoliutsii nuzhna iasnost'," *NAF*, 1930, no. 4, pp. 88-95. Kritsman defended himself against these accusations. L. N. Kritsman, "O kharaktere nashei revoliutsii," *NAF*, 1930, no. 4, pp. 96-115.

32. This strong statement was made by Pavlov, the head of the Sector of State and Law, which had collected the original data for Kubanin's study. See "Analiz krest'ianskogo dvora," pt. 2, p. 84.

33. The "overemphasis on capitalism" was singled out by Pavlov, ibid., p. 85; by Ionov, ibid., p. 93; by Dubrovskii, ibid., p. 96; and by Raevich, ibid., p. 87.

34. For a prime example of such criticism, see the remarks by Dubrovskii, ibid., p. 97.

35. The point was made both by Gaister, ibid., pp. 91-92, and by Vermenichev, ibid., p. 99.

36. It was Sulkovskii who faced this issue head on. Ibid., p. 94.

37. Ibid., p. 103.

38. Ibid., pp. 104-106.

39. M. Sulkovskii, "Opyt postroenie programmy seminarskikh zaniatii po sel'sko-khoziaistvennoi ekonomii dlia sotsial'no-ekonomicheskikh vuzov," *NAF*, 1929, no. 10, pp. 146-155.

40. The full stenographic report of the conference was

published in 1930. *Trudy pervoi vsesoiuznoi konferentsii agrarnikov-Marksistov.* The keynote addresses and other important speeches were carried in the journal of the Communist Academy, *Vestnik Kommunisticheskoi Akademii,* and in the journal of its Agrarian Institute, *Na agrarnom fronte,* during 1930.

41. For the record of that conference, see *Trudy pervoi vsesoiuznoi konferentsii istorikov-Marksistov* (Moscow, 1929).

42. Only a small portion of the delegates spoke at the conference. For a list of the speakers, see *Trudy pervoi vsesoiuznoi konferentsii agrarnikov-Marksistov,* pp. 406-407.

43. *Plan rabot Kommunisticheskoi Akademii na 1929/1930 god* (Moscow, 1930), p. 19.

44. For a report of the pre-conference meeting held in the Urals, see "Pervaia ural'skaia oblastnaia konferentsiia Marksistov-agrarnikov," *NAF,* 1929, nos. 11-12, pp. 211-214; for the report of the analogous meeting held in Belorussia, see "Soveshchanie kommunistov-agrarnikov pro agitprope Tsk VKP (b) Belorussia," ibid., pp. 215-218; for the report on delegate selection in the Ukraine, see *Trudy pervoi vsesoiuznoi konferentsii agrarnikov-Marksistov,* pp. 104-107.

45. For the leadership of the new society, see *Trudy pervoi vsesoiuznoi konferentsii agrarnikov-Marksistov,* p. 430. The assumption by the Kritsman group of the leading roles in the society was hardly surprising, given the extent to which the members of the group dominated the planning of the conference. The Presidium of the December meeting included Kritsman, Gaister, Vermenichev, and Kubanin; the Secretariat included Sivogrivov; and the Mandate Commission included Sulkovskii. Ibid., p. 12.

46. For a good description of Stalin's *Pravda* article, see Lewin, *Russian Peasants,* pp. 455-456.

47. The irony of the timing of the decision to collectivize and the commission on implementation has been pointed out by a Western economic historian. See Alec Nove, *An Economic History of the USSR* (London, 1969), p. 164.

48. Most of the discussion of collectivization stemmed not from Kalinin's speech, but from the controversial speech given

by Iu. Larin, the economist. Larin claimed that the kolkhozy were not fully socialist forms of agriculture. For this he was roundly taken to task by many of the delegates.

49. For the disputes in the Belorussian republic, see the contributions of Pinchuk and Merezhin, *Trudy pervoi vsesoiuznoi konferentsii agrarnikov-Marksistov*, pp. 175-186 and 355-358. For the disputes in the Ukraine, see the speech of Lozovoi, ibid., pp. 104-107. For the dispute in Voronezh, see the remarks by Kuvshinov, ibid., pp. 141-145. For the incidents in Leningrad, see the speeches given by Alekseev, Ignat'eva, and Dektiarev, ibid., pp. 155-162, 347-353, 358-361.

50. The extent to which Dubrovskii's views were similar to those of other members of his Institute is not known.

51. Under the heading "bourgeois" scholars, Miliutin listed Litoshenko, Kondrat'ev, and Vainshtein, the planner and economist. Under the rubric "neo-narodnik" only Chelintsev and Chaianov were mentioned by name. *Trudy pervoi vsesoiuznoi konferentsii agrarnikov-Marksistov*, p. 25. Under Left and Right deviationists, Trotsky, Preobrazhenskii, and Bukharin were cited by name. Ibid.

52. Dubrovskii underscored his institutional affiliation at the 1929 conference. The reasons for his expression of loyalty remain obscure. He had been the deputy director of the International Agrarian Institue since 1925 and simultaneously a member of the editorial board of *Na agrarnom fronte*, the journal of the Agrarian Institute. In the December 1929 issue of the journal, Dubrovskii's name was mysteriously dropped from the board. This raises the possibility that his relations with the Agrarian Institute had reached an impasse, leaving him no base other than the International Agrarian Institute.

53. For the accusation that Dubrovskii was a member of the Right deviation, see *Trudy pervoi vsesoiuznoi konferentsii agrarnikov-Marksistov*, p. 121. For the charge that Dubrovskii held a position similar to that of Chaianov, see ibid., pp. 171, 230-231; for the statement that Dubrovskii had not accorded sufficient priority to industrialization, see ibid., p. 120.

54. Ibid., pp. 230-231. Vermenichev linked Dubrovskii to Sukhanov and termed both "destroyers of Leninist thought."

55. In an interview given forty years after the conference, Dubrovskii explained the logic behind such preemptive attacks. The political climate of the time, he claimed, made it mandatory to prove one's orthodoxy—a necessity that often led scholars to accuse their rivals of deviance in order to avoid similar attacks on their own views. Interview, April 3, 1969.

56. As evidence of this insensitivity, Dubrovskii pointed to a book written by Kritsman in 1926, one in which the author had failed to call for all-out war against the kulak. *Trudy pervoi vsesoiuznoi konferentsii agrarnikov-Marksistov*, p. 322.

57. Dubrovskii's own approach to classification was crude. He insisted that before one could discern a peasant's social class, one had to know in advance what sort of peasant it was who was borrowing or lending land or inventory. Ibid., p. 324. This was tantamount to saying that class analysis was a prerequisite to the analysis of peasants by class.

58. Ibid., p 325. For a contemporary discussion of the problems of identifying kulaks, see Moshe Lewin, "Who was the Soviet Kulak?" *Soviet Studies* 18, no. 2 (1966): 189-212.

59. *Trudy pervoi vsesoiuznoi konferentsii agrarnikov-Marksistov*, p. 323. On this point, Dubrovskii contended, Kritsman resembled Menshevik thinkers.

60. Ibid., p. 317.

61. In the attempt to exonerate himself, Dubrovskii had submitted a series of documents, which were reprinted in the stenographic report of the conference. Ibid., pp. 315-316.

62. Dubrovskii was supported primarily by Ignat'eva from Leningrad. This was plainly a case of war making strange bedfellows. Apparently, Ignat'eva had worked under the well-known professor Kazhanov in Leningrad. Kazhanov was attacked by Sulkovskii for having espoused a view close to that of the "neo-narodniks" and as a consequence lost his position. In retaliation for the destruction of her superior by a member of the Kritsman group, Ignat'eva joined Dubrovskii.

63. Kritsman's illness was announced at the beginning of the four-day conference. See *Trudy pervoi vsesoiuznoi konferentsii agrarnikov-Marksistov*, p. 12. While Dubrovskii announced that he did not want to take unfair advantage of Kritsman's absence, there is no question that Kritsman's illness

provided him with a considerable psychological advantage.
64. Ibid., p. 373. Of course, Kritsman's position was based on Kubanin's research, a fact not raised by Kubanin at this point, probably because he himself had come under attack earlier in the conference and now preferred to hide behind Kritsman.

65. Ibid., pp. 373-374.

66. Gaister associated himself rather than Kritsman with this question of history, although it was known to all that the notion of the agrarian revolution as petit bourgeois had originated with Kritsman. Ibid., p. 403. Gaister's bravery may be explained by the fact that, unlike Kubanin, he felt reasonably secure at the December meeting.

67. Ibid.

68. See, for example, the denial by Kubanin, ibid., p. 365; and that by Gaister, ibid., p. 405.

69. Ibid., pp. 417-426.

70. Ibid., pp. 422-424.

71. Ibid.

72. Ibid., p. 430.

73. Ibid., p. 465. The resolution did say that not all members of the Institue were orthodox in their views, but no individuals were singled out as deviant.

74. Ibid., p. 355. This suggestion was made by Chakhvadze, who claimed that a polemicist such as Dubrovskii was not fit to be deputy director of the International Agrarian Institute.

75. Ibid., p. 246. Gaister suggested the censure because Dubrovskii's institute had published Studenskii's work on German agriculture.

76. The only coverage of Stalin's appearance in an English work is in Lewin, *Russian Peasants*, pp. 476-477. This is preceded by an informative chapter in which Lewin examines the reasoning that led Stalin to deliver his December speech. See Ibid., pp. 446-477.

77. *Trudy pervoi vsesoiuznoi konferentsii agrarnikov-Marksistov*, p. 434.

78. First, he denounced the "theory of balance," according to which both sectors had to develop evenly. Ibid., pp. 434-436. Second, he criticized the theory of spontaneous development.

Ibid., pp. 436-437. Third, he scored the theory of the persistence of the small-scale farm. Ibid., pp. 437-441. Fourth, he castigated those theorists who maintained that the peasants had not gained by the October Revolution. Ibid., pp. 441-444. Finally, he launched a critique against those who maintained that the kolkhozy were not socialist in character. Ibid., pp. 444-446.

79. Ibid., pp. 446-448.

80. Interview with S. M. Dubrovskii, May 6, 1969.

81. "Opyt postroeniia programmy seminarskikh zaniatii." Sulkovskii had prepared this syllabus as part of the discussion on agricultural economics held in the Communist Academy's Agrarian Institute in October 1928.

82. "Programma po sel'skokhoziaistvennoi ekonomii," *NAF*, 1930, nos. 11-12, pp. 160-173.

83. For the stenographic record of the 1930 conference, see "Obzor vsesoiuznogo soveshchaniia rukovoditelei kafedr sel'skokhoziaistvennoi ekonomii," *NAF*, 1930, nos. 11-12, pp. 108-160. It appears that Uzhanskii, the keynote speaker at this meeting, had been responsible for the preparation of the new syllabus. For his analysis of the new period in rural inquiry, see ibid., p. 109.

84. See "V redaktsiiu zhurnala "NAF'," *NAF*, 1930, no. 10, pp. 146-147, for the recantation of Sulkovskii.

85. "O rabote agrarnogo instituta Komakademii," *NAF*, 1930, no. 10, p. 113. Apparently the works of Gaister, Sulkovskii, and Kubanin were slated for scrutiny at the same session.

86. "Ot redaktsii," *NAF*, 1932, no. 1, p. 4.

87. For the biographies of some of the most important and vocal members of this new group, see appendix D.

88. There had always been some grumbling among undergraduates enrolled in the Timiriazev Academy, but until the end of 1929 that grumbling had been sporadic and mild in tone.

89. For example, the Communist University of the Workers of China was the base of two members of the new group.

90. Some of this group hailed from the Timiriazev Academy. In general, the "scholars" who fitted under this category were not major luminaries, but men of second rank. They may have joined the new group because of opportunistic motives or

out of fear of being attacked for heterodox opinions.

Chapter 11

1. The extent to which behavior can be conditioned by the anticipation of developments was discussed in Samuel Stouffer et al., *The American Soldier*, vol. 1, *Adjustment During Army Life* (Princeton, N.J., 1949), p. 411.
2. The extent of that open-endedness was discussed in chapter 2.
3. Sheila Fitzpatrick, "Cultural Revolution as Class War," in *Cultural Revolution in Russia, 1928-1931*, ed. Sheila Fitzpatrick (Bloomington, Indiana, 1977).
4. Joravsky termed the men of the new generation "Bolshevizers." David Joravsky, *Soviet Marxism and Natural Science, 1917-1932* (New York, 1961), pp. 250-271.
5. Moshe Lewin has made a most persuasive argument to the effect that the potential of NEP in economics was not fully mined. See Moshe Lewin, "The Immediate Background of Soviet Collectivization," *Soviet Studies* 17 (October 1965): 162-197.
6. For the extent to which Soviet economic reformers today are drawing upon the NEP premises, see Moshe Lewin, *Political Undercurrents in Soviet Economic Debates* (Princeton, N.J., 1974).

Appendix A

1. Naum Jasny, *Names to be Remembered* (Cambridge, 1972), pp. 200-203; Basile Kerblay, "A. V. Chaianov: Life, Career, Works," in *The Theory of Peasant Economy*, ed. Daniel Thorner, Basile Kerblay, and R. E. F. Smith (Homewood, Illinois, 1966); interview with S. M. Dubrovskii, May 1969, Moscow; *Nauchnye rabotniki Moskvy* (Leningrad, 1930), p. 307.
2. Jasny, *Names to be Remembered*, pp. 197-200; J. A. Newth, "Some Economic Controllers—III," *Soviet Studies* 12 (1960-1961): 290; interview with S. M. Dubrovskii, 1969, Moscow; *Biulleten' Gosudarstvennogo Nauchno-Issledovatel'skogo Instituta Sel'sko-Khoziaistvennoi Ekonomii*, 1928, no. 4, pp. 126-127; *Nauchnye rabotniki Moskvy*, p. 174.

3. Jasny, *Names to be Remembered*, pp. 203-204; *Biulleten' Gosudarstvennogo Nauchno-Issledovatel'skogo Instituta Sel'sko-Khoziaistvennoi Ekonomii*, 1928, no. 4, pp. 127, 135; interview with S. M. Dubrovskii, 1969, Moscow.

4. Interview with S. M. Dubrovskii, 1969, Moscow; *Biulleten' Gosudarsvennogo Nauchno-Issledovatel'skogo Instituta Sel'sko-Khoziaistvennoi Ekonomii*, 1927, nos. 1-2, p. 62; *Nauka i nauchnye rabotniki v SSSR* (Leningrad, 1928), p. 408.

5. *Biulleten' Gosudarstvennogo Nauchno-Issledovatel'-skogo Instituta Sel'sko-Khoziaistvennoi Ekonomii*, 1928, no. 4, pp. 127, 135.

6. A. V. Chaianov, "Peasant Farm Organization," in Thorner, Kerblay, and Smith, *Theory of Peasant Economy*, p. 35; *Biulleten' Gosudarstvennogo Nauchno-Issledovatel'skogo Instituta Sel'sko-Khoziaistvennoi Ekonomii*, 1927, nos. 1-2, p. 62; *Trudy vsesoiuznoi konferentsii agrarnikov-Marksistov*, vol. 1 (Moscow, 1930), p. 144.

Appendix B

1. Interview with S. M. Dubrovskii, 1969, Moscow; E. H. Carr, *The Bolshevik Revolution*, 3 vols. (London, 1952) 2: 376-378; *Vestnik Kommunisticheskoi Akademii*, no. 150 (1930), p. 161; *Nauchnye rabotniki Moskvy* (Leningrad, 1930), p. 147.

2. Interview with S. M. Dubrovskii, 1969, Moscow; *Vestnik Kommunisticheskoi Akademii*, no. 33 (1929), p. 271.

3. Interview with S. M. Dubrovskii, 1969, Moscow; *Vestnik Kommunisticheskoi Akademii*, no. 30 (1929), p. 252.

4. Interview with S. M. Dubrovskii, 1969, Moscow; *Biulleten' Gosudarstvennogo Nauchno-Issledovatel'skogo Instituta Sel'sko-Khoziaistvannoi Ekonomii*, 1927, nos. 1-2, p. 62.

5. Ibid.

6. *Biulleten' Gosudarstvennogo Nauchno-Issledovatel'-skogo Instituta Sel'sko-Khoziaistvennoi Ekonomii*, 1927, nos. 1-2, p. 62; *Nauchnye rabotniki Moskvy*, p. 9.

7. *Biulleten' Gosudarstvennogo Nauchno-Issledovatel'-skogo Instituta Sel'sko-Khoziaistvennoi Ekonomii*, 1927, nos. 1-2, p. 62; *Nauchnye rabotniki Moskvy*, p. 196.

8. Interview with S. M. Dubrovskii, 1969, Moscow.

9. Interview with S. M. Dubrovskii, 1969, Moscow; *Vopro-

sy istorii, no. 1 (1971): 218.
10. *Bol'shaia Sovetskaia Entsiklopediia*, 2d ed. (Moscow, 1954) 29: 414-415.

Appendix D

1. *Nauchnye rabotniki Moskvy* (Leningrad, 1930), p. 277.
2. Ibid., p. 287.
3. Ibid., p. 157.
4. Ibid., p. 79.
5. Ibid., p. 258.
6. Ibid., p. 163.
7. Ibid., p. 70.

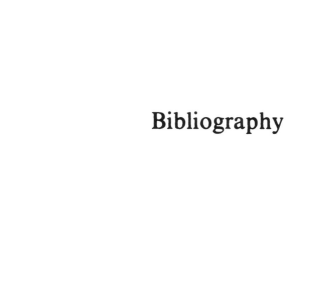

Bibliography

Bibliography

The following abbreviations have been used in citing journals: *NAF* for *Na agrarnom fronte*, *PSKh* for *Puti sel'skogo khoziaistva*, and *VKA* for *Vestnik Kommunisticheskoi akademii*.

Soviet Sources

Periodicals

Agrarnye problemy, 1927-1930.
Biulleten' Gosudarstvennogo Naucho-Issledovatel'skogo Instituta Sel'sko-Khoziaistvennoi Ekonomii, 1927-1928.
Ekonomicheskoe obozrenie, 1923-1930.
Na agrarnom fronte, 1925-1932.
Planovoe khoziaistvo, 1923-1930.
Puti sel'skogo khoziaistva, 1925-1930.
Sel'skoe i lesnoe khoziaistvo, 1921-1924.
Sotsialisticheskaia rekonstruktsiia i sel'skoe khoziaistvo, 1930-1932.
Uspekhi agronomii, 1925.
Vestnik Kommunisticheskoi akademii, 1924-1931.
Vestnik Sotsialisticheskoi akademii, 1922-1923.
Vestnik statistiki, 1925-1929.
Zapiski Leningradskogo Sel'sko-Khoziaistvennogo Instituta, 1924.

Writings of the Organization-Production School

Chaianov, A. V. [Tchayanov]. "Agricultural Economics in Russia." *Journal of Farm Economics* 10 (October 1928):543-549.

———. *Biudzhetnye issledovaniia: istoriia i metody.* Moscow, 1929.

———. *Biudzhety krest'ian Starobel'skago uezda.* Moscow, 1915.

———. [Tchayanoff]. "L'Etat actual de l'économie et de la statistique agricole en Russie." *Revue d'économie politique* 42 (January-February 1928): 82-96.

———. [Ivan Kremnev]. "The Journey of My Brother Alexei to the Land of Peasant Utopia." *Journal of Peasant Studies* 4, no. 1 (October 1976): 63-117.

———. *Kak organizirovat' krest'ianskoe khoziaistvo v nechernozemnoi polose.* Moscow, 1925.

———. *Kratkii kurs kooperatsii.* Moscow, 1915.

———. *Krest'ianskoe svekloseianie tsentral'no-chernozemnoi oblasti.* Moscow, 1929.

———. *Lën i drugie kul'tury v organizatsionnom plane krest'ianskogo khoziaistva nechernozemnoi Rossii.* 2 vols. Vol. 1 (Moscow, 1912). Vol. 2 (Moscow, 1913).

———. "Metody bezdenezhnogo ucheta khoziaistvennykh predpriiatii." *Trudy vysshego seminariia sel'sko-khoziaistvennoi ekonomiki i politiki pri Petrovskoi Sel'sko-khoziaistvennoi Akademii.* No. 2 (Moscow, 1921).

———. "Metody sostavleniia organizatsionnykh planov sel'sko-khoziaistvennykh predpriiatii v usloviiakh sovetskoi ekonomii." *Biull'eten' Gosudarstvennogo Nauchno-issledovatel'skogo Instituta Sel'sko-khoziaistvennoi Ekonomii,* 1928, nos. 1-4, pp. 5-15.

———. *Nomograficheskie elementy ekonomicheskoi geografii.* Moscow, 1921.

———. "O differentsiatsii krest'ianskogo khoziaistva." *PSKh,* 1927, no. 5, pp. 109-122.

———. *Ocherki po ekonomike trudovogo sel'skogo khoziaistva.* Moscow, 1924.

———. *Ocherki po teorii trudovogo khoziaistva.* Moscow, 1912-1913.

―――. "On the Theory of Non-Capitalist Economic Systems." In *A. V. Chayanov on the Theory of Peasant Economy*, edited by Daniel Thorner, Basile Kerblay, and R. E. F. Smith. Homewood, Illinois, 1966.

―――. *Optimal'nye razmery sel'skokhoziaistvennykh predpriiatii*. 3rd ed. rev. Moscow, 1928.

―――. "Optimal'nye razmery zemledel'cheskikh khoziaistv." *Problemy zemleustroistva, optimal'nye razmery zemledel'cheskogo khoziaistva, kolichestvennyi uchet effekta zemleustroistva*. Moscow, 1922.

―――. "Opyty izucheniia izolirovannogo gosudarstva." *Trudy vysshego seminariia sel'sko-khoziaistvennoi ekonomii i politiki*. No. 1 (Moscow, 1921).

―――. *Opyt razrabotki biudzhetnykh dannykh po sto odnomu khoziaistvu Starobel'skago uezda Khar'kovskoi gubernii*. Moscow, 1915.

―――. *Organizatsiia krest'ianskogo khoziaistva*. Moscow, 1925.

―――. *Osnovnye idei i formy krest'ianskoi kooperatsii*. Moscow, 1919.

―――. *Osnovnye idei i formy organizatsii sel'skokhoziaistvennoi kooperatsii*. Moscow, 1927.

―――. *Osnovnye idei i metody raboty obshchestvennoi agronomii*. Moscow, 1918.

―――. "Ot klassovoi krest'ianskoi kooperatsii k sotsialisticheskoi rekonstruktsii sel'skogo khoziaistva." *Sel'skokhoziaistvennaia zhizn'*. February 15, 1929.

―――. "Peasant Farm Organization." In *A. V. Chayanov on the Theory of Peasant Economy*, edited by Daniel Thorner, Basile Kerblay, and R. E. F. Smith. Homewood, Illinois, 1966.

―――. *Petrovsko-Razumovskoe v ego proshlom i nastoiashchem; putevoditel' po Timiriazevskoi sel'sko-khoziaistvennoi akademii*. Moscow, 1925.

―――. "Poniatie vygodnosti sotsialisticheskogo khoziaistva." In *Metody bezdenezhnogo ucheta khoziaistvennykh predpriiatii*. Moscow, 1921.

―――. "Potreblenie i proizvodstvo sel'skokhoziaistvennykh produktov vo Frantsii." 2 pts. *Agronomicheskii Zhurnal*,

1913, no. 1, pp. 20-55; and *Agronomicheskii Zhurnal*, 1913, no. 5, pp. 21-44.

————. *Putshestvie moego brata Alekseia v stranu krest'ianskoi utopii.* Moscow, 1921.

————. *Sebestoimost' sakharnoi svekly.* Moscow, 1928.

————. "Segodniashnii i zavtrashnii den' krupnogo zemledeliia." *Ekonomicheskoe obozrenie*, 1929, no. 9, pp. 39-50.

————. "Vozmozhnoe budushchee sel'skogo khoziaistva." In *Zhizn' i tekhnika budushchego*, edited by A. Kolman. Moscow, 1928.

————, and Studenskii, G. A. *Istoriia biudzhetnykh issledovanii.* 2nd and enlarged ed. Moscow, 1922.

Chelintsev, A. N. *Est'-li zemel'naia renta v krest'ianskom khoziaistve?* Kharkov, 1918.

————. "K metodologii sel'skokhoziaistvennogo mikroraionirovaniia." *PSKh*, 1928, nos. 4-5, pp. 26-45.

————. "K teorii organizatsii sel'skogo khoziaistva massy krest'ianskikh khoziaistv." *PSKh*, 1928, no. 8, pp. 23-32.

————. "K voprosu o differentsiatsii krest'ianskogo khoziaistva." *PSKh*, 1927, no. 4, pp. 114-132.

————. "K voprosu o predmete, zadachakh, i metodakh organizatsii sel'skogo khoziaistva." *PSKh*, 1928, no. 9, pp. 12-21.

————. "O printsipakh stroitel'stva i proizvodstvennykh tipov kolkhozov." *PSKh*, 1928, no. 11, pp. 22-38.

————. "Ocherki po sel'sko-khoziaistvennoi ekonomii." *Sel'skoe khoziaistvo i lesovodstvo*, no. 134 (October 1910), pp. 251-286.

————. *Opyt izucheniia organizatsii krest'ianskogo sel'skogo khoziaistva na primere Tambovskoi gubernii.* Kharkov, 1919.

————. *Russkoe sel'skoe khoziaistvo pered revoliutsii.* Moscow, 1928.

————. *Sel'sko-khoziaistvennye raiony evropeiskoi Rossii kak stadii sel'sko-khoziaistvennoi evoliutsii i kul'turnyi uroven' sel'skogo khoziaistva v nikh.* Moscow, 1911.

————. "Sel'skokhoziaistvennye raiony, poraionnye perspektivy sel'skogo khoziaistva, i napravlenie meropriiatii sel'skokhziaistvennoi politiki." *PSKh*, 1927, no. 9, pp. 35-57.

———. *Sostoianie i razvitie russkogo sel'skogo khoziaistva po dannym sel'sko-khoziaistvennoi perepisi 1916 goda i zhelezno-dorozhnykh perevozok.* Moscow, 1918.

———. "Spetsializatsiia sel'skogo khoziaistva po raionam SSSR." *Sotsialisticheskaia rekonstruktsiia i sel'skoe khoziaistvo*, 1930, no. 2, pp. 54-80.

———. *Teoreticheskie obosnovaniia organizatsii krest'ianskogo khoziaistva.* Kharkov, 1919.

———. *Uchastkovaia agronomiia i schetovodnyi analiz krest'ianskogo sel'skogo khoziaistva.* Samara, 1914.

———. "Zhivotnovodstva i kormovoi vopros." 3 pts. *PSKh*, 1929, no. 2, pp. 35-56; *PSKh*, 1929, no. 3, pp. 20-43; *PSKh*, 1929, no. 4, pp. 21-37.

Makarov, N. P. "Differentsiatsiia krest'ianskogo khoziaistva." *PSKh*, 1927, no. 4, pp. 103-113.

———. *Kak Amerikanskie fermery organizuiut svoe khoziaistvo.* Moscow, 1921.

———. *Krest'ianskoe khoziaitsvo i ego evoliutsiia.* Vol. 1. Moscow, 1920.

———. *Organizatsiia sel'skogo khoziaistva.* Berlin, 1924.

———. *Organizatsiia sel'skogo khoziaistva.* Moscow, 1925.

———. "Problema intensivnosti v sel'skom khoziaistve." *Biulleten' Gosudarstvennogo Nauchno-Issledovatel'skogo Instituta Sel'sko-Khoziaistvennoi Ekonomii*, 1927, nos. 1-2, pp. 11-34.

———. "Problema kul'turnoi revoliutsii v derevne i shkola krest'ianskoi molodezhi." *PSKh*, 1929, no. 5, pp. 103-111.

———. *Usloviia i predely primeneniia traktorov v sel'skom khoziaistve.* Moscow, 1922.

"Sbornik statei po voprosam sel'sko-khoziaistvennogo raionirovaniia i ekonomicheskoi geografii." *Trudy Vysshego Seminariia sel'sko-khoziaistvennoi ekonomii i politiki pri Petrovskoi Sel'sko-khoziaistvennoi Akademii.* No. 1. Moscow, 1921.

Studenskii, G. A. *Intensivnost' i psevdointensivnost' v krest'ianskom khoiziastve.* Samara, 1927.

———. *K. voprosu ob opredelenii i izmerenii intensivnosti*

sel'skogo khoziaistva. Samara, 1926.

————. *Ocherki po teorii krest'ianskogo khoziaistva.* Moscow, 1923.

————. *Ocherki sel'skokhoziaistvennoi ekonomii.* Moscow, 1925.

————. *Opyt issledovaniia organizatsii krest'ianskogo khoziaistva tsentral'no-chernozemnoi oblasti.* Moscow, 1926.

————. *Organizatsiia krupnykh sel'sko-khoziaistvennykh predpriiatii v Germanii.* Moscow, 1929.

————. *Osnovnye voprosy metodiki biudzhetnykh i schetovodnykh issledovanii.* Samara, 1929.

————. *Problemy organizatsii krest'ianskogo sel'skogo khoziaistva.* Samara, 1927.

————. *Renta v krest'ianskom khoziaistve i printsipy ego oblozheniia.* Moscow, 1925.

————. *Tekhnicheskii perevorot v Amerikanskom sel'skom khoziaistve.* Samara, 1930.

Agrarian-Marxist Writing

"Analiz krest'ianskogo dvora." Two parts. *NAF* (1929, No. 7), pp. 96-106; and *NAF* (1929, No. 8), pp. 83-106.

Anisimov, Ia. A. "Differentsiatsiia krest'ianskogo khoziaistva." *PSKh* (1927, No. 6), pp. 126-128.

————. "K postanovke nekotorykh voprosov ob organizatsii sel'skogo khoziaistva primenitel'no k usloviiam SSSR." *PSKh* (1928, No. 4-5), pp. 16-26.

————. "Osnovnye polozhenii organizatsionno-proizvodstvennoi shkoly v uchenie ob organizatsii krest'ianskogo khoziaistva." *PSKh* (1928, No. 2), pp. 3-15.

————. "Postanovka nekotorykh voprosov ob organizatsii sel'skogo khoziaistva v proshlom." *PSKh* (1928, No. 1), pp. 3-17.

————, Vermenichev, I., and Naumov, K., *Proizvodstvennaia kharakteristika krest'ianskikh khoziaistv razlichnykh sotsial'nykh grupp.* Moscow, 1927.

"Diskussiia o klassovykh gruppirovkakh krest'ianskikh khoziaistv v Komakademii." 3 parts. *NAF*, 1928, no. 5, pp. 123-146; *NAF*, 1928, no. 6-7, pp. 178-201; and *NAF*, 1928, no. 8, pp. 102-110.

Gaister, A. "Itogi vsesoiuznoi konferentsii agrarnikov-Marksistov." *NAF*, no. 1, pp. 17-36.

———. *Rassloenie Sovetskoi derevni*. Moscow, 1928.

Gordeev, G. S. *Osnovnye problemy sel'sko-khoziaistvennoi ekonomii*. Moscow, 1929.

———. "Uchenie ob intensivnom i ekstensivnom sel'skom khoziaistve." *NAF*, 1928, no. 3, pp. 34-52.

Iakushkin, I. V., ed. *Vysshaia Sel'skokhoziaistvennaia Shkola v SSSR*. Moscow, 1948.

Kritsman, L. N. "Desiat' let na agrarnom fronte proletarskoi revoliutsii." In Kritsman, *Proletarskaia revoliutsiia i derevnia*. Moscow, 1929.

———. *Geroicheskii period velikoi russkoi revoliutsii*. Moscow, 1925.

———. "K voprosu o klassovom rassloenii sovremennoi derevni." 4 parts. *NAF*, 1925, no. 2, pp. 47-55; *NAF*, 1925, nos. 7-8, pp. 3-37; and *NAF*, 1925, no. 9, pp. 23-32; and *NAF*, 1925, no. 10, pp. 2-46.

———. "Lenin i put' k sotsializmu." In Kritsman, *Proletarskaia revoliutsiia i derevnia*. Moscow, 1929.

———. "O kharaktere nashei revoliutsii." *NAF*, 1930, no. 4, pp. 96-114.

———. *Klassovaia struktura sovetskoi derevni i eë izucheniia*. Moscow, 1926. Reprinted in *Proletarskaia revoliutsiia i derevnia*. Moscow, 1929.

———. "Klassovye gruppirovki krest'ianskikh khoziaistv." *NAF*, 1928, no. 4, pp. 114-144. Reprinted in Kritsman, *Proletarskaia revoliutsiia i derevnia*. Moscow, 1929.

———. *Klassovoe rassloenie v sovetskoi derevni (po dannym volostnykh obsledovanii)*. Moscow, 1926. Reprinted in Kritsman, *Proletarskaia revoliutsiia i derevnia*. Moscow, 1929.

———. "Novyi etap." *Osnovnye nachala zemlepol'zovaniia i zemleustroistva*. Moscow, 1927. Reprinted in Kritsman, *Proletarskaia revoliutsiia i derevnia*. Moscow, 1929.

———. "O statisticheskom izuchenii klassovoi struktury Sovetskoi derevni." 4 parts. *NAF*, 1926, no. 2, pp. 3-10; *NAF*, 1927, no. 7, pp. 3-22; *NAF*, 1927, nos. 8-9, pp. 3-17; and *NAF*, 1927, no. 10, pp. 3-17. All four parts were reprinted in Kritsman, *Proletarskaia revoliutsiia i derev-nia.* Moscow, 1929.

———. "Ot tiagi k zemle k tiage k rynku." *Sotsialisticheskoe khoziaistvo*, 1923, nos. 4-5. Reprinted in Kritsman, *Proletarskaia revoliutsiia i derevnia.* Moscow, 1929.

———. *Proletarskaia revoliutsiia i derevnia.* Moscow, 1929.

———. Review of Chaianov, *Optimal'nye razmery selskokhoziaistvennykh predpriiatii*, in *VKA*, no. 3 (1932), pp. 401-407. Reprinted as "Krupnoe i melkoe khoziaistvo v zemledelii," in Kritsman, *Proletarskaia revoliutsiia i derevnia.* Moscow, 1929.

———. "Soiuz proletariata i bol'shinstva krest'ianstva v SSSR posle pobedy revoliutsii." Kritsman, *Proletarskaia revoliutsiia i derevnia.* Moscow, 1929.

———. "Sovremennaia melkoburzhuaznaia politicheskaia ekonomiia." Kritsman, *Proletarskaia revoliutsiia i derevnia.* Moscow, 1929. Originally published as a foreword to A. V. Chaianov, *Ocherki po teorii trudovogo krest'ianskogo khoziaistv.* Moscow, 1923.

———, ed. *Materialy po istorii agrarnoi revoliutsii v Rossii.* Moscow, 1928.

Kubanin, M. *Klassovaia sushchnost' protsessa drobleniia krest'ianskikh khoziaistv.* Moscow, 1929.

———. "Sotsial'no-ekonomicheskaia sushchnost' problemy drobimosti." *NAF*, 1928, no. 1, pp. 10-32.

———. "Sotsial'no-ekonomicheskaia sushchnost' problemy drobleniia krest'ianskikh khoziaistv." 2 pts. *NAF*, 1928, no. 8, pp. 10-32; and *NAF*, 1928, no. 11, pp.7-27.

Lubiako, V., and Naumov, K. "K voprosu o postroenii organizatsionnykh planov sovkhozov." *PSKh*, 1927, no. 12, pp. 3-8.

Naumov, K., and Shadrin, D. "Opyt postroeniia klassovoi gruppirovki krest'ianskikh khoziaistv." *NAF*, 1928, no. 4, pp. 10-33.

Raevich, G. "K issledovaniiu krest'ianskogo dokhoda." 3 parts. *NAF*, 1926, no. 3, pp. 3-17; *NAF*, 1926, nos. 5-6, pp. 5-15; and *NAF*, 1928, no. 1, pp. 40-49.

———. "K popytkam obosnovaniia teoreticheskoi sistemy sel'sko-khoziaistvennoi ekonomii. *NAF*, 1929, no. 1, pp.

14-20.
———. "K voprosu o priemakh izucheniia sotsial'no-ekonomicheskikh tipov sovremennoi derevni." *Vestnik statistiki*, 1927, no. 1, pp. 104-113.
———. "Teoriia krest'ianskogo khoziaistva i poniatia 'rabotnik.'" *NAF*, 1925, nos. 11-12, pp. 23-34.
Sivogrivov, A. "Predmet, metod, i zadachi organizatsii sel'skogo khoziaistva." *PSKh*, 1928, no. 3, pp. 3-21.
Sulkovskii, M. "A. V. Chaianov, *Optimal'nye razmery sel'skokhoziaistvennykh predpriiatii*." *NAF*, 1928, no. 4, pp. 145-149.
———. "Dokhody, ikh obrazovaniia i ispol'zovaniia v razlichnykh klassovykh gruppakh krest'ianskikh khoziaistv." *NAF*, 1929, no. 7, pp. 60-77.
———. "Evoliutsiia i raspad neonarodnichestva." *NAF*, 1929, nos. 11-12, pp. 76-97.
———. "Nakoplenie v krest'ianskikh khoziaistv." *NAF*, 1929, no. 8, pp. 45-62.
———. "Opyt sotsial'no-klassovoi gruppirovki krest'ianskikh biudzhetov podsolnechnogo raiona." *NAF*, 1928, no. 5, pp. 52-63.
———. "Predmet i metod sel'sko-khoziaistvennoi ekonomii." *NAF*, 1928, no. 12, pp. 36-48.
Uzhanskii, S. T. "Differentsiatsiia krest'ianstva." *PSKh*, 1927, no. 6, pp. 129-136.
———. "Sel'sko-khoziaistvennaia ekonomika kak akademicheskaia distsiplina. *NAF*, 1928, no. 12, pp. 49-59.
Vermenichev, I. "Klassovoe rassloenie i klassovye pozitsii burzhuaznykh i melkoburzhuaznykh teoretikov." 2 pts. *NAF*, 1927, no. 4, pp. 78-87, and *NAF*, 1927, no. 7, pp. 37-53.
———. "O differentsiatsii krest'ianstva." *PSKh*, 1928, no. 1, pp. 105-113.
———, Gaister, A., and Raevich, G. *710 khoziaistv Samarskoi derevni*. Moscow, 1927.

Other

Bastrakova, M. S. *Stanovlenie Sovetskoi sistemy organizatsiia nauki (1917-1922)*. Moscow, 1973.

Chagin, B. A. *Ocherk istorii sotsiologicheskoi mysli v USSR 1917-1969.* Leningrad, 1971.

Deiatel'nost' Kommunisticheskoi Akademii. Moscow, 1928.

"Deiatel'nost' Kommunisticheskoi Akademii za ianvar'-iiun', 1926." *VKA*, no. 18 (1926), pp. 301-320.

Figurovskaia, N. K. "Bankrotstvo 'agrarnoi reformy' burzhuaznogo vremennogo pravitel'stva." *Istoricheskie zapiski* 81 (1968): 23-67.

Ikonnikov, S. N. *Sozdanie i deiatel'nost' ob"edinennykh organov TsKK-RKI v 1923-1934 gg.* Moscow, 1971.

Khriashcheva, A. I. *Gruppy i klassy v krest'ianstve.* Moscow, 1924.

———. "K kharakteristike krest'ianskogo khoziaistva revoliutsionnogo vremeni." *Vestnik statistiki*, 1920, nos. 5-8, pp. 84-106.

———. "K voprosu ob izuchenii rassloeniia krest'ianstva." *NAF*, 1925, no. 1, pp. 80-85.

———. *Krest'ianstvo v voine i revoliutsii.* Moscow, 1921.

———. "Usloviia drobimosti krest'ianskikh khoziaistv." *Ekonomicheskoe obozrenie*, 1928, no. 9.

Knipovich, B. N. *K metodologii rainonirovaniia.* Moscow, 1921.

Kondrat'evshchina. Moscow, 1930.

"Kratkii obzor tsentrov ekonomicheskoi mysli v oblasti sel'skogo khoziaistva v Evrope i drugikh stranakh." *Biulleten' Gosudarstvennogo Nauchno-Issledovatel'skogo Instituta Sel'sko-Khoziaistvennoi Ekonomii*, 1927, nos. 1-2, pp. 53-61.

"Kratkii otchet o deiatel'nosti Kommunisticheskoi Akademii." *VKA*, no. 15 (1926), pp. 326-338.

Kratkii otchet o rabote Kommunisticheskoi Akademii za 1928-1929 gg. Moscow, 1929.

Larin, A. "K voprosu o sotsial'no-proizvodstvennoi sushchnosti protsessa drobleniia krest'ianskikh khoziaistv." *Ekonomicheskoe obozrenie*, 1929, no. 8, pp. 72-84.

Lenin, V. I. "Eleventh Congress of the R. C. P. (B.) March 27." *Collected Works* 32: 259-326.

———. "Left-wing Childishness and the Petty-bourgeois Mentality." *Collected Works* 37: 323-354.

————. "Letter to the Fifth All-Russian Congress of Trade Unions." *Collected Works* 33: 370-371.

————. "On Cooperation." *Collected Works* 33: 467-475.

————. "Political Report to the Central Committee of the R.C.P. (B.) March 27." *Collected Works* 33: 280-285.

————. "Report on the Substitution of a Tax in Kind for the Surplus-Grain Appropriation System." March 15, 1921. *Collected Works* 32: 214-228.

————. "The Agrarian Programme of Social Democracy in the First Russian Revolution, 1905-1907." *Collected Works* 13: 217-431.

————. *The Development of Capitalism in Russia.* Moscow, 1956.

————. "The International and Domestic Situation of the Soviet Republic." *Collected Works* 33: 219-221.

————. "The New Economic Policy and the Tasks of the Political Education Departments." *Collected Works* 33: 60-80.

————. "The Tax in Kind (The Significance of the New Policy and its Conditions)." *Collected Works* 32: 329-366.

————. "To the Fourth Congress of the Communist International." *Collected Works* 33: 417.

Liashchenko, P. "Predmet i metod sel'sko-khoziaistvennoi ekonomii." *NAF*, 1928, no. 2, pp. 11-27.

Litoshenko, L. N. *Evoliutsiia i progress krest'ianskogo khoziaistva.* Moscow, 1923.

Liviant, Z. "V osnovnom voprose revoliutsii nuzhna iasnost'." *NAF*, 1930, no. 4, pp. 88-95.

"Materialy po nauchnoi rabote Instituta Sel'sko-Khoziaistvennoi Ekonomii." *Biulleten' Gosudarstvennogo Nauchno-Issledovatel'skogo Instituta Sel'sko-Khoziaistvennoi Ekonomii,* 1928, nos. 1-4, pp. 126-136.

Meerson, G. "Semeino-trudovaia teoriia i differentsiatsia krest'ianstva na zare tovarnogo khoziaistva." 2 pts. *NAF*, 1925, no. 3, pp. 33-53; and *NAF*, 1925, no. 4, pp. 137-145.

Mesiatsev. P. A., ed. *Programmy i uchebnyi plan fakul'teta sel'skokhoziaistvennoi ekonomii i politiki Petrovskoi Sel'sko-Khoziaistvennoi Akademii.* Moscow, 1923.

"Mezhdunarodnyi agrarnyi institut i ego rabota za iztekshii

god." *Agrarnye problemy*, no. 2 (November, 1927), pp. 185-192.

Miroshkin, Ia. "O predmete i metode sel'sko-khoziaistvennoi ekonomii." *NAF*, 1929, no. 2, pp. 20-33.

Moskovskaia Sel'skokhoziaistvennaia Akademiia imeni Timiriazeva 1865-1965. Moscow, 1969.

Nemchinov, V. S. "O statisticheskom izuchenii klassovogo rassloeniia derevni." *Biulleten' ural'skogo oblastnogo statisticheskogo upravlneiia*, 1926, no. 1, pp. 24-38.

"O rabote agrarnogo instituta komakademii."*NAF*, 1930, no. 10, p. 113.

"Obzor vsesoiuznogo soveshchaniia rukovoditelei kafedr sel'-skokhoziaistvennoi ekonomii. *NAF*, 1930, nos. 11-12, pp. 108-160.

Organizatsiia nauki v pervye gody Sovetskoi vlasti (1917-1925). *Sbornik dokumentov*. Leningrad, 1968.

Organizatsiia Sovetskoi nauki v 1926-1932 gg. Sbornik dokumentov. Leningrad, 1974.

Osnovnye nachala zemleispol'zovaniia i zemleustroistva. Moscow, 1927.

Osnovy perspektivogo plana razvitiia sel'skogo i lesnogo khoziaistva. Moscow, 1924. Published as *Trudy Zemplana*, no. 5 (1924).

"Osnovy perspektivnogo plana razvitiia sel'skogo i lesnogo khoziaistva." 6 pts. *PSKh*, 1925, no. 4, pp. 186-214; *PSKh*, 1925, no. 5, pp. 162-192; *PSKh*, 1926, no. 1, pp. 185-219; *PSKh*, 1926, no. 2, pp. 213-228; *PSKh*, 1926, no. 3, 120-140; and *PSKh*, 1926, no. 4, pp. 137-167.

"Ot redaktsii." *NAF*, 1928, no. 2, p. 11.

"Ot redaktsii." *NAF*, 1932, no. 1, p. 4.

"Otkrytie Mezhdunarodnogo agrarnogo instituta." *Agrarnye problemy*, no. 2 (July 1927), pp. 174-178.

Perspektivy razvërtyvaniia narodnogo khoziaistva SSSR na 1926/27-1930/31. Moscow, 1927.

"Pervoi ural'skoi oblastnoi konferentsii Marksistov-agrarnikov." *NAF*, 1929, nos. 11-12, pp. 211-214.

Plan rabot Kommunisticheskoi Akademii na 1929/1930 god. Moscow, 1930.

Pokrovskii, M. "O deiatel'nosti Kommunisticheskoi Akademii." *VKA*, no. 22 (1927), pp. 5-18.

"Preniia po dokladu o differentsiatsii derevni." *PSKh*, 1927, no. 9, pp. 118-133.

"Preniia po dokladu o differentsiatsii krest'ianskogo khoziaistva." *PSKh*, 1927, no. 8, pp. 103-127.

"Programma po sel'skokhoziaistvennoi ekonomii. *NAF*, 1930, nos. 11-12, pp. 160-173.

Prokopovich, S. N. *Krest'ianskoe khoziaistvo.* Berlin, 1923.

"Protokol obshchego sobraniia chlenov Kommunisticheskoi Akademii 2-ogo iuniia 1925 goda." *VKA*, no. 12 (1925), pp. 363-390.

Rudakova, E. "O predmete sel'skokhoziaistvennoi ekonomii." *NAF*, 1930, no. 10, pp. 70-91.

"Soveshchanie kommunistov-agrarnikov pri agitprope TsK VKP(b) Belorussii." *NAF*, 1929, nos. 11-12, pp. 215-218.

Sukhanov, N. N. *K voprosu ob evoliutsii sel'skogo khoziaistva.* Moscow, 1909.

———. *Ocherki po ekonomike sel'skogo khoziaistva.* Petrograd, 1923.

———. "O differentsiatsii krest'ianskogo khoziaistva." *PSKh*, 1927, no. 6, pp. 137-147.

Svavitskii, N. A. *Zemskie podvornye perepisi: obzor metodologii.* Moscow, 1961.

———, and Svavitskii, Z. M. *Zemskie podvornye perepisi, 1880-1913 gg.* Moscow, 1926.

Targulian, O. M. "Akademiia za desiat' let." *PSKh*, 1927, no. 10, pp. 50-66.

———. "Kolkhoznoe stroitel'stvo po Chelintsevu i samokollektivizatsiia po Chaianovu." *PSKh*, 1930, no. 9, pp. 8-25.

Trudy pervoi vsesoiuznoi konferentsii agrarnikov-Marksistov. Vol. 1. Moscow, 1930.

Udal'tsov, A. "Ocherk istorii Sotsialisticheskoi Akademii." *Vestnik Sotsialisticheskoi Akademii*, no. 1 (1922), pp. 13-39.

Ulasevich, V. "Predmet i metod sel'sko-khoziaistvennoi ekonomii." *NAF*, 1929, no. 4, pp. 64-81.

"V redaktsiiu zhurnala 'NAF.'" *NAF*, 1930, no. 10, pp. 146-147.

Volkov, E. *Agrarno-ekonomicheskaia statistika Rossii.*

Moscow, 1923.

Western References

Azrael, Jeremy. *Managerial Power and Soviet Politics.* Cambridge, Mass., 1966.

Barber, Bernard. "Resistance by Scientists to Scientific Discovery." *Science* 134 (1961): 596-602.

————, and Hirsch, Walter, eds. *The Sociology of Science.* New York, 1962.

Bauer, Raymond. *The New Man in Soviet Psychology.* Cambridge, Mass., 1952.

Ben David, Joseph. *The Scientist's Role in Society.* Engelwood Cliffs, New Jersey, 1971.

Ben David, Joseph, and Zloczower, Abraham. "Universities and Academic Systems in Modern Society." *European Journal of Sociology* 3 (1962): 45-84.

Bennet, Merrill K. *Farm Cost Studies in the United States.* Stanford, Calif., 1928.

Boeke, J. H. *Economics and Economic Policies of Dual Societies.* New York, 1953.

————. *The Structure of the Netherlands Indian Economy.* New York, 1942.

Brown, Edward J. *The Proletarian Episode in Russian Literature, 1928-1932.* New York, 1953.

Bruner, Edmund de S. *The Growth of a Science: A Half-Century of Rural Sociological Research in the United States.* New York, 1957.

Carr, E. H. *The Bolshevik Revolution.* 3 vols. London, 1952.

————. *Socialism in One Country.* 2 vols. London, 1958.

————, and Davies, R. W. *Foundations of a Planned Economy.* 3 vols. Vol. 1 in 2 pts. London, 1969.

Case, H. C. M., and Williams, D. B. *Fifty Years of Farm Management.* Urbana, Illinois, 1957.

Chisholm, Michael. *Rural Settlement and Land Use.* London, 1968.

Cohen, Stephen F. *Bukharin and the Bolshevik Revolution.* New York, 1973.

Cole, Jonathan R., and Cole, Stephen. *Social Stratification in Science.* Chicago, 1973.

Cole, Stephen. "Continuity and Institutionalization in a Science: A Case Study of Failure." In *The Establishment of Empirical Sociology*, edited by Anthony Oberschall. New York, 1972.

Crane, Diana. *Invisible Colleges*. Chicago, 1972.

Day, Richard B. *Leon Trotsky and the Politics of Isolation*. Cambridge, England, 1973.

Dupree, A. Hunter. *Science in the Federal Government: A History of Policies and Activites to 1940*. New York, 1957.

Elesh, David. "The Manchester Statistical Society: A Case of Discontinuity in the History of Empirical Social Research." In *The Establishment of Empirical Sociology*, edited by Anthony Oberschall. New York, 1972.

Ellison, Herbert J. "The Socialist Revolutionaries." *Problems of Communism* 16 (1967): 2-14.

Erlich, Alexander. *The Soviet Industrialization Debate*. Cambridge, Mass., 1960.

Fauser, Immanuel. "German Approach to Farm Economic Investigations." *Journal of Farm Economics* 8 (1926): 389-397.

Fitzpatrick, Sheila. "Cultural Revolution as Class." In *Cultural Revolution in Russia, 1928-1931*, edited by Sheila Fitzpatrick. Bloomington, Indiana, 1977.

———. "Cultural Revolution in Russia, 1928-1932." *Journal of Contemporary History* (1974): 33-52.

———. *The Commissariat of Enlightenment*. Cambridge, England, 1970.

———. "The 'Soft' Line on Soviet Culture and its Enemies: Soviet Cultural Policy, 1922-1927." *Slavic Review* 33 (1974): 267-288.

Forman, Paul. "Weimar Culture, Causality, and Quantum Theory, 1918-1927: Adaptation by German Physicists and Mathematicians to a Hostile Intellectual Environment." *Historical Studies in the Physical Sciences* 3 (1971): 1-115.

Frauendorfer, Sigmund von. "Development, Methods, and Results of Agricultural Economic Research in the United States." *Journal of Farm Economics* 10 (1928): 286-311.

Gillespie, Charles C. *The Edge of Objectivity. An Essay in the History of Scientific Ideas*. Princeton, New Jersey, 1969.

Gouldner, Alvin. "Cosmopolitans and Locals: Toward an Analysis of Latent Social Roles." *Administrative Science Quarterly* 2 (1957): 281-300, 444-480.

Graham, Loren. *The Soviet Academy of Sciences and the Communist Party 1927-1932.* New York, 1967.

Hagstrom, Warren O. *The Scientific Community.* New York, 1965.

Hobson, Asher. "Agricultural Economics in Europe." *Journal of Farm Economics* 9 (1927): 421-423.

―――. *The International Institute of Agriculture: An Historical and Critical Analysis of its Organization, Activities, and Policies of Administration.* Berkeley, Calif., 1931.

Isard, Walter. *Location and Space Economy.* Cambridge, Mass., 1962.

Jasny, Naum. *Names to be Remembered.* Cambridge, England, 1972.

Joravsky, David. "The Construction of the Stalinist Psyche." In *Cultural Revolution in Russia, 1928-1931*, edited by Sheila Fitzpatrick. Bloomington, Indiana, 1977.

―――. *The Lysenko Affair.* Cambridge, Mass., 1970.

―――. *Soviet Marxism and Natural Science 1917-1932.* New York, 1961.

Karcz, Jerzy. "Thoughts on the Grain Problem." *Soviet Studies* 18 (1967): 399-434.

Kerblay, Basile. "A. V. Chaianov: Life, Career, Works." In *A. V. Chayanov on the Theory of Peasant Economy*, edited by Daniel Thorner, Basile Kerblay, and R. E. F. Smith. Homewood, Illinois, 1966.

Kuhn, Thomas. *The Structure of Scientific Revolutions.* Chicago, 1962; 2d. enlarged ed. Chicago, 1970.

Lewin, Moshe. *Lenin's Last Struggle.* New York, 1968.

―――. *Russian Peasants and Soviet Power.* London, 1968.

―――. "Who Was the Soviet Kulak?" *Soviet Studies* 18 (1966): 189-212.

Male, D. J. "The Village Community in the USSR: 1925-1930." *Soviet Studies* 14 (1963): 225-248.

Marcson, Simon. *The Scientist in Industry.* New York, 1960.

Medvedev, Roy A. *Let History Judge.* New York, 1971.

Mendel, Arthur P. *Dilemmas of Progress in Tsarist Russia:*

Legal Marxism and Legal Populism. Cambridge, Mass., 1961.

Merton, Robert K. "Insiders and Outsiders: A Chapter in the Sociology of Knowledge." *American Journal of Sociology* 78 (1972): 9-48. Reprinted as "The Perspectives of Insiders and Outsiders." In Merton, *The Sociology of Science*, edited by Norman W. Storer. Chicago and London, 1973.

――――. "The Matthew Effect in Science." *Science* 149 (1968): 56-63. Reprinted in Merton, *The Sociology of Science.*

――――. "Paradigm for the Sociology of Knowledge." In *The Sociology of Knowledge*, edited by James E. Curtis and John Petras. New York, 1970. Originally published as "Sociology of Knowledge." In *Twentieth Century Sociology*, edited by Georges Gurvitch and Wilbert Moore. New York, 1945. Reprinted in Merton, *The Sociology of Science.*

――――. "Science and the Social Order." *Philosophy of Science* 5 (1938): 321-337. Reprinted in Merton, *The Sociology of Science.*

――――. "Priorities in Scientific Discovery: A Chapter in the Sociology of Science." *American Sociological Review* 22 (1957): 635-659. Reprinted in Merton, *The Sociology of Science.*

――――. "Science and Technology in a Democratic Order." *Journal of Legal and Political Sociology* 1 (1942): 115-126.

――――. "Science, Technology and Society in Seventeenth Century England." *Osiris* 4 (1938): 360-632.

――――. "Singletons and Multiples in Scientific Discovery: A Chapter in the Sociology of Science." *Proceedings of the American Philosophical Society* 105 (1961): 470-486. Reprinted in Merton, *The Sociology of Science.*

――――. "Social Conflict over Styles of Sociological Work." In *Transactions of the Fourth World Congress of Sociology.* Vol. 3. Louvain, 1959. Reprinted in *The Sociology of Knowledge*, edited by James E. Curtis and John W. Petras, New York, 1970; and in Merton, *The Sociology of Science.*

――――. *Social Theory and Social Structure.* Rev. and enlarged ed. New York, 1957.

———. "The Sociology of Knowledge." In *Social Theory and Social Structure*. Rev. and enlarged ed. New York, 1957.

———. *The Sociology of Science*. Edited by Norman W. Storer. Chicago, 1973.

Miller, Robert F. "Soviet Agricultural Policy in the Twenties: The Failure of Cooperation." *Soviet Studies* 27 (1975): 220-244.

Millar, James. "A Reformulation of A. V. Chayanov's Theory of the Peasant Economy." *Economic Development and Cultural Change* 18 (1969-1970).

Mullins, Nicholas C. "The Development of a Scientific Specialty." *Minerva* 10 (1972): 51-82.

Nelson, Lowry. *Rural Sociology: Its Origin and Growth in the United States*. Minneapolis, Minn., 1969.

Nove, Alec. *An Economic History of the USSR*. London, 1969.

Pipes, Richard. *Struve: Liberal on the Left, 1870-1905*. Cambridge, Mass., 1970.

Ponsard, C. *Histoire des Théories Economiques et Spatiales*. Paris, 1958.

Popper, Karl. *Conjectures and Refutations*. New York, 1965.

Radkey, Oliver. *The Agrarian Foes of Bolshevism*. New York, 1958.

Research in Farm Management: Scope and Method. Publications of the Advisory Committee on Social and Economic Research in Agriculture of the Social Science Research Council, no. 13. Edited by John Black. New York, 1932.

Research Method and Procedure in Agricultural Economics. A Publication of the Advisory Committee on Economics and Social Research in Agriculture of the Social Science Research Council. 2 vols. N.p., 1928.

Robinson, Geroid Tanquary. *Rural Russia under the Old Regime*. New York, 1961.

Roth, Walter. "Farm Budgeting in Germany." *Journal of Farm Economics* 11 (1929): 623-632.

Schad, Suzanne P. *Empirical Social Research in Weimar Germany*. The Hague, 1972.

Schapiro, Leonard. *The Communist Party of the Soviet*

Union. New York, 1964.

Schwarz, Solomon. "Populism and Early Russian Marxism on Ways of Economic Development in Russia." In *Continuity and Change in Russian and Soviet Thought*, edited by Ernest Simmons. Cambridge, Mass., 1955.

Shanin, Teodor. *The Awkward Class: Political Sociology of Peasantry in a Developing Society: Russia 1910-1925.* Oxford, 1972.

Shteppa, Konstantin F. *Russian Historians and the Soviet State.* New Brunswick, New Jersey, 1962.

Smith, T. Lynn. "Sorokin's Rural-Urban Principles." In *Pitirim A. Sorokin in Review*, edited by Philip J. Allen. Durham, North Carolina, 1963.

Sorokin, Pitirim A. *Leaves from a Russian Diary.* Boston, 1950.

Sorokin, P., Zimmermann, C. C., and Galpin, C. *A Systematic Source Book in Rural Sociology.* 3 vols. Minneapolis, Minn. 1930.

Stouffer, Samuel, et al. *The American Soldier.* Vol. 1. *Adjustment During Army Life.* Princeton, New Jersey, 1949.

Taylor, Henry C. *Agricultural Economics.* New York, 1919.

Taylor, Henry C., and Taylor, Anne Dewees. *The Story of Agricultural Economics in the United States 1840-1932.* Ames, Iowa, 1952.

Thunen, Johann H. von. *Von Thunen's Isolated State.* Edited by Peter Hall. Oxford, 1966.

Toulmin, Stephen. *Human Understanding.* Vol. 1. Princeton, New Jersey, 1972.

Vucinich, Alexander. *Science in Russian Culture, 1861-1917.* Stanford, Calif., 1970.

Weinberg, Elizabeth Ann. *The Development of Sociology in the Soviet Union.* London, 1974.

Wreckers on Trial. London, 1930.

Yaney, George L. "Agricultural Administration in Russia from the Stolypin Reforms to Forced Collectivization: An Interpretive Study." In *The Soviet Rural Community*, edited by James Millar. Urbana, Illinois, 1971.

Znaniecki, Florian. *The Social Role of the Man of Knowledge.* New York, 1940.

Unpublished Sources

Figurovskaia, N. K. "Razgrom burzhuaznykh i melkoburzhuaznykh agrarnykh teorii, 1917-1930." Candidate's thesis. Moscow State University, 1961.

Fitzpatrick, Sheila. "Stalinism and Culture." Paper prepared for the Research Conference on Stalinism, held in Bellagio, Italy, July 25-31, 1975.

Swanson, James. "The Bolshevization of Scientific Societies in the Soviet Union." Ph.D. dissertation. Indiana University, 1968.

Yaney, George L. "The Imperial Russian Government and the Stolypin Land Reforms." Ph.D. dissertation. Princeton University, 1961.

A series of interviews with S. M. Dubrovskii, senior historian at the Institute of History of the USSR Academy of Sciences and a participant in many of the events described in this book.

Index